STREETWISE

24 HOUR
MBA

Books in the Adams Streetwise® series include:

Adams Streetwise® Business Forms (with CD-ROM)

Adams Streetwise® Business Letters (with CD-ROM)

Adams Streetwise® Business Tips

Adams Streetwise® Complete Business Plan

Adams Streetwise® Customer-Focused Selling

Adams Streetwise® Do-It-Yourself Advertising

Adams Streetwise® Finance and Accounting

Adams Streetwise® Hiring Top Performers

Adams Streetwise® Independent Consulting

Adams Streetwise® Managing People

Adams Streetwise® Marketing Plan

Adams Streetwise® Motivating and Rewarding Employees

Adams Streetwise® Relationships Marketing on the Internet

Adams Streetwise® Small Business Start-Up

Adams Streetwise® Small Business Turnaround

Adams Streetwise® Time Management

STREETWISE

24 HOUR MBA

Power Workshops for
Business Success, including:

Leadership, Marketing,
Finance, Motivating
Employees, and Business
Communications

by Alexander Hiam

Adams Media Corporation
Holbrook, Massachusetts

Published by Adams Media Corporation
260 Center Street, Holbrook, MA 02343. U.S.A.
www.adamsmedia.com

ISBN: 1-58062-256-9

Printed in the United States of America.

J I H G F E D C B A

Library of Congress Cataloging-in-Publication Data
Hiam, Alexander.
Streetwise 24 hour MBA : power workshops for business success, including leadership,
marketing, finance, motivating employees, and business communications / by Alexander Hiam.
p.   cm.
ISBN 1-58062-256-9
1. Industrial management. I. Title.
HD31.H478 2000
658–dc21   00-035592

This publication is designed to provide accurate and authoritative information with regard to
the subject matter covered. It is sold with the understanding that the publisher is not engaged
in rendering legal, accounting, or other professional advice. If legal advice or other expert assistance is required, the services of a competent professional person should be sought.
— From a *Declaration of Principles* jointly adopted by a Committee of the American Bar
Association and a Committee of Publishers and Associations

Cover illustration by Eric Mueller.

This book is available at quantity discounts for bulk purchases.
For information, call 1-800-872-5627.

Visit our exciting small business Web site: www.businesstown.com

CONTENTS

COURSE I: THE BUSINESS COMMUNICATIONS COURSE

COURSE II: THE LEADERSHIP COURSE

CONTENTS

COURSE VI: THE ETIQUETTE OF BUSINESS SHORT COURSE

COURSE VII: SEXUAL HARASSMENT SHORT COURSE

COURSE VIII: INNOVATING TO LEAD YOUR MARKETS SHORT COURSE

COURSE IX: MANAGING CRITICAL INCIDENTS IN SALES AND MARKETING SHORT COURSE

A day is a long time in the world of business.

In the average 24 hour period, General Motors sells about $500 million dollars worth of vehicles and Wal-Mart Stores sell about $350 million worth of all sorts of stuff.

But big companies aren't the only ones who are very busy in the average day. In the U.S. alone, approximately 2,000 new businesses are formed in each 24 hour period, including several dozen new Internet startups. And, simultaneously, about 200 established businesses fail.

What are the people in this busy world of business doing in the average 24 hour period? Well, more of them are working more hours than ever before according to labor statistics. They have to work long hours to handle the average of 178 communications they receive each working day. And to polish their resumes—the average employee now stays at his or her job for only a few years at most before moving on.

And to satisfy these increasingly mobile employees' demand for housing appropriate to their location, tastes, and income, between 4 and 5 thousand new homes are completed each day and between 13 and 14 thousand existing homes are resold.

If it's a weekday, then we can also say that the average individual earns about $80 dollars in that same 24 hour period. Far short of the $500 million brought in by GM, to be sure—and also not very impressive compared to the earnings of the highest paid individuals in the country. For instance, last year Robert F. Young, founder of Red Hat Inc., a software company that went public, saw his stock options soar and achieved a personal net worth of $2 billion. That worked out to earnings of about $7.7 million each working day, and also earned him the accolade of Top Entrepreneur of the Year according to *Business Week* magazine's January 10, 2000 issue.

There is a fairly large gap between the average employee's daily earning of less than $100 and top entrepreneurs' earnings in the millions of dollars. In fact, to be honest, it is a shockingly large gap. But the economy has been good and the average employee can expect to earn a bit more each day than the day before. In fact, yearly growth in the cost of compensation in the U.S. is running at 3.2% at the time of this writing. That works out to a 98 cent raise each day for the average

> There is a fairly large gap between the average employee's daily earning of less than $100 and top entrepreneurs' earnings in the millions of dollars.

worker. So if the average employee waits 8 million years, he or she will be earning just as much as today's top entrepreneurs and executives.

Somehow I don't think the average raise is going to close the gap between average earnings and the performance of top entrepreneurs and executives any time soon. In fact, statistics show that the gap between those who are doing well and those who are working average jobs is growing each and every day. The most economically successful ten percent are in fact pulling ahead of the average person by thousands of dollars a day right now as they take advantage of a hot economy and opportunities to exploit the growth of the World Wide Web.

> The average employee is struggling just to keep up with a more rapid pace of work than ever.

Keeping Up?

In fact, the average employee is struggling just to keep up with a more rapid pace of work than ever. Studies of a wide variety of organizations, both in the U.S. and abroad, show that the working environment is less stable and predictable and more full of surprises and change than ever before.

Maybe that's why in the same 24 hour period $171 million dollars is spent on training in U.S. businesses of more than 100 employees. Companies are rushing to orient, train, and retrain their people. My own company is part of that growth industry—we develop and distribute training materials and curricula to thousands of North American and European companies. And what we see is two related complaints:

- *First*, we often encounter employees (or entrepreneurs) who feel like they are unable to get ahead of the curve and tap into the explosive economic growth enjoyed by the economic elite. Perhaps that's why individuals are seeking their own training at record numbers right now by participating in seminars and workshops as well as returning to school.
- *Second*, we constantly hear complaints from senior managers and human resources executives that they cannot find the

leaders they need to step up and help them expand their businesses. That's why both recruitment and training budgets are growing in corporations.

So on the one hand, many people feel frustrated that they are not moving ahead as quickly as they'd like in their careers. On the other hand, the managers of hot companies of all sorts are complaining they cannot find the people they need to promote into fast-track positions. Maybe we can work something out.

Maybe We Can Help

Some things take a little longer than a day. New companies arise to displace old companies on that most prestigious of business lists, the Fortune 500, only once every 12 to 20 days. And it takes a bit more than a day to move yourself onto a faster career track than whatever one you may now be on (and no matter how successful you are, there always seems to be a faster track beckoning, doesn't there?). But there should always be a way for anyone with the motivation and desire to participate more actively in the business opportunities that surround us each and every day. That is in fact the purpose and focus on this unusual book.

This book is really a collection of "virtual" day-long and half-day professional workshops or seminars—the kind of seminars leading companies are prescribing for their hottest up-and-comers.

If you wanted to really bone up on your management skills and prepare yourself to shift lanes in your professional career, you'd be smart to attend as many good professional training sessions as you could. In fact, you probably do already. But there is only so much time in a day, and only so much money in your corporate and personal training budgets. Most people manage to find time for no more than a few days of live training a year at the most—which works out to less than three minutes of professional training per day. For the average employee, probably less than a single minute. That's not a very big investment in one's future, is it?

> There should always be a way for anyone with the motivation and desire to participate more actively in the business opportunities that surround us each and every day.

An Alternative Formula for Success

Here's what I think. I think that *if you could spend at least a half hour each day on professional training and development*–about ten times the average–then you would find it far easier to move toward your personal and professional goals rapidly and effectively. But how could you do that without devoting ten times as much money and time to such events?

That is the creative challenge we posed to ourselves when we sat down to think about this book. We didn't want to write or publish just another book on business. I'd already written more than a dozen, and my editor and publisher had produced hundreds. What was unique about *this* effort that would justify a year of our hard work and the breaking of one of your hard earned twenty dollar bills?

The answer we came up with was that we wouldn't write just another business book. In fact, we decided not to create a book at all. At least not in the conventional sense.

We decided to *create a series of self-training courses*, modeled on the training curricula and activities that my firm develops for managers at leading companies and other organizations (like the armed forces). We decided to create a collection of workshops and seminars, each comparable in their approach and coverage to the best one-day and half-day training events in their fields. And we decided to provide coverage of many of the hot topics that seem to be associated with go-ahead success in management, entrepreneurship, and sales.

In short, we decided that there was an easy way to help you benefit from the content of those many workshops and seminars you won't have time to attend this year. You can simply study them on your own, right here between the covers of this book. And I'm convinced that if you make a habit of studying content such as this for at least, say, 25 minutes each day, you will notice a significant change in your own preparation and performance.

> We decided to create a collection of workshops and seminars, each comparable in their approach and coverage to the best one-day and half-day training events in their fields.

The Contents at a Glance

By the way, I ought to explain what the title's acronym means, just in case you are unfamiliar with it. The MBA is the most common graduate degree in business, the Master's in Business Administration. I have one myself, and I have taught in several MBA programs too, so I don't have anything against this degree. It's great preparation for a successful business career. However, when you take the idea of mastering business and combine it with my publisher's concept of a "streetwise" approach, you get an interesting variation.

Instead of focusing on the conventional core courses of a two-year business management program, our *Streetwise MBA* focuses on the real-world issues and subjects that are holding people back in their careers. The sort of topics that leading corporations are prescribing through their corporate universities. And the sort of topics that many savvy entrepreneurs and salespeople are seeking individual training in through workshops and evening courses as well.

So a streetwise MBA is one that prepares you to succeed by showing you what to do (and what not to do) to achieve success in the real world of business—whether as a corporate manager, salesperson, or entrepreneur.

That's considerably different from what a traditional MBA does. A Master's degree in Business Administration, as offered by most business schools, includes in-depth study of the fields of economics, accounting, marketing, management, and finance. It focuses on technical details of these fields, and often draws on what professors study and publish, rather than on what people do to succeed in the real world.

That's why most people end up seeking additional training, even if they have earned an MBA at a leading business school. And that's why major corporations invest millions in workshops and trainings for their star performers. Every Fortune 1000 company has a corporate training department with a budget in the millions, dedicated to grooming the next generation of star employees.

What do star performers learn in these corporate training workshops and seminars, and in the "school of hard knocks," that makes them more successful than someone without a real-world MBA?

> A streetwise MBA is one that prepares you to succeed by showing you what to do (and what not to do) to achieve success in the real world of business.

They learn that success in any business enterprise, large or small, requires a different constellation of skills from the ones taught in schools. Things like superior communication skills, leadership ability, and motivation make all the difference in the real world.

And if you stop to look closely at leading entrepreneurs, executives or salespeople, you will find they all have superior communications skills. They all are good leaders and supervisors, able to organize and direct the work of others with ease. They are highly self-motivated, and are great motivators of other people. They know to keep themselves out of trouble by avoiding legal and ethical pitfalls in areas such as discrimination, bribery, sexual harassment, and workplace romances. And they are good with money—they all have a practical, real-world understanding of how to raise and manage funds. For example, successful managers, executives, and salespeople all know the value of good cash flow and are careful to manage their finances accordingly.

Where do you acquire such real-world skills? Until now, it wasn't easy. You had to cobble together your own course by learning from mentors, attending expensive seminars and workshops, and integrating some of that "hard" knowledge from business-school courses as well. It is going to be pretty hard to bone up on all these important streetwise skills in the one to three minutes of formal training available to the average employee in the average 24-hour day!

That's why we decided to bring together a series of "virtual" workshops. Here, in an innovative, user-friendly format, you will find nine popular workshops in one book. These workshops give you access to the kind of training that leading businesses are teaching their best employees to groom them for advancement. They give you access to the kinds of knowledge that entrepreneurs need to get ahead in business. And they give you practical training that can help boost a sales career as well.

Much of the contents of these workshops falls into the "what they don't teach you at any business school" category. You might short-cut your own streetwise learning by many years if you study each of these workshops carefully. Many of the secrets of success in business are contained in these simulated workshops, each with its series of short training sessions and activities:

> These workshops give you access to the kind of training that leading businesses are teaching their best employees to groom them for advancement.

1. The Business Communications Course
2. The Leadership Course
3. The Employee Motivation Course
4. The Organization Course
5. The Financial Management Course
6. The Etiquette of Business Short Course
7. The Sexual Harassment Short Course
8. Innovating to Lead Your Markets Short Course
9. Managing Critical Incidents in Sales and Marketing Short Course

You can decide what order you wish to take these courses. Or, if you wish, feel free to look within them to select one of the many specific, short training sessions that make up each workshop. However you choose to pursue your studies, you will certainly find much that is new and applicable to your daily work! Good luck, and congratulations in advance for your future successes.

Skill, Attitude, and Knowledge

Remember, success is simply a combination of skills, attitudes, and knowledge. You've already proven you have a positive attitude by picking up this book. By adding some "streetwise MBA" skills and knowledge, you will be providing that attitude with the nutrients it needs to grow and prosper, bringing you to a higher level of success. And helping you make each and every day a more profitable and personally rewarding one than the day before. If you let the law of averages do its work, you will probably achieve an earning power tomorrow that is 98 cents higher than your earning power today. Give it a few million years and you'll be the next Bill Gates. Or, if you want to take the bull by the horns, you can do some preparation, improve your skill, attitudes, and knowledge, and beat the curve by being worth significantly more tomorrow than you are today.

A lot can happen in 24 hours. What are you waiting for? Better get started right away!

> Remember, success is simply a combination of skills, attitudes, and knowledge.

The Business Communications Course

Overview of Course I

My uncle, Alex Watson, used to joke about a sergeant he had in the army who always told him, "Every time you think you weaken this organization." That's a common perception today among executives who like to believe they are the only ones with the insight to make difficult decisions. They're wrong, and in truth, most employees strengthen their organizations every time they think. Thinking is good. And most people have enough common sense to add some value every time they think. On the other hand, I've come to realize that the old line is right when applied to communications.

In fact, in today's businesses, it is fair to say to most employees, "Every time you communicate you weaken this organization."

Poor communications lead to conflicts instead of cooperation, hurt employee motivation instead of building it, and produce confusion and keep people in the dark when they really need to know what is going on. Communications can have so many affects on so many aspects of business performance that it is hard to overstate its importance in business.

Yet most managers are poor communicators. They fail to keep their employees, bosses, associates, and customers properly informed. They don't explain their ideas or instructions clearly. They alienate employees and drive away prospects through poor or inappropriate communication. They freeze up in front of audiences and deliver shaky, unintelligible speeches and presentations. And their writing, well, their writing is painful to read.

In short, the average manager is a poor communicator who is more likely to cause trouble than not when it comes to communicating with others. But enough about the typical manager. You're goal is to be an exceptional manager or a successful entrepreneur, so I know you won't tolerate the typical communication abuses. Communication is an incredibly powerful tool for those who know how to use it effectively. In this chapter I'll show you how to become an exceptional communicator through these seven sessions:

Session 1: What, to Who?

Session 2: Pen Power

Session 3: Advanced Business Writing

Session 4: From Writer's Block to Writing for Fun

Session 5: Communicating with Voice Mail Systems

Session 6: Giving Killer Presentations
(Instead of Getting Killed by Them)

Session 7: What to Say to Employees Who
Badmouth You

Introduction

INTRODUCTION

Some communications workshops use an amusing exercise to teach us to attend carefully to inflection and emphasis in the spoken word. Whether you are listening or speaking, the use of emphasis can hold the key to meaning, and this exercise, which you can do yourself, helps make us aware of that important point. Simply say the following sentence seven times, each time emphasizing a different word:

"I never said you stole the money."

If you emphasize the first word, it goes like this: "*I* never said you stole the money." Which means that somebody else said so. If you emphasize the second word, it goes like this: "I *never* said you stole the money," which sounds like you are protesting against their accusation that you said so. Emphasize the third word and the meaning is different again: "I never *said* you stole the money," which means you think they did but didn't say so. Or how about "I never said *you* stole the money." Now you're saying someone else did, perhaps a co-conspirator. If it's "I never said you *stole* the money," then you mean that they did take the money but perhaps not by stealing. If it's "I never said you stole *the* money," you imply they might have stolen other money instead. Finally, if you say "I never said you stole the *money*," it sounds like you think they stole something else.

Seven dramatically different meanings from the exact same words. Communication is a subtle art, isn't it!

The subtleties of good communication are just as important in written as in spoken English. When you write, it's not the word emphasis, the nonverbal cues, and other face-to-face issues. It's things like spelling, punctuation, grammar, and style—all those little rules and tips they try to teach us in grade school when we couldn't really care less. Now we care. At least we should care deeply, because how we present ourselves in writing is an important contributor to our professional success or failure. As you'll see in this chapter, writing is, paradoxically, more and more important in business in spite of the rise of computer, fax, e-mail, voice mail, and other new media and systems. To many people, you are how you appear on paper. Vital relationships are built or lost through the written word. We all need to bone up on our writing skills to succeed in the modern world of business.

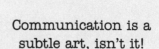

Communication is a subtle art, isn't it!

Transform yourself into one of the (all too few) really great presenters.

Then there are the presentations. Do you like getting up in front of an audience and holding forth? Do you have complete confidence that you can win over a tough audience and wow them with your presentation skills? Well, maybe you do, but most managers do not. Almost all managers are poor presenters, and the vast majority of people suffer from stage fright. Top that off with the sad fact that typical training seminars and advice *do not help you overcome stage fright*, and it's a miracle anybody makes presentations at all. In this chapter I'll also show you how to overcome your anxiety, for real, so that you can begin to transform yourself into one of the (all too few) really great presenters.

But before we dive into these more specific skills, let's start with a session on something that is so fundamental most people overlook it entirely. I'm talking about what you should say—the message itself. And I'm talking about who you should say it to—the audience. Too often, we all blunder into communications without thinking systematically about what the message should be and who needs to hear the message. As a result, the majority of business communications are communicating the wrong information to the wrong people. No amount of refining your skills will make that formula into a winner!

What, to Who?

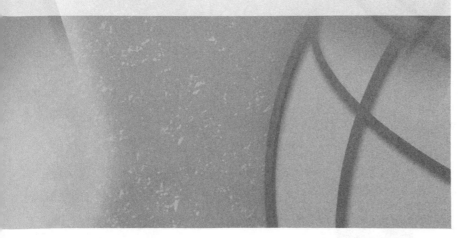

A grammarian might edit the title of this lesson to read, "What, to whom," but I don't care. The most important thing in communications is to get the right message to the right person. If you don't have the right message and the right receiver, it doesn't matter how you communicate that message. Your presentation, letter, e-mail, or whatever can be brilliant. It won't matter. Good communications are wasted on the wrong message and the wrong audience. Let's make sure your communications are effective by being clear on what you should communicate, and to who. Or whom.

I do a lot of work in the area of employee motivation, and I keep running into cases in which employee motivation has been hurt by poor communications. This linkage is not obvious to most people, but once you look closely at it you can see that how managers communicate is probably the single biggest driver of motivation levels in their people. It all comes down to communicating the wrong things or not communicating anything when you should have.

When Communications Destroy Motivation

Motivating employees is a high priority these days, as well it should be. High job mobility, a tight labor market, and markets demanding fast-paced innovation all add up to a growing performance challenge. Managers everywhere are rushing to implement new rewards and recognition systems, and trainers are working overtime to keep up with the demand for new programs. But in truth, these initiatives are running into barrier after barrier. And often it's because managers have not communicated well with their people. Here are a few of the more common communications errors that are destroying employee motivation in organizations all around the world:

Abusing

Most bosses are verbally abusive; it's the tradition. Criticizing or blaming employees, ordering them around like children, withholding key information from them, trivializing their contributions, or diminishing their worth by ignoring them or talking down to them are all commonplace behaviors. And sometimes managers lose their tempers and get angry at employees as well. Too bad all these behaviors destroy motivation.

> Grasp the subject, the words will follow.
> —CATO THE ELDER,
> *ARS RHETORICA*

"Inconsidering"

You've heard of consideration and empathy. Well, inconsideration is their opposite, and employees say it is how most supervisors are. Managers feel too busy to worry about how their people feel, and they seldom realize how much influence they have on employee emotions. But here's something else most managers don't know: The amount of consideration shown by managers is one of the most powerful predictors of bottom-line financial performance! Consideration builds motivation and boosts performance. Inconsideration destroys motivation and limits profit potential. And often the difference is simply a matter of how you speak or write to your people. For example, it's considerate to ask employees how their work is going before telling them what to do. It's rude and inconsiderate if you don't.

Talking

Most managers damage employee motivation by accident every time they speak to their people. They interrupt, fail to ask sincere or open questions, and demonstrate poor listening skills. As a result, employees rank communications as their number one complaint. Managers think they are communicating, but until they rethink their interpersonal skills and apply some new techniques, they aren't. They are damaging employee motivation instead.

Vacuuming

A failure to communicate essential feedback to employees is very damaging to their motivation and performance levels. But most employees operate in a performance vacuum in which management has accidentally sucked away most of the important feedback information. Employees lack the details of why their tasks are important, and they do not receive rapid, accurate feedback about how they perform. If you tell employees who, what, when, and where, as most managers do, you are overlooking the most vital part: *why*. Employees need a clear view from their tasks to the overarching purpose or plan. And if you provide infrequent performance reviews you are leaving out the most important part of feedback: information they can use to evaluate themselves and learn by doing. Because of these common errors, employees often do "no-splash" tasks. It's as if their

> Truth is not merely what we are thinking, but also why, to whom and under what circumstances we say it.
> —VÁCLAV HAVEL

work is tossed into a bottomless pit. They listen and listen but never hear it hit bottom.

Because managers routinely make these common communication errors, employees typically operate at low levels of job motivation. Most people feel far more motivated about a hobby, sport, or cause they pursue than about their own work, even though their work offers much more potential for personal growth, development, and accomplishment. By recognizing and avoiding such errors, managers can learn to harness the natural motivation and enthusiasm of their people. The results can be astonishing.

Thinking about Who Needs to Hear What, When

The key to getting the right message to the right person is to focus on who needs to hear what, when. People have communication *needs*. Fill their needs and you get communications right. Fail to and you don't.

The management grid gives us one valuable clue as to who needs to hear what, when. It tells us that employees sometimes need you as a manager to focus on people issues and sometimes on task issues. Most managers instinctively favor one orientation. So they overlook the other orientation. They focus on task and not on people. Or vice versa. To avoid this common communication error, stop and ask yourself whether employees need *information* about how to do their work, or if they need *support* in order to feel better about their work. It's one or the other. Got to be. So just ask yourself which, and you are far more likely to pick the right message than most managers. See the employee communications grid in Figure 1-1, for help in crafting the right approach to your message content.

Getting the Content Right in Persuasive Communications

In communicating with customers and prospects, audiences for your presentations, and anyone else you wish to persuade or *wow*, you can use a very similar analysis. Basically, they have two kinds of communication needs too, just like employees. Except where employees need information about the task, your audience needs logical

> Employees sometimes need you as a manager to focus on people issues and sometimes on task issues. Most managers instinctively favor one orientation.

FIGURE 1-1. EMPLOYEE COMMUNICATIONS GRID

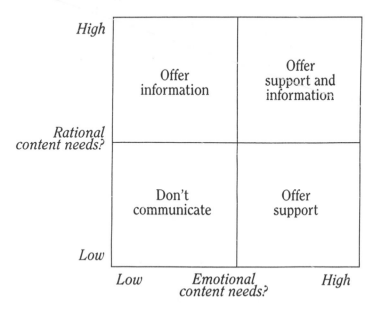

(Used by permission of Alexander Hiam & Associates.)

arguments. And where employees would need emotional support, your audience needs you to get emotionally involved.

For example, let's say you are speaking to a group of buyers from companies about your new business service. Your presentation needs to build both a logical and an emotional case. You need to provide hard information to get them rationally involved. But a logical appeal alone won't make the sale. People also have to get emotionally involved. So your presentation needs to warm them up with appeals to their feelings. Make them smile. Remind them of how frustrating it is when the competitor's service messes up. Tell them a personal story about yourself.

These emotional involvement devices are appropriate when you sense that your audience is emotionally withdrawn or uninvolved. Then you need to get warm and human with them. But when you feel that they are emotionally engaged and like you, but lack full

> A logical appeal alone won't make the sale.

rational involvement, then you've got to switch gears again and give them facts and logical arguments.

These two forms of content—logical and emotional—are very different. They require different styles and approaches. Most presenters naturally favor one or the other because of their personalities. But to be a good persuasive communicator, you must learn to alternate between the two types of content. Build some of both into your script or plan for any persuasive communication. And switch from one to the other when you sense the audience needs you to balance your content for them. That way you will build up their involvement and truly persuade them on all levels, emotionally and intellectually.

Analyzing Their Information Needs

People often have specific information needs that you must consider. Too often, we forget to communicate with people and thereby fail to fill their information needs. Informational communications are a lot easier than persuasive or motivational communications. But only if you remember to actually communicate!

Changes create information needs, so whenever something changes you need to think about who should be informed of what. For example, when there is a significant change, employees (or anyone affected by it) will have a sequence of information needs. First, they will want to know what the change is—they need basic information to assess its relevance and define it. Then they want to know how it will affect them personally. Their next natural question is what they will need to do to protect themselves and cope with the change. Only when employees have had these content needs met by your communications are they ready to think about how the change will affect the organization and how to get the most benefit out of the change for the business.

If you fail to recognize that employees naturally need information about the personal impact of a change first, then you will waste your time talking about how the change is good for your business and never meet their basic information needs. The following table, based on a presentation by Ken Blanchard, makes the sequence of information needs clear. Make sure you answer each question in sequence or you won't be communicating effectively:

THE SIX STAGES OF CONCERN IN THE CHANGE PROCESS

Stage	Employee Information Need
1. Information	"What's going on?"
2. Personal	"How will it affect me?"
3. Management	"What do I need to do?"
4. Consequences	"How will it affect our organization?"
5. Collaboration	"What can I do to help implement the change?"
6. Refocus/Refinement	"What else can we change to get even more benefits?"

(Based on Exhibit 27 of Hiam, *The Portable Conference on Change Management*, HRD Press.)

Remembering to Communicate with *All* Interested Parties

Are you involved in activities or events that concern other people? You bet. Yet you probably don't communicate your news about these activities or events with all who have a stake in the outcomes. Most managers fail to keep everyone fully informed. It's not that they mean to leave people out of the loop. It's just that they forget.

But the consequences of leaving people out of the loop are disastrous. The single biggest complaint of employees in a wide variety of opinion surveys is that their managers do not communicate well with them. So employees certainly feel like they are left out of the loop too often. And customers often complain too. They feel like changes aren't shared with them. They want to know about anything that affects them. Then there are bosses. If you have an employer, or even (if you run your own business) a board of directors, you need to provide more information about your activities and any problems you encounter than most managers do. Don't neglect to keep your superiors informed!

It's hard to remember to communicate with all interested parties because there are so many of them. Way to many. The average Fortune 1000 employee sends out approximately 100 communications a day in one form or another, ranging from water cooler chats to formal business letters. Even so, lots of interested parties are left out—and probably others are included who don't really have a legitimate interest. It's

> Most managers fail to keep everyone fully informed.

hard to think clearly about who needs to know what. So let's apply a simple but powerful tactic to fix this all-too-common communications problem. I call it the Who Cares? list.

Who Cares?

The Who Cares? list is simply a list of all the people who have a legitimate interest in any event or action in which your involvement gives you access to useful information. And the point of a Who Cares? list is to make sure you get that information to all the people who might care about it.

How do you compile and use a Who Cares? list. Efficiently, very efficiently, or you'll waste all your time writing lists. I recommend making a single alphabetical list of all the people in your file of cards or your electronic address book. Just their names will do unless you want to get fancy and build a full database of contact information. This master list of everyone you already communicate with becomes the core of your Who Cares? list. But it isn't a complete list yet, because you need to ask yourself if there are some people missing from the list. Perhaps you don't have cards or addresses for some of your customers, teammates, or superiors. Add them in so they are available for Who Cares? analyses.

Now you've got a master list of people who *might* care. But do they? Use the list by scanning it and marking all who care about a specific activity or event you have new information about. A fancy way to do this is to make a big table of names down the left hand side and events or topics across the top. Check each intersection where someone would care about the event. They need a communication from you. And nobody else does.

If you get in the habit of doing a formal Who Cares? analysis, or at least an informal mental check of who might care, you will be able to focus your communications. You'll find you are wasting time communicating to lots of people who don't have a real need for your information. And you will also find you are forgetting to communicate information to many people who care about it and would definitely benefit from it. Aligning your communications to make sure

Take care of the sense, and the sounds will take care of themselves.

—LEWIS CAROLL, *Alice in Wonderland*

you get the right information to the right people is a powerful strategy. Too bad so few people use it!

Are You Making Sense?

There is one additional fundamental to keep in mind whenever you communicate. Perhaps the most fundamental fundamental of all. It is that communication can only be as good as the ideas it conveys. The famous philosopher Ludwig Wittgenstein once wrote that, "What can be said at all can be said clearly; and whereof one cannot speak thereof one must be silent." Translating this into streetwise business advice, the point is to shut up if you don't have something important to say! Too often, communications seem to be an end in and of themselves. When there is no clear or compelling idea that requires communication, people communicate all the more.

I don't want to harp on this point, because to do so would require a separate course on thinking. Let's just put it this way. If you don't have a well-developed idea or thought, don't communicate. Stop and think. Clear your head. Get focused. Figure out what the point really ought to be. As one of the Roman scholars of old once put it, "Grasp the subject, the words will follow."

What we all need to work on is to develop our own BS filter. Call it a *sense screen* if you prefer something more civilized. Whatever you call it, you'll know you have one when you stop for a fraction of a second before speaking or writing and think, "Okay, what am I going to say here, and *is it worth saying?*"

You'll be amazed how much this simple filter catches. And when you develop the mental habit of making sure you make sense, you will become more aware of how little sense most people really make. Too many people in business seem to be throwing away trash ideas or uncontrolled feelings when they communicate, instead of sharing something of value.

Perhaps the best single piece of streetwise advice I can give anyone who wants to be a great communicator is to *communicate less.* That way, what you do communicate will be just the good stuff, not the trash.

> Too many people in business seem to be throwing away trash ideas or uncontrolled feelings when they communicate, instead of sharing something of value.

Session 2

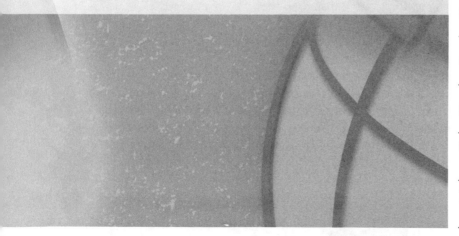

Pen Power

The word processor is mightier than the missile.

The pen is mightier than the sword, and, in this modern age, the word processor is mightier than the missile. Certainly in business the written word is still a dominant force, and, in fact, far more writing is done now that we have personal computers to write with. I bet there will never be a truly paperless business. And even if there is, there will be lots of virtual paper because people have to write and have to read.

Putting it in writing is essential when you have to communicate something complex, when you want to create a record of the communication, or when you need to make a good impression at a distance. The average employee in a Fortune 1000 business writes and sends fifteen message slips, seven faxes, eleven interoffice letters, ten e-mail messages, and eleven letters a day, according to a recent survey. But by the time you read these statistics, they will be far too low, because each time I see a survey of this type the number of messages sent goes up. I'd guess that the typical employee currently sends thirty or more e-mails a day, for example. That's a lot of business writing!

It's an interesting paradox that the introduction of new information technologies increases instead of decreases the amount of writing we must do. In fact, it's such an interesting paradox that researchers at Harvard have been studying and writing on it for years. Everyone assumed that computers and e-mail would make paper unnecessary. Not so. We generate more printed and hand-written notes than ever. And everyone assumed that cheap long-distance telephone calls, cell phones, and pagers would replace written communications. Not so. Often those calls end in a "send me something in writing" request. The more we communicate—and we certainly are communicating more than ever—the more we must write.

There are letters, faxes, memos, reports, plans, e-mails, Web pages (they are largely written content after all), brochures, catalogs, instructions and user's manuals, postcards, award certificates and plaques, thank-you notes and invitations, press releases, and probably many more written communications, but I need to pause for breath. So let's face it. To succeed in business today, *you need to be a better and faster writer than ever before*. Yet few people view themselves as good writers. Most find writing a difficult and unpleasant chore. And many people suffer from writer's block. Let's do something about those problems. Right now.

Writing Dos and Don'ts

Business writing is perhaps one of the best oxymorons ever coined. An oxymoron, in case you've forgotten, is a combination of contradictory words. And in business, it is almost impossible to find good writing. The average memo, e-mail, plan, proposal, or pitch letter is so poorly written that it certainly hurts business instead of helping. Few would call such stuff writing in the true sense of the term.

I think the low standards in business writing are a natural result of the importance of writing in business, which may sound funny. If writing is so important, why don't people make an effort to write well? But the reality is somewhat different from that ideal. In truth, business writing is so important that *everyone* has to write, and that includes lots of people who are not very good at writing. Most people don't see themselves as writers. They don't write lots of letters, poems, and stories at home, or take writing workshops for fun. Most people don't even read for pleasure any more. But when they get to work they are suddenly expected to write.

Fortunately, the low standard of writing in business is an advantage to you as it offers you an easy way in which to stand out as superior to the average. A little investment in your writing skills can go a long way toward positioning yourself as more sophisticated and polished than others. And it will permit you to communicate more effectively and efficiently, which has many subtle benefits to your career.

It's not that hard to look good on paper in the world of business since most people don't. I'll give you some simple guidelines in this lesson to help you produce superior business writing, starting with one that is a no-brainer but that most people nonetheless overlook. It is to *check your work* before sending it off to represent you to the world of business.

Check your work!

A vast majority of business letters, memos, and e-mails are dashed off in a hurry, permitting lots of errors to slip through that the authors could have fixed. You probably know how to proofread and correct, but do you apply these skills to business writing? Not unless you make a point of not only spellchecking but carefully proofreading everything you write.

Most Common Error?

Perhaps the most common error in business writing is to confuse its and it's. It's is a contraction for it is. It's only appropriate where you want to say "it is" but are in a hurry. Its is a possessive form of it. Quite different. Use its in a sentence such as "when the company was acquired, half of its employees were laid off." If you write "half of it's employees were laid off," you will look pretty stupid to anyone who knows how to write. By the way, there is a foolproof way to avoid this error. *Never ever use "it's"* in business writing. In formal written English you should avoid the it's contraction and spell out "it is" instead. If you follow that simple rule, you will never be tempted to misuse the contraction. Happily, it's—I mean it *is*—easy to avoid this most common of errors.

It can be surprisingly hard to find every "obvious" error, so you need to adopt a process that gives you more than one chance. There are two keys to good editing and correcting:

1. Set the writing aside for at least a short while before proofing it.
2. Read it carefully, with pencil or mouse in hand, fixing every problem you see.

> It can be surprisingly hard to find every "obvious" error, so you need to adopt a process that gives you more than one chance.

You can repeat this process to see if you find even more errors the second time around. Some writers need to subject their work to three or four rounds before it is really good. Others can do it in only one round of correction. (And some writers really need help with proofing. If that's true of you, you've got to find someone to review and correct your writing!)

In applying these two steps, make sure you design a system that works easily for you. For example, if composing on a computer, read your writing through and spellcheck it on screen. Then print it out and cue it up for proofreading later in the day. (You might try scheduling a half hour for proofing and improving your written materials. Save them in a pile or file until you have time to look at them.)

A time delay between writing and proofing does wonders. It makes errors more visible and leads you to improve upon or clarify your wording because it gives you enough distance to view the writing objectively.

Blow off the less important writing

Too busy to check your work? Many people say they are too rushed to bother correcting or even reading their own writing at work. That's like saying you're too busy when you get up to see what clothes you select from your closet and drawers so you just wear any random combination to work. It says a lot more about your lack of care for how you present yourself than it does about your schedule. You need to treat how you present yourself and how well you communicate as *high-priority issues* because they have a large impact on your progress in business. And writing is all about both factors; in writing you make a strong impression about yourself as well as communicating a message. Therefore, you need to realize that:

If you feel you have too much writing to take the time to proof and correct it, then you are probably writing too much.

Fewer, better-written communications will do a lot more for you and your business than many poor ones.

Stop and rank the things you must write in terms of importance to the business and to you. Then write the most important ones carefully and well, and blow off the others. Perhaps a phone message would do, or a one-sentence e-mail, or even better, try doing nothing at all! It's easy to waste time on letters, reports, and proposals that no one ever reads or that will prove to be of little or no consequence. Why bother? Better to concentrate on the things that really matter so you can do them well. Applying the basic principles of good time management to your writing will help you improve its quality.

Check your spellchecker

A common problem in this computerized age is for business writing to incorporate errors spellchecking programs don't catch. You have to be smarter than a spellchecker if you want to write well.

Your computer doesn't know whether a word should be possessive or plural, for example, which explains why so many unnecessary apostrophes appear in business writing today. "The company's vehicles do not carry accident insurance" is correct, but "Five company's will be represented at the meeting" is not. You'll be surprised how often such errors creep in once you start to look for them. I often see signs outside of otherwise respectable businesses in which a gratuitous apostrophe appears. Anybody who notices this error thinks the writer is stupid. And that's not a good impression to give others if you want to succeed in business.

Similarly, beware of words with more than one spelling, since spellcheckers aren't. Do and due; to, too and two; sight, site, and cite; canvass and canvas; current and currant; pare, pair, and pear; principal and principle; serial and cereal; capital and capitol; seller and cellar; fair and fare; cell and sell; blue and blew; stationery and stationary; all are examples of what the experts call *homophones*: words that sound alike but have different meanings. I run into trouble with them often because I don't think to check my spelling in a dictionary (a real one, not the spellchecker on my computer).

> Stop and rank the things you must write in terms of importance to the business and to you. Then write the most important ones carefully and well, and blow off the others.

It doesn't look very good to write,

"I think we should check to sea if the plain service will cell better at a lower fair"

if you are proposing to reduce the fare for a plane trip in order to see how many more seats you'll sell. Even if your idea works out, you will have made a pore (oops, I mean pour, or is that poor?) impression on anyone who reads your proposal.

(If you are enterprising and good with computers, you might want to compile a database of homophones and train your spellchecker to flag them so that you can check them to make sure you've got the right one. And if you work at Microsoft, maybe you can put this capability into the next Word release so I can use it too!)

Do you have *time* to be right?

Yes, this process will take you a little longer. So where will you get the extra time? By not responding to the least important e-mails and by sticking to one-word responses to less-important e-mails. Many messages can be handled with a simple "Yes," "No," "Agreed," or "Receipt acknowledged." Try it!

Also look out for topaz (oops, I mean typos) that produce a real, but not the right, word. It is easy and common to transpose or drop a letter and end up with an unintended word. Your spellchecker may not notice, but the reader will wonder what's the matter with you. Both of these sentences were passed by my spellchecker with flying colors, but one is going to go over a lot better with the boss than the other:

The sales figures are in for last quarter and they look better than we expected.

The salts figures arc on for lust quarter end they lock butter then au expectorated.

When spellcheckers make Freudian slips

Another common problem with spellchecked documents is that typos can transform words to less desirable but similarly spelled ones, such as trust to lust or tryst, manager to manger or mange, sox (sometimes people spell socks that way by accident) or six to sex, botch or batch to bitch, best to breast, boot to boob, pens or pennies to penis, sit

> Many messages can be handled with a simple "Yes," "No," "Agreed," or "Receipt acknowledged." Try it!

to shit, as to ass. Your spellchecker won't see anything strange about the appearance of such words in a memo to your boss or customers. It lacks an embarrassment checker. (Hey, programmers, can you add an embarrassment checker to the next Word release too? Thanks!)

Using the wrong word is only mildly embarrassing if it's just some random word, but when it's something inappropriate or shocking, then you're in big trouble. So the errors of this type to watch out for are ones that slip something inappropriate into your business communications, such as a slang term, an insulting word for some ethnic group, or something bedroom or bathroom oriented.

The best defense against these errors is to be aware that they do occur and to look for them in your own writing. And check your work! If you give yourself even a half hour between writing and rereading a report, memo, e-mail, or letter, you will notice such errors with ease.

E-mail Tip:
Never Compose!!!

Most people respond quickly to each e-mail, right there within their e-mail program or system. Which generally means they write and send responses without thinking, proofing, or spellchecking. As a result, the quality of business communications took a nose dive with the rise of e-mail. But you can avoid this common error by simply shifting over to a word processing file to draft your responses. (I keep two windows open, my e-mail window and a window with a new Word word processing file.) Then follow this process:

1. Write each e-mail response first in Word, WordPerfect, or whatever word processing software you prefer to use.
2. Run your spellchecker and whatever other editing programs you use. (Don't be tempted to switch this step with step 3, thinking you can avoid the need to spellcheck twice. The reason you spellcheck here in step 2 is to give the message time to incubate in your mind before you try to edit it. Without at least a few seconds of incubation, you won't be able to edit efficiently.)
3. Review each message by re-reading and making any obvious improvements (try to cut unnecessary ideas and words and anything that might offend the recipient).
4. If you made any edits on step 3, re-run that spellchecker just to be sure!
5. Copy (cut and paste) the whole message into your e-mail program's message screen. Now you have a perfect response instead of an off-the-cuff one.

Interesting Fact

Almost all resumes and job letters contain one or more errors, and roughly one in ten contain a misspelling in the candidate's name or address. Would you hire someone who can't get his or her name and address right on a resume?

Don't rush to distribute your writing. Admit that you are not superhuman and will hardly ever write something perfectly the first time through.

Don't misspell a name!

I just had lunch with a manager who complained bitterly about the continuing problem of her employees sending out letters to clients with the client's name or company misspelled or with an incorrect title. Sometimes even the name of the *writer's* company was misspelled. For some reason, many people forget to check the spelling of names and the accuracy of titles, addresses, and contact numbers. But the recipient takes great offense at such errors.

Since names aren't in the spellchecker you get with your word processing program, it's up to us humans to make sure they are right. I always make a point of checking the names, titles, and contact information against my source—a business card, letter, or whatever—especially if I've had an employee generate a letter or pile of letters. It just takes a second to do, and I'm surprised at how often I catch an error—about 10 percent of the time in my experience with various professional word processors.

Tip: If your employees keep making errors of this type, consider entering the names and numbers of your key business contacts or customers into the dictionaries for their spellcheckers. You can add any words you wish to a spellchecker: Just type them in a regular file, run the spellchecker, and select the add option when the checker doesn't recognize a name. It's a nice goal to make yourself more careful or your employees smarter, but if there is an easy way to make your computers smarter instead, that's the surest bet by far!

Advanced Business Writing

I could (and sometimes do) go on for hours and hours about how to write well. It's a big topic. Some people devote their lives to the pursuit of great writing. You don't want to do that, I bet, but you certainly want your writing to be good enough to advance your career, not hold it back. So one more round is definitely a good idea. Let's look at some additional ways you can achieve mastery of written business communications.

Please Use Standard Written English

People rarely speak in formal English, so it is a challenge to write using standard sentence structures and word usage. But people expect more polish and sophistication in written than in spoken English. A formal business letter, proposal, or plan certainly demands standard written English.

Let's start by straightening out the old I/me issue. I'm going to advocate a modern, nonstuffy policy in which you avoid only the most egregious errors, because rules of usage are loosening and "me" is acceptable in more places than it used to be. But usage still demands an "I" in certain situations. When you are the actor, the subject of the sentence, then use an I:

"I will be going to the meeting next week with you."

When somebody else is the main actor or subject of the sentence, then you step back to the end and become me:

"Are you going to the meeting with me?"

But that's not very difficult. Most people can construct those two sentences correctly by ear. Where our ears begin to fail us is when the sentences get more complex. For example, when other people enter the picture, it is easy to forget to put yourself after them. I and me go after any other people if there is a list, not before:

Wrong: "I and Joe will be going to the meeting." "Will you be going with me and Joe?"

Right: "Joe and I will be going to the meeting." "Will you be going with Joe and me?"

> A formal business letter, proposal, or plan certainly demands standard written English.

And when I or me is part of a list including the names of others, most people lose track of whether to use I or me. For example, the following error is common:

Wrong: "Joe and me will be going to the meeting."

Your ear would catch the error if you wrote "Me will be going," but the error is disguised by the addition of Joe. So when you proof your sentences, leave the other names out and say the sentence out loud with only the I or me in it. If you drop the Joe and say "Me will be going" your ear will correct it to I with ease.

Danger! Sentence Under Construction

You also need to watch out for poorly constructed sentences of all sorts. I don't expect you to write poetic prose, although it's nice if you can. But I certainly expect you to *write complete sentences that are easy to follow*. This is not a difficult requirement, but it is frequently violated in business writing. When you combine a few typos with some incomplete sentences and awkward sentence structures, you are not really communicating. And you certainly don't look like a pro who is on the way to the top.

Take the following sample from a memo announcing a new teamwork initiative:

"As you may have heard we are switching to a team system as last month's announcement made clear. That team leaders will be holding initial meetings to determine team roles and structures. If you are a team leader you should have attended the orientation session and pick up your packet and list of team members from me."

What exactly is this manager trying to say? Hasty writing has jumbled her sentences and concealed her meaning. Her second sentence is alarming because it is not actually a complete sentence, so the reader worries that something important has been left out. She would do well to use simpler, shorter sentences, each with one clear message.

Simple sentence structures make it easy to avoid trouble, especially if you are in a hurry. Starting with "As you may have heard" sets you up for a complex structure, one that many people have trouble writing their way out of. Actually, I could have said that better

> Sentence structure is innate but whining is acquired.
>
> —WOODY ALLEN

myself! How about this way of putting what should be a basic rule of all business writing:

Start with your main point to avoid confusing sentence structures.

Every sentence should have but one clear point. Any sentences lacking a clear point should be cut.

It is simpler and easier for all involved to say, for example, "We are switching to a team system." That's how I'd edit the first sentence of the above quote, which originally read, "As you may have heard we are switching to a team system as last month's announcement made clear." It isn't really relevant that some may have heard about this switch, or that they should have heard about it at last month's meeting. All the writer really needs to do is make the point that this switch is required. Then the rest of the communication can get down to explaining how to make the switch. Writing is not as complicated when you focus on the key points and keep the sentences simple, is it?

Note also that the writer's use of lengthy, complicated sentence structures led to considerable ambiguity. The meaning gets lost if the sentences are complicated. Take this sentence:

"If you are a team leader you should have attended the orientation session and pick up your packet and list of team members from me."

It's long enough that the author failed to notice an inconsistency in tense. "You should have attended" is in the past tense, but "pick up your packet" is in the present tense. The meaning is unclear as a result. Were they supposed to pick up their packets at the orientation session (and if so, what should they do if they didn't get one)? Or perhaps the author means to say that team leaders can *now* pick up packets. There is no way to be sure about how to interpret this sentence. If it were confined to the main point, however, it would stand a far better chance of being clear. For instance, it could be rewritten to say, "I hope leaders have the packets we handed out at the last orientation." And once the author managed to write a sentence as clear as that, it would be obvious that another sentence was also needed. Something like, "But leaders missing their packets can get copies from me this week."

Let's see how the initial quotation looks now that we've simplified each of its sentences. It now reads,

> Writing is not as complicated when you focus on the key points and keep the sentences simple.

"We are switching to a team system. I hope leaders have the packets we handed out at the last orientation. But leaders missing their packets can get copies from me this week."

It's so much easier to write simple sentences well. Try it, you'll like it!

Is Isn't Okay?

Standard written English also avoids slang and contractions. Contractions aren't appropriate in a formal business letter, a resume, a loan application, or a business plan. They cheapen the feel of the communication. But standards are evolving, and contractions are increasingly appropriate in less formal writing, such as e-mails and memos. I've started using contractions in my books, since I write informally as if speaking to my reader. So use your judgment about contractions and slang. Avoid them if you feel formality is appropriate. Use them if you want to capture a less formal feeling. Formal writing is written for the eye, therefore, it follows the rules of written language. Informal writing is written for the ear and can follow the rules of spoken language instead. But either way, make sure you *follow* those rules.

Clarify Your Thoughts First

You simply cannot write well if you haven't thought well first. Most writing suffers from a lack of clear thinking. That's why your English teachers used to make you write outlines. But formal outlines are a hassle, so try writing a simple *idea list* before drafting your business writing.

An idea list is a short list of the ideas you need to convey in your writing, in the order you want to convey them. For example, the manager wanting to write a memo to employees about a new team work structure might write the following idea list:

- Need to start teams this month.
- Leaders need packets.
- Get from me if don't have.
- Leaders should set up meetings.

> Good heavens! For more than forty years I have been speaking prose without knowing it.

Ideas often need to be clarified and untangled.

- Packets explain how to run the first meeting.
- I need a report from each leader after first meeting.
- Report should identify any problems so we can work on them.

A list like this is clear and easy to write from. But it might not start out as clear. Ideas often need to be clarified and untangled, so the idea list can take longer than the actual writing. For instance, the first draft of the above idea list might have looked more like this:

- Were they at last month's meeting?
- Packets have instructions, so leaders who don't have packets need them. Get from me?
- They may run into problems, which I need to hear about.

The first idea on the list isn't very helpful, so it can be cut. (You'll find that happens frequently.) The second and third are important but need work. Both are not as clearly thought through as they could be, and both could be broken out into more than one idea to make them clearer. When you work on this idea list, you get something much clearer and more helpful—as we saw a moment ago.

It's easy to write from a clear idea list. Much of the difficulty people say they have with writing is really difficulty with thinking. Do the thinking up front and the writing takes care of itself.

Write Active Sentences, Not Passive Ones

Anyone who writes or speaks in the passive voice gets my vote for least likely to succeed. It is a dreadful but increasingly widespread habit. Passive sentence constructions obscure the meaning and make you sound stuffy and standoffish. Not sure what I'm talking about? Just click on CSPAN and listen to any politician speaking and you'll get an earful of passive constructions in a hurry.

Here are some examples:

"The teamwork program has been redesigned."

"There have been some quality errors in production this week."

"A problem has come to my attention."

These are dreadful sentences. They are passive, meaning that you can't tell who took what action. Passive sentences hide the actors. They make it sound like YOU have something to hide. Maybe you did something wrong and don't want to be found out. Or perhaps you just don't know what happened and are concealing your ignorance.

Look at each of those examples of passive sentences again. Who did what? It's not clear. In the first sentence, somebody has redesigned the teamwork program, but you can't tell who. Why not? Are they ashamed of their work? Afraid of the consequences? That is the clear implication, and so it puts everyone hearing it on the defensive. They will assume that the new design is bad and will react negatively. With passive sentences, resistance to your message is guaranteed! (Oops, I mean, *I* guarantee resistance. That's the active form.) Passive sentences always create more resistance and negative feelings than active ones.

Let's redesign those three dreadful sentences by making them active. It's easy. Just figure out who did what and put them into the sentences:

"I have redesigned the teamwork program."

"My work group ran into some quality problems this week."

"The president brought a problem to my attention."

Much better! Now we know where we stand. Active sentences communicate, whereas passive sentences confuse and conceal. Leave that game to the politicians. (Oh, and if you are an ace programmer, can you teach my computer to search for and flag all uses of "would," "has been," "has come to," and similar has and have phrases? These are sure indicators of passive sentences.)

> One of our defects as a nation is a tendency to use "weasel words." When a weasel sucks eggs the meat is sucked out of the egg. If you use a "weasel word" after another, there is nothing left of the other.
> —THEODORE ROOSEVELT

From Writer's Block to Writing for Fun

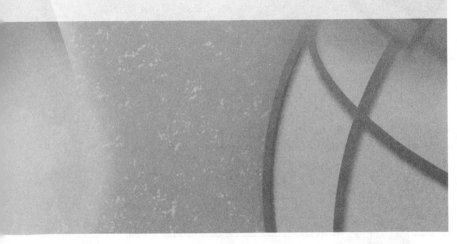

In this session I want to share two things that I think are extremely valuable. One is a simple trick I use to overcome writer's block. I don't want you sitting and staring at a blank page or screen when you could be cranking out good writing. Life's too short to tolerate writer's block! The other thing I want to share with you is the idea that writing can be an exciting, rewarding journey of personal discovery and development. When you stop treating it like a chore and start treating it like the fascinating challenge it is, writing can become a wonderful adventure.

> Writing is easy. All you do is sit staring at a blank sheet of paper until the drops of blood form on your forehead.
>
> —GENE FOWLER

Overcome Writer's Block with One Easy Trick!

I estimate that a million hours a year are wasted in U.S. businesses by people who are stuck on how to get their writing started. If we could overcome the problem of writer's block, most managers could work at least an hour less each week.

Writer's block is generally experienced at the beginning of the writing process. Do you ever sit and stare at a blank Word document file on your computer screen? Do you spend time starting, then crossing out, numerous attempts at a first sentence of a draft memo? Ever stare at an e-mail wondering where to start your response to it? Most people do.

I also know for a fact that many managers spend weeks and weeks obsessing about how to get started on writing a business plan or marketing plan. Some of these people with writer's block call me every week after reading one of my books. And I find that they are happy *once I get them started*. The hard part is knowing where to start.

One of the causes of writer's block is a failure to think before writing. You can't start writing if you don't know why you are writing or what you want to say. So do that idea list I described earlier. Then you'll know why you are writing.

And also try this easy but highly effective trick. Start by saying,

"I am writing to..."

Tell them why you are writing. It's a simple, straightforward beginning, and it gets you off in the right direction right away. Here are some of the forms it can take:

"I am writing to ask you if you will meet me to discuss our new product line."

"I am writing to update you on the progress of our team."

"I am writing to ask you about the raise you said I would qualify for at the beginning of this month."

"I am writing to report a projected shortfall in inventories of product X."

"I am writing to share the ideas generated in our brainstorming session."

"I am writing in response to your request for an analysis of the department's budget."

"I am writing to request a loan from your bank to fund the acquisition of new vehicles for my business."

"I am writing to complain about the poor service we received and request a refund."

"I am writing to ask you to pay the back balance you owe us."

It's wonderful how letters, memos, e-mails, and reports seem to write themselves when you start with that simple phrase, "I'm writing to. . . ." Not only that, but the result is shorter and better written as well. The magic of this trick is that it gets you to the main point in your opening sentence. And that's good writing, especially in business where everyone is in such a hurry to find out what you have to say.

If you cannot finish the "I am writing to . . . " sentence, then perhaps you don't have a good reason to be writing. Sometimes that happens. For example, you might feel that it is appropriate to respond to someone because they wrote you. But if there is really nothing to say, you won't be able to tell them why you are writing. In which case, don't bother. No point sending a communication that begins, "I am writing to write you."

> The magic of this trick is that it gets you to the main point in your opening sentence.

Learn From Your Writing

Most of us don't improve our writing skills because we do not seek out feedback about our writing. For example, how often do you look back at documents you wrote and reflect upon the quality of your writing?

What? You don't save copies of your business writing to analyze later on? Well, neither do most people, but unless you look back and learn from your past performance *you will never improve*. Apply the principles of feedback and learning to your business writing and it will soon be well above average.

Here's another even more radical suggestion. *Find a real editor to help you out*. Why not hire an expert to review and mark up some examples of your writing? People with Ph.D.s in English are among the least employable of all human beings, so you should have no trouble finding an expert who'll give you a quick tutorial or some editing for a very modest price. (Maybe just a dinner at the nearest

Allegory:
When Giants of Industry Write

I occasionally work with one of those people who just seem to know how to grow businesses and make money. His name is Tom LeDuc, and he has built a number of successful businesses over the years. His latest venture involves the creation and marketing of video courses, and to do that he needs to write good scripts. But he freely admits that writing isn't his strong suit. In fact, he says he cannot even type. So how can he produce great video scripts? He solves this problem in two ways.

First, he does something he is better at than writing; he talks. As are many managers, he is accustomed to speaking and presenting and can talk a blue streak. So he often dictates his ideas instead of struggling to write them all down.

Then he turns them over to a writer. As a result, Tom is able to create some of the most compelling writing I've ever seen. He may not "be" a writer, but he sure knows how to write! The point is that if you are a manager, you should be able to manage any task to a good end result, whether it's something you do yourself or something you find others to do for you.

restaurant!) Try calling nearby business schools and asking them for the names of the people who teach their students how to write. Or call the nearest English department of a liberal arts or community college and ask for the names of underemployed experts.

Ever Hang Out with Real Writers?

There is another radical step you can take if you really want to improve your writing. Join a writer's group or sign up for a writing workshop. There are such things in your town, but you may not have encountered them because they cater to writers, not business people.

But since you are in the business world, your income is probably five to fifty times as high as the average fiction writer or poet in your community, and you will find the cost of writer's workshops and events to be trivial. Not only that, but you will find it surprisingly entertaining to get out of your business box and spend some time with people who sit around a room reading their short stories or journal entries to each other. Beats watching TV when you get home from work, that's for sure!

Help is out there in many forms and places. You just need to use it. Furthermore, you *can* afford it if you know where to look to find underemployed experts or tap into the writing community in your area. And if you think about it in terms of opportunity costs, you can't afford *not* to. Business writing is simply too important to overlook.

Writers, like teeth, are divided into incisors and grinders.

—WALTER BAGEHOT
(By the way, which are you?)

Session 5

Communicating with Voice Mail Systems

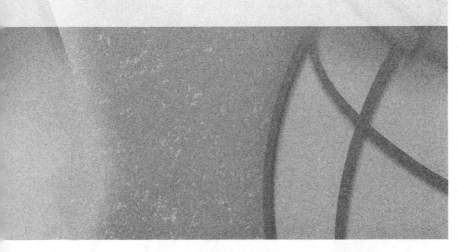

I n this electronic age we may still do business with people, but much of the time we have to communicate with machines.

Answering systems block our telephone access to the people we wish to speak with, and when we try to end-run this problem we often find ourselves communicating with their computers or fax machines instead. Often the best strategy is to grit your teeth and simply communicate through voice mail messages. I find I increasingly have business relationships maintained largely or even entirely through exchanged messages. It seems a bit impersonal, but on the other hand it is quite efficient. And for routine exchanges, efficiency is probably the priority anyway.

But what about those many times when you want to try to talk to someone in order to enlist their help or make a sale? Leaving a voice mail message doesn't seem like a viable option, but if you refine the message, it can be highly effective. One of the things I always try to do is to find out whether a key contact I'm courting prefers the phone, letters, or e-mail. Everybody has a favorite channel, and with many executives it's verbal communications. If so, then you are far better off leaving a brief voice mail message than writing the ultimate business letter.

But how do you communicate effectively through the voice mail maze? There are some tricks to it. In fact, phone mail systems are so important these days that some firms are hiring communications specialists to train people in how to use these systems more effectively! For example, Steve Kaye, president of the business skills training firm Personal Quality, offers training on communicating via voice mail.

Here are some tips to keep in mind when preparing to tackle a phone mail system:

> Everybody has a favorite channel, and with many executives it's verbal communications.

- Make sure you obtain extensions so you can make your way to the right voice mail in the first place. As Kaye observes, "If you know a person's extension, voice mail systems can facilitate an efficient connection. Otherwise, many voice mail systems are a disgrace to the organizations that installed them." And a barrier to your communicating your message. So make it a practice to ask for and collect extension numbers. They are more valuable than phone numbers these days!

- If you don't have and can't find the right extension, bypass voice mail systems by pretending you don't have a touch-tone phone. Wait for a human being to tell you the extension or make the connection for you.

- What do you do if there is no way to talk to a human? Many of the newer systems actually bump you out if you don't input a correct extension. Not very friendly. One way to cope with this is to try dialing a zero. Even if it's not offered as an option, it will often lead you to a live secretary somewhere. Another way is to select any option that promises to lead you to a live person, then ask that person for the extension of the person you want. Then there is the fallback option of communicating by e-mail, fax, or letter a request for someone to give you his or her extension. Sometimes it comes down to that.

- When you do succeed in getting into someone's voice mail, it's easy to mumble, stutter, and bumble your way through a confused message. The problem is we naturally tend to prepare ourselves for a conversation, not a one-way message. Yet in today's communication environment, you have to face the fact that most of your calls will be to voice mail systems, not to people. To leave a good message, you have to prepare it. If you aren't prepared, you won't give a good voice mail performance.

- How do you prepare for a great voice mail performance? Start by writing a simple list of the points you need to communicate, such as:
    - your name
    - your phone number and e-mail
    - reminder that they said they'd try a sample of your new product
    - request for them to call to schedule the delivery
    - a suggested time when they can reach you in person if they wish to

That's a communications plan. It only takes a moment to create, but it will dramatically improve the effectiveness of your call. Oh, but there is one more thing you have to do to be fully prepared. You have to run through your plan, pretending you are leaving the mes-

> To leave a good message, you have to prepare it. If you aren't prepared, you won't give a good voice mail

> Effective, well-planned voice mail messages are a great communication form in their own right.

sage and talking to each of the points on your list. Why? Because *you have to be sure you can get your message recorded in less than two minutes*. Many systems cut you off at the two minute mark, and that spoils your performance and keeps you from communicating everything you need to get across. So just check the timing of your message before making the call and recording that message.

If you follow the approach I just described, you will leave clear, powerful, well-spoken voice mail messages. This puts you in a very small minority, the top one percent of business communicators! And you will find that effective, well-planned voice mail messages are a great communication form in their own right. They can make sales, collect receivables, build networks, generate enthusiasm for projects, or simply stimulate return calls.

But What if They Actually *Answer* Their Phone?

Of course, you might go to all the trouble of planning a wonderful one-and-a-half minute voice mail performance, only to find that the person picks up the phone instead of letting it go through to the voice mail system. Don't worry! The planning you did to prepare your message guarantees you a better telephone conversation too. You will be more focused and clear, and you will take less of their time to communicate your message. They will appreciate that. And if they have the time to chat, you can let them draw you into a more extended conversation after you've made your key points. But should they be in a hurry, you will be assured of an effective conversation. Whatever is going on at the other end of the telephone line, your preparations will lead you to be (no surprise here) better prepared!

The Medium of the New Millennium?

The Internet is hot, plain-paper fax machines are a great leap forward over the old technology, and overnight mail is still a viable option. But let's face it, none of them are a good substitute for the human voice when you need to make real contact with someone important. That's why voice mail is emerging as one of the most important new media for business communications.

One study commissioned by Pitney Bowes concluded that the average employee in a U.S. business leaves ten voice mail messages each day—which comes out to hundreds every month.

Rather than grumbling about phone systems, why not admit we have a new medium on our hands and learn how to master it? Any new communications medium can be seen as an opportunity. This one certainly is. Heck, if you know what you're doing and dig around for the right extensions, you can deliver a personal message to the CEO of every Fortune 500 company. They might not talk to you in person, but you can probably get them to listen to two minutes of your voice. That's enough to pitch your latest great idea and then some if you take the time to design a good voice mail message.

I like this new medium. I can work with it. By the way, what's your extension?

> You can deliver a personal message to the CEO of every Fortune 500 company.

Giving Killer Presentations (Instead of Getting Killed by Them)

As managers, we have to present constantly. Whenever you need to speak in a formal or pressured setting, you are giving a presentation. It might be as simple as your boss asking you to come into her office and give you a report on your team's progress. Or it might be a situation in which you have to make a sales presentation to a client, give a tour to a visitor, or stand up in a staff meeting to give a report on a project. All of these situations rely on your presentation skills. And all of them put you in the spotlight, which means that you will make a lasting impression on your audience—for good or for bad—depending upon how well it goes.

Then there are the less frequent but even more important major presentations. You have to give a speech at a conference or sales meeting, lead a session at a training event, or represent your company on a panel or in a televised interview. Maybe it's just a within-company event at which you have to hand out some employee rewards. Regardless of the context, the fact that you are presenting to an audience of significant size in a somewhat formal, stage-like setting makes it a major presentation that requires considerable skill and often considerable preparation as well.

How well do you handle these many and varied presentations? Are you comfortable, natural, and engaging so that your audience is sad to see the presentation end? Nothing personal, but I seriously doubt it. At least from a statistical perspective, the odds are very slim that you are a master of the presentation arts, because so few managers are.

In fact, the large majority of managers suffers from presentation anxiety. They get stage fright. Their palms sweat, their vision clouds, their ears ring, the blood rushes to their face, they perspire freely under their shirts or dresses, their hands shake, their legs may even shake and shiver, they may suffer from nausea or need to go to the bathroom, and they typically feel weak and disoriented. The audience of course picks up on their anxiety, which makes it even worse.

The Honest Truth About Performance Anxiety

I once saw the results of a survey that asked people what their greatest fears were. Fear of death was in the top ten, naturally. Fears of illness and injury were high, too. But at the very top, the number one fear, was *public speaking*. On average, people are more afraid of public speaking than of dying! It's no wonder people have such a hard time giving good presentations.

Nobody can give a good presentation—or even remember what the heck they said—when they are suffering from presentation anxiety. Stage fright is the single biggest cause of poor presentations, so it stands to reason that you've got to lick any presentation anxiety you feel in order to improve your performance significantly.

Yet no business school I've ever heard of offers courses aimed at eliminating stage fright, and even the corporate training courses on presentation skills don't deal with this key issue very effectively. In general, the advice people get falls into the "mind over matter" camp.

For example, one of the leading presentation guides advises you to reduce anxiety by visualizing yourself as feeling relaxed, by breathing to loosen your muscles, by flexing and moving your major muscle groups to release tension, and by making eye contact with the audience.

Sorry, but that just won't work! The more you try such methods, the more panicked you are likely to get.

I remember distinctly when, in my early years as a manager and consultant, I was terrified of public speaking. Even though I have since given hundreds of presentations and now feel completely comfortable in front of an audience or camera, I still recall the terrible feelings of anxiety I used to have. I remember those feelings distinctly because they were so intensely unpleasant that I could not possibly forget them. I remember those feelings more distinctly than I remember the pain I felt when I broke my leg, or when I had my wisdom teeth out. I've never given birth, but my wife tells me that her initial public speaking experiences were scarier even than childbirth. So I want to be perfectly honest with you about presentation anxiety. It is a terribly powerful thing and *you cannot conquer it through will power alone*!

You cannot "get those butterflies in your stomach to fly in the same direction" as one old saying puts it. No amount of breathing, wiggling limbs, or visualizing yourself as relaxed will stop you from feeling

Stage fright: nervousness felt at appearing before an audience.
—*Webster's Dictionary*

like hell. And if you try looking members of your audience in the eye, you will probably feel a sudden attack of panic rather than relaxation.

It's scary when you aren't used to presenting. I can't talk you out of that fear and you can't talk yourself out of it. The fear is very real. So when a trainer tells you, as one book I'm looking at right now puts it, to "learn to make the stress work for you," don't feel bad that you can't do it. Nobody can. Stress doesn't work for you, it works *against* you in a presentation. If you are uncomfortable with the situation, face the reality that you are going to suffer some or all of those terrible performance anxiety symptoms. No way around it.

So the first thing to do when preparing for a presentation is to anticipate how anxious the situation will make you. As Figure 1-2 shows, stress varies directly with the size of your audience. You are used to talking to people one-on-one, so an audience of one cannot produce very high levels of anxiety. Even if it's your boss, a job interview, or something else of major importance, there is no way that audience of one can make you as rattled as an audience of five or ten. Similarly, when audience size jumps up into the tens or hundreds, the anxiety is likely to be far higher. So audience size is a simple, easy predictor of anxiety. You can and should anticipate higher anxiety levels with larger audiences. This means you need to prepare so as to give yourself more support when you face a larger audience rather than a smaller audience—a technique I'll explain in detail in a few minutes.

Anxiety levels are also higher if the subject of the presentation is less familiar to you, if the setting is uncomfortable and new, if the context is more formal, and if you do not know the people in the audience very well. So consider all of these secondary factors, and if some of them apply, then figure you will have even more anxiety than you normally would with an audience of that size. *You need to make a realistic assessment of how anxious you are going to feel.* Don't deceive yourself on this point.

Look once more at Figure 1-2. The good news it presents is the powerful relationship between experience and comfort. The more times you have presented to a similar sized audience, the lower your stress will be. In fact, the only way to overcome presentation anxiety is to give lots of presentations. Sorry, I know that's not a pleasant

> You need to make a realistic assessment of how anxious you are going to feel. Don't deceive yourself on this point.

FIGURE 1-2 PRESENTATION ANXIETY

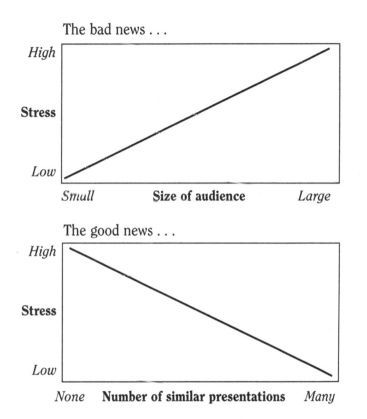

The bad news . . .

The good news . . .

cure, but at least it works. I can guarantee results. I know it worked for me and for every other person I know who now gives presentations with ease. (They all started out with stage fright, by the way. *Everybody* does.)

When I first started teaching business school classes, for example, I was terrified. I would arrive hours early and slink around, sweating and worrying about how it would go. I'd check the room and switch the overhead projector on and off ten times to make sure it worked. I'd suddenly think that I had left my notes behind and have to pull them out and check them. Ten minutes later, I'd have to check them again. And when I first walked into the classroom and saw all those people sitting there staring at me, my mind would go blank and I'd feel a strong urge to run away and never come back. But the amazing thing was that these feelings got a little better with each class until I felt reasonably comfortable in that classroom by the end of the semester. Experience had worked its magic.

Of course, the first time I taught in a big lecture hall I went through the whole process again. And the first time I gave a speech at a large convention hall it happened again. And the first time I was interviewed for a radio program I re-experienced some of those same symptoms. Then when I went on a TV talk show for the first time it happened all over again. But over time, each of these contexts became more familiar until the stress levels were low enough that I could concentrate on what I said and how I said it, instead of being preoccupied by fear.

To anticipate your stress level, then, you need to factor in your level of experience with an audience of the type you must face in your next presentation. If you have only worked with an audience of this size and type once or twice, you can expect to feel considerable performance anxiety. If you've been in front of such audiences a dozen times, your anxiety will be moderate. And if you've worked this sort of audience twenty or more times, it should be a piece of cake.

Prepare for Your Level of Anxiety

Now that you've considered audience size, your past experience, and other factors, you can realistically predict how anxious you will be for a specific presentation. If it's an unfamiliar situation, you know you'll feel performance anxiety. So plan on it. Prepare for it. Make sure you have all the props, crutches, and supports you need to make it through an unpleasant, anxious situation. That's the only realistic way to tackle performance anxiety. First, face the fact that you will feel it. And second, plan your presentation so as to make it possible to do a good job in spite of your performance anxiety.

How do you prepare for performance anxiety? There are lots of little tricks that will help you get through an anxious performance. In general, they involve the use of props to help you out. Props are great. You can lean on them. They take much of the burden off of you, thereby making your presentation job easier and reducing the anxiety. Use as many of them as you think your feelings and the situation warrant:

- Written script to read (use large type; staple pages in order)
- Flip chart with pre-written notes and pre-drawn diagrams
- Lectern you can hide behind and hold onto
- Overheads with an outline of your points (use really large type and number them to help avoid confusion over order)
- Slides with an outline of your points (so you can present in the dark)
- Handouts that summarize, illustrate, or support your talk (get them reading so they aren't staring at you!)
- Index cards, each with key facts or words for a section of your talk
- A video you can show to reduce the amount of presenting you have to do
- A guest speaker or second presenter to reduce the amount of presenting you have to do
- A Powerpoint or other computer-based presentation
- A chair or stool to sit in while you speak (if this makes you feel more comfortable)
- Music you can play at the beginning of your presentation (if this makes it easier to get started)
- Posters or other displays you can put around the room (to get people milling around instead of staring at you)
- Any activity you can ask the audience to do (to take the heat off of you and reduce the amount of speaking you must do)
- Breakout formats in which you give your presentation to smaller groups in a smaller room. (If you can control the schedule and format, it's better to give your presentation three times over, once to each of the divisions of your company for example, than to give it once to an audience three times the size.)

All of these tactics are designed to make *you* feel better. Hopefully you can find ways to make them work for the audience too.

There are lots of little tricks that will help you get through an anxious performance.

> It's not what I do, but the way I do it. It's not what I say, but the way I say it.
>
> —MAE WEST

In theory at least, any one of these tactics might be good as a presentation method. But in truth, the focus here is on making you happy, because if you aren't happy, you'll never make the audience happy.

It would be nice not to have to worry about your emotional state, but that's unrealistic if the situation is one that you know will produce performance anxiety. So instead of following the usual advice, which pushes you to get up there without any props and deliver a rousing speech from memory, you had better plan on using lots of props. When anxiety is an issue, the streetwise rule to follow is:

The more you can hide behind your presentation tactics, the better!

I hope you don't think I'm being cynical when I say that. I'm really quite serious. When anxiety is likely, the rules of presenting are very different from when it is not. Let the pros who are used to big audiences do it their way. Until you gain their experience, our way should be the secure way. Do everything you can to make it an emotionally viable, livable experience for yourself. If you can control the context with less anxiety by making your job easier, then you will do a better job. That's all there is to it.

I'm not going to tell you to give up your current props and work on delivering a more animated, professional, ad lib presentation if you are still struggling with fear. What you need to do is deal with that fear. By using fear-reducing props and tactics, you will be better able to meet at least minimum performance standards. You can realistically plan to do a competent job in spite of your fear. And that means you will be willing to make presentations. You will seek out opportunities to present and receive more invitations to present as well. Which will get you up your experience curve and help you get over your stage fright the only way anyone really can—by practicing. Once you reach the point where you are comfortable with the kind of audience and situation in which you must present, then you can begin to think about how to improve your style and approach. You can switch gears and start working on the quality of your presentation skills instead of working on your fears. Let's make that switch now and focus on how to improve presentations when you are feeling comfortable enough to think about the fine points.

Improving Your Presentation Style

There are two schools of thought when it comes to style. One holds that style needs to be refined and developed until you have a well-learned role you play in front of audiences, rather like an actor playing a part. In this approach, your presentations become highly stylistic and you are truly a different person when you present. If you develop a good role for yourself, this approach can produce success. You can learn to be humorous, dramatic, emotional, forceful, or charismatic as a speaker. Some people go as far as to watch videos of their favorite speakers over and over, imitating inflection and mannerisms until they can "do" the style with ease. (Politicians often choose this approach to refining their presentation skills.)

The other approach to style is to relax and let your own natural personality and style emerge. An old spiritual tune epitomizes this philosophy with the line, "This little light of mine, I'm gonna let it shine. Not gonna make it shine, Lord, just gonna let it shine." The idea is that a natural, comfortable, honest style is the most likely to win over your audience and the easiest for you to do really well. Just let you own light shine through. Don't try to be somebody you aren't.

Which approach to style is right? I think it simply comes down to individual personalities. In some people, the theatrical, showy style is what they feel most comfortable with. They may not be ready or willing to be honest and natural with an audience. Or they may not feel the audiences they address are ready for that. In which case they should go ahead and "put on" the style they think best suits the occasion.

But in most business presentations, an artificial style is inappropriate and will not make as good an impression as a more natural style. You don't have to act. You just have to act like yourself. Creating a role that isn't you makes it much harder to play the role well. I'm generally in favor of honest, natural approaches in which you don't worry overly about style.

> When we see a natural style, we are quite surprised and delighted, for we expected to see an author and we find a man.
> —BLAISE PASCAL
>
> • • •
>
> He does it with a better grace, but I do it more natural.
> —WILLIAM SHAKESPEARE, *TWELFTH NIGHT*

Refining Your Style

My earlier remarks concerning the value of a natural, honest style address the problem of finding your style. But once you find a comfortable, appropriate style for your presentations, the next step is to learn to execute that style with ease and skill. It's not enough to just be yourself in front of an audience. You have to be yourself *well*. You want to show them your best side, not your average or worst. So once you've found your style, it's time to start refining it. You need to take a closer look at what you do and say. You need to analyze your own presentation style.

To analyze your own presentation style, you can ask yourself questions such as the following (based on Dorothy Grant Hennings's *Mastering Classroom Communication*):

- Is my speaking voice monotonous?
- Do I use gestures to speak for me?
- Am I physically overactive in communicating? Underactive?
- What messages do I send through my facial expressions? Do my facial expressions add to or distract from my message?
- Are my words, body, and voice sending the same message, or do I send conflicting messages?

Questions such as these help you begin to see yourself as the audience does. They increase your awareness of your style and approach, and they help you target areas in need of improvement. In general, when we begin asking such questions, we discover that we are not nearly as expressive as we could be. In fact, the unpleasant reality is that almost all managers give boring presentations. So the best way for most of us to refine our style is to work on becoming more expressive.

Expressing Yourself

Most of us are fairly inhibited when it comes to presentations. We speak in a monotone and hold ourselves rigid and still. As a result, we bore our audiences to death. Nervousness accentuates this tendency toward boredom. When you're nervous, it's hard to speak in an animated manner or gesture as naturally as you normally do. You need to work on overcoming any nervousness you feel about public speaking—we talked about that already. But you also need to practice being animated and interesting when you speak. You need to work on being *expressive*.

> You need to analyze your own presentation style.

Self-awareness is the key to improved communications. Any activities or exercises you do to make yourself more aware of how you express yourself will help you become more expressive and effective as a public speaker, and as a communicator in general. I really mean any exercises. Listen to a tape recording or phone message of your voice. Talk to yourself in the mirror. Set up a cheap video recorder on a tripod in the back of the room and record your next presentation. Or simply practice your presentation in front of a video recorder at home. All such activities produce a dramatic rate of learning and improvement. They are well worth the trouble and the initial embarrassment you may feel.

There are also plenty of structured training activities that can help. Professional trainers who coach public speakers and actors have lots of great activities, but some of them may seem a bit "out there" to you if you aren't used to the world of actors. For example, it's a great training activity to pretend you are a tree, jellyfish, or dog, and act out this role through body movements. But it's pretty silly and not something you're likely to do in the office. So I tend to favor simpler, more presentation-related training activities.

Here are a few good self-training activities I think you'll find easy and helpful. Each of them involves reading a simple paragraph or list out loud in different ways. Pick something without much inherent interest. A page of the phone book or dictionary or an encyclopedia entry are all ideal for your first efforts. Their lack of inherent meaning or interest allows you to focus on how you perform, not what you say. If you grow tired of reading dull content, however, you can allow yourself to "graduate" to something more interesting. I recommend the text of a lengthy print advertisement torn from a magazine.

In each of the following activities, your goal is to practice a specific presentation skill by exaggerating your use of it while reading out loud:

> *Lesson 1: Tone training.* Practice using tone by making your voice go up and down the musical scale while reading. If this is hard for you, first say the notes of the scale in a singsong voice: "Doe re me fa so la ti doe" or "La la la la la la la la." Now repeat the same tones while reading the words, one

> **Self-awareness is the key to improved communications.**

word per tone. Go up the whole scale, then back down. Keep traveling the scale as you read. A few minutes of this and you will have tuned your ear and voice to the tone of your voice as you speak. Now go back and read the same words in a more natural, pleasant manner, only varying tone as you think you need to make your words and sentences sound interesting. Listen to the tone specifically and experiment with using it in subtle ways to make your speaking more pleasant to listen to.

Lesson 2: Volume training. Practice varying the volume or loudness of your voice by pretending that you are a radio that someone is slowly turning all the way up, then slowly turning down. Read out loud, starting with a very quiet voice and gradually getting louder with each word until you are speaking as loudly as you possibly can without shouting. Now gradually reduce the volume. Repeat this sequence multiple times until you feel you are more aware of the volume of your voice and comfortable with your control over it. Then go back and read the same material again, this time varying volume only as much as you think you need to in order to make the reading sound interesting (whether it is or not).

Lesson 3: Emotion training. Now read your material out loud with the goal of expressing a particular emotion through your reading. Start with one emotion. Then reread trying to express another emotion. Here are a series of emotions you can use for this exercise:

> Round 1: Fear and anxiety
>
> Round 2: Boredom
>
> Round 3: Contentedness, enjoyment
>
> Round 4: Excitement and enthusiasm

I picked this particular sequence on purpose because I think it represents the typical emotional progression people go through as they gain experience with public speaking. At first they are very anx-

> You need to make your words and sentences sound interesting.

ious, and they unintentionally convey this emotion to their audiences! With more practice, they overcome that anxiety, but their presentation is dull and they convey boredom instead. If they begin to get really good and start feeling up for presentations, their enjoyment of the experience comes through and the audience feels happy too. Then, if they get really good, they learn to infuse their speaking with the enthusiasm they feel for the subject and that comes through loud and clear in their speaking style. By practicing each of these emotions, you can learn to avoid conveying first two to your audience.

Lesson 4: Gesture training. In this activity, read your material out loud while maintaining an absolutely still and rigid posture. Try not to move your body or face at all. Then think about how it feels to speak without any gestures or nonverbal components. Which nonverbal elements did you miss the most? Facial expressions? Hand movements? Arm gestures? The ability to pace around while speaking? When we force ourselves not to do any of these things, we become strongly aware of their loss. We feel the natural urge to incorporate gesture and expression into our speaking because they are, after all, a natural and very important part of person-to-person communications. So this exercise helps us get in touch with our natural gestures. It reminds us to use them.

Finish the activity by taking it to the other extreme. Try reading out loud while using as many and as exaggerated gestures as you possibly can. It will take you a while to loosen up and really go for it, so read your material several times over. Try to be as dramatic and silly as you can. You will know you've mastered this activity when you reduce yourself to hopeless laughter!

When it comes to learning to use gestures effectively, the best thing you can do is *practice in normal conversation*. Make a point of working more animation and gesture into your routine conversations, then when you make a presentation, you'll have a store of natural, comfortable gestures to fall back on. The best gestures are the ones that arise naturally from the speaker's subject and feelings. But gestures can't "bubble up" out of you if you haven't got any habits of gesture in the first place!

> The best gestures are the ones that arise naturally from the speaker's subject and feelings.

Finally, read the piece through again, this time attending to gesture and facial expression with the intent of using them appropriately and well. Stay away from either extreme. Find the gestures that feel comfortable for you and seem to fit the words and make them appealing.

These lessons don't take all that long, but they do help you get in touch with your natural style and become more expressive and interesting as a presenter. Given the importance of presentations in management, that's a very beneficial thing, both for your audiences and for you.

Hot Presentation Tip: Try Smiling!

A psychologist interested in facial expressions asked mothers *not to smile* while holding their infants. Instead, they tried to look sad or depressed. At first, the babies tried to elicit a positive response from their mothers. They smiled, reached out toward them, and gurgled. But after a short while, they gave up. They just couldn't sustain the interaction without positive facial expressions from their mothers. They quickly became withdrawn. And after the experiment ended (it lasted only three minutes), the mothers found it hard to stimulate a response from the babies. It took some time for the effect to wear off.

Why is this relevant to your behavior at work as a manager and presenter? Aren't we far removed from the baby stage and far more self-sufficient? Yes and no. In fact, people are generally quite emotionally withdrawn at work. They all wear the mask of business. They don't smile easily or often. They act like those mothers in the experiment, holding back and not allowing their emotions to be expressed in natural, instinctive expressions and postures, especially in presentations. Most managers maintain a serious demeanor when they present to an audience. And the audience responds just the way those babies did. It becomes withdrawn. When you break this pattern and make a point of smiling often in a presentation, your audience smiles too. It acts happy and interested. People are more likely to ask supportive questions and agree with your points. Smiling has a very powerful impact in presentations. Try it sometime!

> Smiling has a very powerful impact in presentations. Try it sometime!

Designing an Appropriate Presentation

When people plan a presentation, they usually focus on questions like "Should I use charts, slides, a Powerpoint presentation, or other audio-visual aids?" And people also tend to think about whether they should use activities, take questions, or do something else to gain or inhibit audience involvement. It is easy to get lost in a jungle of details, from what to wear to whether an introductory joke is appropriate. But there is a simpler way to design the right presentation for every audience and event.

When you start designing your presentation, the key thing to think about is what type of presentation you want it to be. This decision will shape other decisions and make the design task simpler by far. Once you select a basic type of presentation, that decision will make it a lot easier and simpler to get all the details correct.

A good way to think about types of presentations is to *consider two key dimensions*: the extent to which a presentation is informative versus persuasive, and the extent to which it is serious versus entertaining. Your presentation needs to be defined on both these dimensions. Once you decide what profile is appropriate for the presentation, the design decisions will be simple and clear. So let's look at Figure 1-3 and give some thought to what types of presentations are possible.

If you think about it, your presentation will have to be a combination of the variables in the presentations grid. It will have to be either serious or entertaining. And it will have to be either informative or persuasive. So it must fall into one of the four cells of the grid. In Figure 1-3, each cell is labeled with a basic objective to help you decide how to design a presentation of that type.

For example, a presentation that you want to be both *entertaining and persuasive* has as its basic purpose the goal of winning the audience. You want them to "buy into" your presentation and really love it. So you need to use design elements intended to sell the audience by making your presentation entertaining and persuasive.

Exciting graphics and visual images are appropriate, good stories and jokes work well, and any showmanship you can come up with is appropriate as well. You need to focus on entertaining and persuading, so you can pull out all the stops and really give it to them.

> Once you select a basic type of presentation, that decision will make it a lot easier and simpler to get all the details correct.

On the other hand, a presentation that ought to be *serious and informative* should use none of these devices. They would seem out of place to the audience and would not go over at all. Instead, you should take an instructive approach in which you emphasize clear, well-presented facts and figures. Your style needs to be serious and professional. Jokes aren't appropriate. Audio-visual support, if used, should be simple and factual: tables of statistics, lists, graphs, or simple bulleted outlines of main points are fine. And your personal style should be less animated and more calm and professional. You don't need to stride around the room. Just standing comfortably at a podium will do.

The other two options are also clearly defined by the grid. If you feel that an *informative but entertaining* presentation is called for, then your objective is to liven up those facts a bit in order to leave the audience feeling inspired, not just informed. Your style will therefore be somewhere between the two extremes just described. You will use some entertaining elements but will keep closer to the subject and make sure you communicate the core information in a professional and logical manner.

Finally, a *serious, persuasive* presentation needs to take a very professional approach and focus on convincing the audience of your point. A political campaign speech usually takes this form, as does a presentation to a potential investor or business partner you want to get on board. Your style will be serious and focused, and you will use aids that help make you look more prepared and convincing. High-quality audio-visual aids, perhaps even prepared by a professional designer, are appropriate for this type of presentation. And you will certainly want to wear your most expensive and subdued business suit or outfit. If you can control the venue, you'll pick a "power platform" from which to speak—a richly appointed boardroom or a ballroom or conference room with an impressive stage and a very professional feel to it.

You should choose one of those four basic presentation styles.

FIGURE 1-3 THE PRESENTATIONS GRID

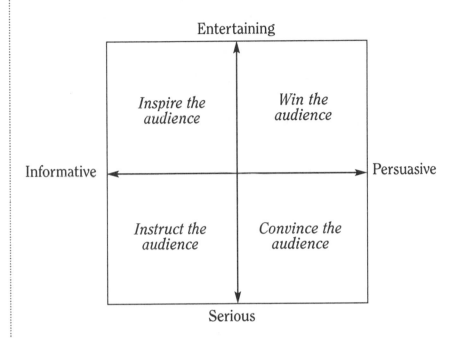

Here is a table that identifies some of the more common uses for each of the four types of presentations:

WHEN TO USE WHICH TYPE OF PRESENTATION

Informative/Entertaining	Employee trainings, new program kickoffs, new product launches
Persuasive/ Entertaining	Recruiting events, fun-oriented events, some sales presentations
Informative/Serious	Presentations to senior managers, stockholders, regulators, judges
Persuasive/Serious	Presentations to major buyers or prospects, teams, investors, some sales presentations

Sometimes it's hard to decide which type of presentation you need to design, even with the grid and the table to look at. If you have difficulty, there is another trick you can use. Simply refer to the next table and select the outcome you think is most desirable. What do you want the audience to think when the presentation is over?

Objectives of Each Type of Presentation

Type	Desired audience reaction
Informative/Entertaining	*Interested:* "I never knew that subject was so fascinating!"
Persuasive/ Entertaining	*Convinced:* "That presenter is really wonderful! Where do I sign up?"
Informative/Serious	*Informed:* "I see. Now I understand."
Persuasive/Serious	*Decided:* "The presenter is right. I agree."

> Whatever business presentation you design and deliver, it needs to create one of these four audience reactions.

Whatever business presentation you design and deliver, it needs to create one of these four audience reactions. Otherwise, it is liable to create one of the many undesirable reactions that result from inappropriate or poorly done presentations. You really don't want the audience to think, "That sure was boring," "That presenter doesn't know what's going on," or "I'm not convinced." Yet unless you set out with a more positive and appropriate result in mind, you are likely to get an undesirable result by accident.

Okay, now you're ready! I can't wait to see your next presentation.

What to Say to Employees Who Badmouth You

t's an all-too-common problem. You are out of the office for a business trip or meeting, and a faithful assistant or helpful associate lets you know that your employees back at the office are making jokes about you and backstabbing you right and left. At first you are angry. And then frustration and disappointment creep in. Do you have to baby-sit these people? What use are they if they can't respect the work you do and don't seem to be committed to their own work? Don't they realize they have good jobs and compensation packages and, in fact, may be overpaid given the quality of work they've been producing lately?

Your first instinct may be to fire the offenders as soon as you get back to the office, maybe even *before* you get back so you don't have to face them in person. Hold on! Don't speak or act in anger or you'll create new and bigger problems for yourself.

If you want to say or do something about the problem of employees badmouthing you, you need to do some preparations first.

> Make sure you have clear, well-documented evidence of the behaviors in question.

Preparations

1. Make sure you have clear, well-documented evidence of the behaviors in question (evidence), then
2. Figure out exactly what harm they do to the organization through this behavior (negative impacts), and
3. Determine whether they have been given clear notice about the need to avoid behaviors that cause such harm (notifications), and finally
4. Find out whether there are other issues on the minds of these employees, which may be root causes of their negative attitudes and behaviors (root causes).

Specifics

Here are some of the likely options for these steps:

Evidence
- Write up, date, and file your own notes from your conversations with those who have observed the negative behaviors.
- Get hold of and file any written evidence of negative behavior, such as e-mails or notes.

- Ask employees who are willing to cooperate to write you a quick memo describing what they have observed.
- Keep a journal describing what you hear and see of relevance to the behaviors in question, including inappropriate responses or comments made directly to you.

You need to collect good evidence of any behavior before you can take action to correct it or remove those responsible for it. Rumors need to be substantiated. If they can't be, then you will have to ask the individuals implicated whether the rumors are true. If they admit to inappropriate behavior, you need to quickly write up notes on your conversation with them in order to document the conversation. If they don't and you don't have any other solid documentation, you need to *drop the issue* before you get yourself in trouble.

Negative Impacts
- Hurts office morale, thereby reducing productivity or quality.
- Makes it hard for you to do your work effectively.
- Creates tension that makes other employees unhappy and could drive them away.
- Makes it hard to bring in and develop new employees.
- Distracts employees from their work.
- Leads employees to blame management for problems instead of finding ways to take ownership of them and solve them.
- Undermines your ability to lead other employees by encouraging them to disrespect your instructions.

> Backstabbing hurts your feelings, but that's not a serious offense from a management perspective unless it also hurts the *business*.

Note that these negative impacts are impacts on the organization and its work, not on you personally. Sure, the backstabbing hurts your feelings, but that's not a serious offense from a management perspective unless it also hurts the *business*. Make sure you frame your words in terms of how their behavior hurts the organization, not you personally!

Notifications
- The employee manual or their job description requires them to behave in an appropriate, professional manner.

- The employee manual or their job description makes creating a positive, constructive team climate an objective of their work.
- The employee manual or their job description provides appropriate processes for bringing complaints to their manager and/or others in the organization.
- Well-known policies or strategies exist concerning the need for open, collaborative communication within the organization.
- They have received negative feedback about similar behaviors in the past, either in writing or in a face-to-face setting.
- There is a documented pattern of inadequate job performance in a variety of areas for these employees.

Note that you or the organization have probably communicated performance expectations that are relevant to the backstabbing behaviors you've heard about. And in the future, you can certainly strengthen any existing notifications by sending out a memo on team spirit, open communication, or some such goal (see models later in this chapter).

Root Causes

- Employees feel they have been passed over for promotions.
- Employees do not have as much support and direction as they need from you or other managers.
- Employees are angry about a recent event in which they feel they were mistreated.
- Employees don't like their jobs and take out their frustrations on you because you are the nearest authority figure.
- Employees have recently had to take on significantly more work without an increase in resources or compensation.
- Employees do not get along well with each other because of personal problems, which leads to a negative interpersonal environment in the office.
- Employees are poorly matched to their work and find it frustrating because they are not doing the things they are best at and most want to do.

There is often a perceived injustice behind employee back talk.

- You have not spent much time building rapport within the office because you are too busy with your own work to spend time on the people side of management.
- You generally give them more negative than positive feedback (so they feel an urge to give you negative messages in response).

Note that an understanding of the root causes of the negative behavior will help greatly in preventing recurrences of that behavior. If there are legitimate concerns or problems in employees' minds, you will need to generate open discussion of these problems. Let them know you recognize and respect their complaints. If it is not feasible to correct the problems, let them know that too and focus your communications on showing that you do empathize but that you also recognize that the work must go on. If, however, you can easily remedy a root problem, go ahead and do that, making sure to communicate your expectation that their behavior will improve too.

> Understanding the root causes of the negative behavior will help greatly in preventing recurrences of that behavior.

Model Letters

How do you say it? Once you have done the appropriate preparations, you are ready to confront the employees in question and communicate your concerns about their inappropriate behavior. You have two possible paths depending upon the circumstances:

Communication path #1: Notify that behavior is inappropriate.

If the evidence is weak, or notification unclear or inadequate, then you need to constrain your communications to providing clear notification of the problem. Your communication goal should be to make clear what you expect and why (in terms of impact on the organization). Then in the future you can monitor their behavior and use communication path #2 if there are continuing problems.

Communication path #2: Reprimand for inappropriate behavior.

If the evidence of wrongdoing is clear, the impact significant, and your preparations reveal that employees have been clearly notified in advance that this sort of behavior is wrong, you can communicate more strongly and can even consider disciplinary action.

Sample Notification

Dear Staff:

It has come to my attention that employees have been making negative and rude comments about their managers. This pattern of behavior is destructive to the organization because it . . . *(pick one or more appropriate phrases from Negative Impacts)* hurts office morale, thereby reducing productivity and quality, and creates tension that makes other employees unhappy and could drive them away.

I want to make it clear that your jobs require an appropriate level of conduct in which you avoid unreasonably negative and critical behavior in order to maintain the professional, team-oriented, cooperative work atmosphere required for us all to do our work well. I expect employees to find more constructive ways to let off steam if that is what they feel they must do. And I expect, and welcome, direct, private communications if employees feel they have legitimate, serious concerns or complaints to air. These expectations are consistent with existing company policies and with your job descriptions, and are relevant to the proper performance of your work.

If you have any questions, please let me know.

Sincerely,

XXXX XXXXXXX

(This message can be delivered in the form of an internal memo or e-mail, and can also be delivered verbally in a one-on-one setting or a staff meeting. If delivered verbally or by e-mail, you should provide a written backup in the form of a memo. And the memo should be copied and filed carefully to provide proof of notification.)

Try these model letters.

Sample Reprimand

Dear (individual name):

Specific evidence has come to my attention that you have been making negative and rude comments about your managers. This pattern of behavior is destructive to the organization because it . . . (*pick one or more appropriate phrases Negative Impacts*) hurts office morale, thereby reducing productivity and quality, and creates tension that makes other employees unhappy and could drive them away.

As you know, your job requires an appropriate level of conduct in which you avoid unreasonably negative and critical behavior in order to maintain the professional, team-oriented, cooperative work atmosphere required for us all to do our work well. I expect employees to find more constructive ways to let off steam if that is what they feel they must do. And I expect, and welcome, direct, private communications if employees feel they have legitimate, serious concerns or complaints to air. These expectations are consistent with existing company policies and with your job description, and are relevant to the proper performance of your work.

Optional: Because I view your behavior as serious and as part of a well-documented pattern of inadequate performance, I am compelled to put you on probation from now until your next scheduled performance review (or until month/day/year, when we will do a formal performance review). What this means is that I expect you to make a significant improvement in your conduct, and especially to avoid future problems in the areas in which I have communicated my concerns in the past. If not, it is entirely possible that you will be asked to leave the company.

I believe that you are fully capable of performing your work at a high level, and I know you have many relevant qualifications and experiences. It is my hope and belief that you can easily avoid future problems and will be able to build upon the many positive aspects of your current job performance. You are capable of being a very valuable member of the team, and your commitment means a lot to the organization and to me.

Sincerely,

XXXX XXXXXXX

(This message should be delivered in the form of an internal memo or letter, and should be copied and filed carefully to provide proof of notification.)

> You are capable of being a very valuable member of the team.

Verbal Responses

If you wish to take a less formal and more personal approach, you can simply speak "off the record" to the employees you believe are involved in inappropriately critical behaviors. You can use an approach such as the following:

Sample Script

"I am concerned about the level of venting and critical talk I hear is going on in the office. It creates a negative environment that some employees find difficult and stressful. It also can have a negative effect on the organization. (Optional: bring in one or more reasons from Negative Impacts). But rather than respond formally, I've decided just to talk to you and let you know that I'd like to see some improvement in the atmosphere in the office."

Let employee respond, but don't be drawn into an argument or sidelined by defensive responses or denials. After listening respectfully to their responses, reiterate your main point and make it clear you expect them to communicate any legitimate concerns to you directly:

"I appreciate that you may have some concerns of your own, and that there are always tensions and stresses to cope with. And I agree that I don't always get as detailed or accurate information about what goes on behind my back as I would like to. Also, I know that I am often busy and may not seem as available or easy to talk with as people would like. But the reality is, *we need to create and maintain a professional, cooperative atmosphere in the office*. If I permit negative behavior patterns to be established, it will only hurt all of us in the long run. I'd like you to help me work out this problem by doing what you can to improve the climate and create a positive work environment for everyone. Can you help me out with this goal?"

Employee should give either an unqualified or a qualified yes. If any yes answer, say:

> If you wish to take a less formal and more personal approach, you can simply speak "off the record."

"Good! I knew I could count on you. I'll check in with you in a little while to see how everything is going, and in the meantime, please feel free to talk to me or e-mail me with any concerns of your own. I'd like to stay in touch with you about this and any other important issues. Thanks very much for your help."

Very rarely an employee may simply say no, refusing to cooperate. If so, then say something like the following, which permits you to avoid immediate conflict and lets you take the time to come up with an appropriate response.

"Well, I'm sorry you see it that way. Your refusal to cooperate makes things much more difficult. I'm not sure what I should do about that right now, but I'll think about it and get back to you soon. In the meantime, please let me know if you change your mind. Thanks for your time."

Well, now you're ready to handle the most difficult and awkward of employee communication challenges. When employees grumble about or criticize their boss, it's bad for the organization's morale. In fact, it's very bad. And when you are the boss in question, it's bad for your morale too!

Perhaps that's why this problem is one I am often asked how to handle. Over the years, many managers (including many good managers who don't deserve to be scapegoated by difficult employees) have approached me seeking help and advice. So you may as well be prepared.

Being in a management role sets you up. Some employees will focus any negative feelings they have on you. They will see you as the problem, not themselves. They will not stop to think that you are simply doing your job and that they have to do theirs as well. They will instead start grumbling behind your back.

Often when you respond promptly with appropriate notifications such as those covered in this session, the grumbling stops. You can nip most of these problems in the bud. But if not, if you have to go all the way and reprimand, perhaps even fire, a very negative employee, well, at least now you know how to do it!

Being in a management role sets you up. Some employees will focus any negative feelings they have on you.

The Leadership Course

Overview of Course II

In this chapter, you will focus on your ability to excel in the leadership of employees, team members, and other groups of people. Leadership is the art of accomplishing important goals through the commitment and competence of others. To master this art, you need to study the following topics:

Session 1: Why Lead When You Can Just Manage?

Session 2: What Kind of Leader Are You?

Session 3: Focusing on People and Tasks

Session 4: Focusing on Commitment and Competence

Session 5: Leading to Build Commitment

Session 6: Leading to Build Competence

Session 7: Putting It All Together

Why Lead When You Can Just Manage?

As I said in the overview of this workshop, leadership is the art of accomplishing important goals through the commitment and competence of others. What makes leadership different from normal management, from business as usual? Well, three things are often missing in the typical workplace:

1. People aren't excited about accomplishing an important goal. Without this inspiration, they perform routinely rather than pushing themselves toward excellence.
2. People don't feel fully committed to their workplace and work. They may feel they are just doing it for the money. They may justify their daily grind by telling themselves "It's a good steppingstone job; it'll look good on my resume." Or they may say, "If I just stick it out a little longer, I'll qualify for unemployment/my pension/a better job when I leave." These sorts of attitudes reflect ambivalence about the work. In typical workplaces, leadership is lacking and the people aren't fully committed to what they are doing. They have one toe in the water and aren't sure they like the feel of it.
3. People aren't fully qualified to do their work well. They probably can and will do a decent job, but they aren't likely to do the best job possible. In fact, they aren't really on a learning path at all. They aren't given good opportunities or reasons to strive for mastery. As a result, they never seem to rise to the top of their professions. And they never do as good of a job as they might.

So, there is a lot leadership can offer in the workplace, whether it is a small entrepreneurial growth company, an established small business, a nonprofit organization like a school or hospital, or a big corporate office or factory where managers supervise people by the hundreds. I've worked with managers in all sorts of organizations. Whether they are executives, entrepreneurs, doctors, teachers, team leaders, or coaches, they all find the leadership path a rewarding and exciting one. The opportunity exists in any group of people to build commitment and competence and strive for superior performances.

> The opportunity exists in any group of people to build commitment and competence and strive for superior performances.

Becoming a Strong Leader (the Easy Way!)

When you create sufficient commitment to a cause or course of action, you are providing strong leadership for your people. And when you design appropriate tasks for your people, you are providing strong leadership of their work. In this chapter you will learn to do both—to provide strong leadership of both people and tasks. The pleasant effects of this leadership include the benefits of creating a more happy and productive group of people.

Good leadership produces happy *and* productive people. It does so without creating a personality cult around the leader or demanding unrealistic changes in the personality of the leader or followers. And good leadership of the kind you're going to learn in this chapter makes the workplace (or classroom or playing field) a more happy and productive one.

Surprisingly, happiness and productivity do go hand in hand when there is good leadership. Why? Because the wise leader makes sure everyone is working effectively toward compelling goals. Good leadership creates a true alignment of interests. Everybody *wants* to do the right things well. The leader creates the necessary conditions for forward motion, then sits back and enjoys the ride.

Let's Get Clear on What Leadership *Isn't*

Too often, however, managers (and teachers and parents and coaches) confuse direction with leadership. Direction is when you give directions and expect them to be followed.

If you own your own firm or have been appointed to a supervisory position in someone else's firm, your direction will often be followed. People will endeavor to do what you say, within reason, out of deference to your position of power. So it's easy to go on for years and years believing you are leading when all you are doing is giving orders.

Who cares? What's wrong with just telling people what needs to be done and letting them figure out how to do it? Nothing, if you don't care how much they do, or how well they do it. But if you care, if effort and achievement matter, then you need to provide real leadership.

And real leadership is not about your positional power, nor is it about your personal power (this chapter isn't about how to become a dominant, charismatic personality any more than it is about how to

> The wise leader makes sure everyone is working effectively toward compelling goals.

become an autocratic, dictatorial one!). Leadership is simply a set of practices and a perspective that you can integrate naturally into your daily behavior.

The Personal Benefits of Leadership

Some of you are probably accustomed to getting decent results from your people by using your personal or positional power to drive them. That's what I call the sheepdog style of leadership. The beady eye and sharp canines of a good sheepdog, combined with its speed and understanding of the desired direction, give the power to drive a flock of sheep into its pen. In traditional business organizations (and many other organizations as well), this sheepdog style of leadership is the norm. And when someone emerges with enough extra bark that they really can stand out from the sheep and play the role of sheepdog, he or she tends to rise in the ranks and assume a leadership role.

And when I've trained or consulted to sheepdog leaders, I've found them to be quite attached to their leadership style. After all, the sheep do run whenever they see the sheepdog coming. Now, that's real power!

But it is a kind of power that leaves much to be desired in today's challenging business environment. Unfortunately, it reduces the organization to a flock of sheep.

Sheep don't think. They don't solve problems. They don't find good new opportunities. They don't ever develop the skills and vision to become sheepdogs. They just eat green stuff and produce some simple, low-value commodities: wool, mutton, lanolin. Know any multimillionaire shepherds?

If, however, you are driving your people so hard that you get reasonably good results (they return to their pens each evening), you may not realize you are in need of more and different leadership. You may not realize just how hard it is to get good results by driving your people. It's just too hard to get good results by pushing. And without real leadership, performance comes down to pressure.

How much pressure can you exert? How much pressure does the power of your position and your own strength make possible? And how long can you lean on your positional and personal power before you wear them down?

> You may not realize just how hard it is to get good results by driving your people. It's just too hard to get good results by pushing.

So in addition to the bottom-line benefits of leadership, there are the personal benefits to consider. Managers who master the art of leadership are able to accomplish wonderful things with apparent ease. Those who don't are worn out at the end of each day. (Sheepdogs put on a great many more miles than the sheep!)

Management is a challenging endeavor. Let's not do it the hard way.

Case in Point

John was trained as an engineer, but now he runs a hospital supply company he founded five years ago. Business is good and the company now employs almost 200 people. For the first time, John doesn't know all of them by name, and that bothers him because he sees himself as a very people-oriented manager.

"I really try to treat each employee as an individual," he says. "I make a point of recognizing everyone's birthdays, and I try to put each person in the position that's right for them. This is a very friendly place to work."

But John was speaking about his leadership style because he was having increasing trouble retaining good employees. If he was such a personal, friendly boss, why were his top people deserting him?

When employees filled in an assessment of John's leadership style, a very different leadership profile emerged. John's employees saw him as autocratic and distant, unwilling to share key information or permit others to participate in key decisions. And employees did not know where John planned to take the company or what his goals or vision were. They also felt that he provided too little support and guidance for them as they tried to develop their own capabilities and take on more responsibilities.

John was shocked and hurt at first by this feedback. But after a few days he began to agree with it. "I just assumed they knew what I was thinking and feeling," he said. "Now I'm making an effort to be more aware of how I relate to them."

Over time, John's leadership matured. And his employee retention problem went away. Now employees really do see their leader as concerned and people-oriented, the way John wanted to be in the first place!

> Managers who master the art of leadership are able to accomplish wonderful things with apparent ease.

What Kind of
Leader Are You?

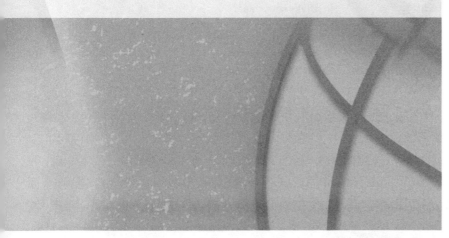

> You have to *choose* how you'll lead in each and every leadership situation.

Self-awareness is the heart of great leadership. It sounds corny, I know, but you really do have to know yourself before you can lead others. You need to see yourself as others see you. If you don't know how your leadership looks on the outside, how can you get the inside part right?

It's not that leadership is acting. It isn't. It has to be genuine. It's just that leadership involves, well, *leadership*. You have to be the one who defines the tenor of your interactions with your people. You have to have a plan in mind, and you have to shape your actions to that plan. You have to *choose* how you'll lead in each and every leadership situation. Then you have to really *do it*.

For example, let's say you are in charge of assembling a team of employees to redesign your department and cut costs by 25 percent. There's no choice about that—as unpleasant as it is—because your company is losing money and newer competitors operate on a lower cost basis. But you can choose who you'll put on this team and how you'll get them started. What should you say and do first? Second? Third?

Most of us tackle such leadership challenges in a fairly predictable way. We do what we usually do, what we've seen others do, which may not be—and usually isn't—the right thing from a leadership perspective.

For instance, many people in the above cost-cutting situation would send a memo to the most technically expert or experienced employees, telling them they have a new assignment. The memo would probably be serious and businesslike. A "we've got an unpleasant job to do but we've got to do it so let's get started okay you two work on that part, you do this, and you do that" tone would be typical. But will it work? How will they react? Is this the right leadership style in the circumstances? What sort of leadership is this, anyway?

Delegation and Leadership

Actually, this example illustrates the delegate style of leadership. That's when you presume your people know how to play their role. And you presume they are willing, even eager, to do so. You may not really believe they are ready and willing, but whenever you hand them the baton in that style, you act as if they are. (Hint: never hand anyone a baton unless they are already running faster than you in the right direction!)

I chose to illustrate the delegate style for a good reason: It's by far the most common style used by managers in all sorts of organizations. In fact, most managers rely largely on this one leadership style.

Yet there are many possible styles of leadership. Some are a bit contrived and won't feel natural enough for you to really use them. But others are quite simple and natural once you get the hang of them. In fact, you probably make some use of other styles already and can increase your mastery of them with relative ease, that is, if you make a conscious effort to be more aware of what leadership style you use.

> Never hand anyone a baton unless they are already running faster than you in the right direction!

Assessing Yourself

So let's find out! Let's actually examine *your* leadership style by finding out which styles you use and how much you use them.

To do so, you simply have to fill in a brief survey and enter the results on a chart. I've chosen to use an assessment from the C-Lead program my firm developed for use by corporate trainers at leading U.S. companies. I know from personal experience that the results are always illuminating, so let's do it!

Leadership Style Self-Assessment

Instructions: Please read through the assessment statements. How well do they describe your current leadership behavior? Rank each one using the 1-to-5 scale of agreement below. Answer as honestly and accurately as possible.

You can focus on your general approach to leadership or assess your leadership of a specific person. If you are concerned about your style with an individual, record his or her name first as a memory aid.

Employee :_____

1	2	3	4	5
STRONGLY DISAGREE	**DISAGREE**	**IN THE MIDDLE**	**AGREE**	**STRONGLY AGREE**

As a leader, I commonly . . .

_____ 1. Give people help and support to ease their fears or concerns.

_____ 2. Try to recharge people by giving them a little rest and encouragement.

_____ 3. Sympathize with people's individual concerns and worries.

Sum of questions 1 through 3 = Score 1

_____ 4. Challenge people by setting tough goals and imposing strict consequences.

_____ 5. Share negative information, rather than shield people from it.

_____ 6. Require performance improvements.

Sum of questions 4 through 6 = Score 2

_____ 7. Do my best to understand people's perspectives.

_____ 8. Devote time to building friendly relations with people.

_____ 9. Prove that I really care through my questions and actions.

Sum of questions 7 through 9 = Score 3

_____ 10. Explain the reasoning behind my goals and objectives.

_____ 11. Inform people about the "big picture" plans, not just their own tasks.

_____ 12. Share information about our goals.

Sum of questions 10 through 12 = Score 4

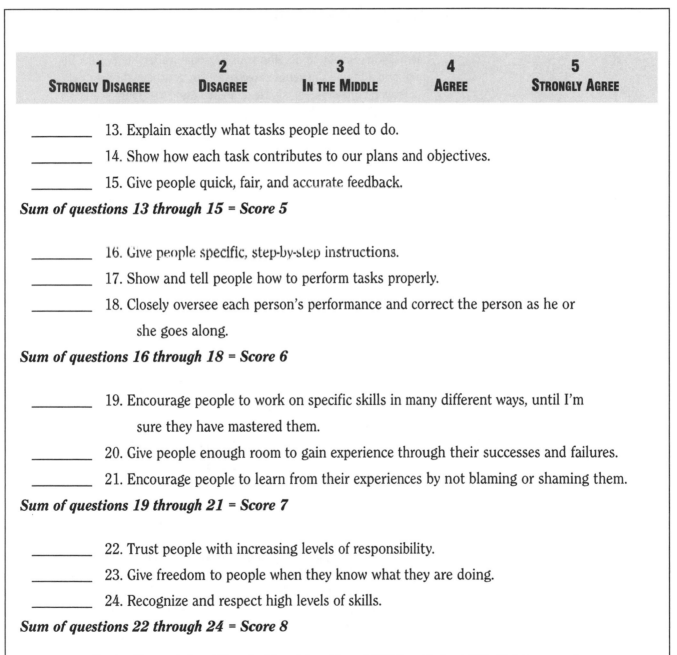

1	2	3	4	5
STRONGLY DISAGREE	**DISAGREE**	**IN THE MIDDLE**	**AGREE**	**STRONGLY AGREE**

_____ 13. Explain exactly what tasks people need to do.

_____ 14. Show how each task contributes to our plans and objectives.

_____ 15. Give people quick, fair, and accurate feedback.

Sum of questions 13 through 15 = Score 5

_____ 16. Give people specific, step-by-step instructions.

_____ 17. Show and tell people how to perform tasks properly.

_____ 18. Closely oversee each person's performance and correct the person as he or she goes along.

Sum of questions 16 through 18 = Score 6

_____ 19. Encourage people to work on specific skills in many different ways, until I'm sure they have mastered them.

_____ 20. Give people enough room to gain experience through their successes and failures.

_____ 21. Encourage people to learn from their experiences by not blaming or shaming them.

Sum of questions 19 through 21 = Score 7

_____ 22. Trust people with increasing levels of responsibility.

_____ 23. Give freedom to people when they know what they are doing.

_____ 24. Recognize and respect high levels of skills.

Sum of questions 22 through 24 = Score 8

Let's Plot Your Profile

Okay, now that you've rated yourself on all twenty-four statements, you're ready to develop your personal leadership profile. Go back and add up each set of three scores to get the eight subtotals if you haven't already done so. Next, create your leadership profile by filling in the bars in Figure 2-1 up to the number corresponding to each of your scores.

FIGURE 2-1 C-LEAD STYLE PROFILE.

	Low			MediumLow			MediumHigh			High		
Score 1	3	4	5	6	7	8	9	10	11	12	13	14	15
Score 2	3	4	5	6	7	8	9	10	11	12	13	14	15
Score 3	3	4	5	6	7	8	9	10	11	12	13	14	15
Score 4	3	4	5	6	7	8	9	10	11	12	13	14	15
Score 5	3	4	5	6	7	8	9	10	11	12	13	14	15
Score 6	3	4	5	6	7	8	9	10	11	12	13	14	15
Score 7	3	4	5	6	7	8	9	10	11	12	13	14	15
Score 8	3	4	5	6	7	8	9	10	11	12	13	14	15

> Your profile indicates at a glance your strongest and weakest styles.

Your profile indicates at a glance your strongest and weakest styles. Most people find their scores are in the low to medium range on the majority of styles. Is that true for you? And most people find they are stronger in one or two styles because they tend to rely on these styles more than the others.

The delegate style is most common among managers. At the other extreme, managers typically score lowest on the empathize style. Which are your most and least used styles?

Before we go further, it is helpful to review each of the eight styles the C-Lead survey measures. Here is what each style means:

1. *Reassure.* The leader helps followers cope with the stresses and challenges of work life by being supportive.
2. *Challenge.* The leader pushes the follower to "wake up" and get more involved in critical issues and concerns.
3. *Empathize.* The leader listens to follower's side, understands how follower feels, and works with follower to choose appealing goals.
4. *Inform.* The leader provides information about the circumstances and big picture plans that guide follower's work.
5. *Explain.* The leader clearly explains what followers must do and why, then provides informative feedback on how well the followers do it.
6. *Direct.* The leader oversees followers in whole units of work, telling them what to do and supervising and correcting as they do it.
7. *Guide.* The leader guides development by helping followers pursue stretch goals and try new things to improve skills.
8. *Delegate.* The leader trusts followers to take on full responsibility for meaningful tasks.

> Great leadership involves using the appropriate style in each circumstance.

As these descriptions of styles illustrate, you can lead in many different ways. Great leadership involves using the appropriate style in each circumstance. And that often means changing your style from one situation to the next. There is no one "right" way to lead, but in any situation there are at least seven wrong ones!

The needs of your people change often, so you need to be flexible as a leader and able to use each of the eight C-Lead styles at a high level. For most managers, the first step toward improved leadership is to increase your knowledge of and comfort with different leadership styles.

Listening Harder

For instance, many managers find they need to practice listening to their people and paying close attention to how they feel. These behaviors are necessary for the empathize style, and also helpful for the explain, reassure, and guide styles. To become more empathetic toward employees, managers can try any one of the following:

- Keep an "Attitudes & Feelings" journal in which you make note of how each employee is feeling each day. This exercise forces you to actually attend to their attitudes and feelings, increasing your sensitivity dramatically over time.
- Make an effort to ask each employee how they are feeling each day—and then listen respectfully to their responses.
- When you ask people how they are, listen to the tone of their answer, not the words. It is not so much what they say in answer to your "How are you?" question, but how they say it. To improve your ability to read tone, try saying "Fine" as if you are really feeling fabulous. Now say it as if you are doing pretty well. Now say "Fine" as if you are not really quite sure how you are. And now say the same word, this time with the feeling that you aren't really doing too well. Finally, say "Fine" as if you are feeling really terrible. The same simple word, so often used, can convey a host of meanings depending upon how it is said. How many of those meanings do you pick up on and respond to?
- Let your people know that you believe people do the best work when they feel good about their work. (I hope you really do believe this simple but powerful truth!) When you tell them that feeling good about their work is a key goal for you as their leader, then it's okay for everyone to work toward this goal.

People do the best work when they feel good about their work.

Focusing on
People and Tasks

I f you make an effort to listen more carefully to your people, you'll become a more considerate, people-oriented manager. A people orientation is one of two key orientations you need to use in order to lead effectively in the modern workplace. And the reassure, empathize, explain, and guide styles all share this focus on how your people are doing.

The other essential orientation in good leadership is a focus on the tasks you want your people to perform. When you define and structure people's roles, explain what they should do and why, and give them clear feedback about their performances, you are being a good task-oriented leader. The challenge, inform, direct, and delegate styles all share this focus on what your people are doing.

To improve your leadership, you need to practice being both more people oriented and more task oriented. Those are the two frontiers for any manager who wants to be a more effective leader. (And why be a more effective leader? Because you get more effective employees.)

> You need to practice being both more people oriented and more task oriented.

How People-Oriented Are You?

You can easily use your C-Lead score (from Session 1) to measure your people orientation. Just add up your individual scores from the four people-oriented styles:

Score 1, Reassure: _____

+

Score 3, Empathize: _____

+

Score 5, Explain: _____

+

Score 7, Guide: _____

= People Score: _____

What does your score mean? You can interpret it using the following scale:

$$12-24 = \text{very low}$$

$$25-36 = \text{low}$$

$$37-48 = \text{medium}$$

$$39-60 = \text{high}$$

Managers fall into the low range, on average, when rated by those they lead. They are on average in the medium range when rating themselves. So you can compare your people-orientation score with these norms. But wherever your score falls, keep in mind that increasing it will boost the performance of your people. When it comes to leadership, more is better!

How Task Oriented Are You?

You also need to be task oriented as a manager. How task-oriented are you? Again, your scores can easily answer this question for you. Just add up the four style scores below, each representing a task-oriented leadership style:

Score 2, Challenge: _____

+

Score 4, Inform: _____

+

Score 6, Direct: _____

+

Score 8, Delegate: _____

= Task Score: _____

> When it comes to leadership, more is better!

Again, you can interpret your score using the following scale:

12–24 = very low

25–36 = low

37–48 = medium

39–60 = high

It's surprising how often employees operate in a vacuum, unsure of what they should do, why they should do it, or how well they are doing.

Managers typically score in the low to medium range on their task orientation, just as they do on the people orientation. To improve, you need to raise your task score into the high range. To raise your score, you need to structure people's work. You need to give them challenging goals, help them pursue those goals, and give them clear feedback about how they do.

It's surprising how often employees operate in a vacuum, unsure of what they should do, why they should do it, or how well they are doing. Perhaps that's why one series of Harvard Business School studies found that salespeople who had the clearest feedback about the effectiveness of their own work were more motivated even than those who had the biggest commissions! Leading by providing clear tasks and feedback about performance on those tasks is a very powerful thing indeed.

Focusing on Commitment and Competence

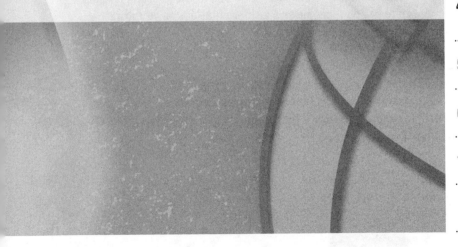

In the previous session, we measured the degree to which you have an orientation toward your people and toward their tasks. And, in performing these measurements, you learned that half of the leadership styles in the C-Lead method are people-oriented, and the other half are task oriented. That is an important way to think about leading, but it is not the only way.

Another powerful insight that will help you select the right approach in any situation is this: Sometimes people need more commitment, and sometimes they need more competence.

In fact, you can even say that commitment and competence are the two causes of good or poor performances. If your people aren't performing as well as you'd like them to, then the problem must either be that they don't want to or that they don't know how to. Commitment or competence; it's really that simple! And as a leader, all you need to do is raise the levels of commitment and competence in your people in order to produce great performances.

Yet it can be difficult to raise people's commitment or competence levels. How do you get them motivated to do their work? How do you teach them to do it better?

That's where your leadership comes in. If you simply manage by telling whom to do what then you're stuck with the current levels of commitment and competence. But if you lead by using the right C-Lead styles in the right sequence, you can build commitment and competence levels naturally.

And when you are building commitment or competence, you are simply using those same eight styles. You are simply focusing on the people or the task sides of leadership. In fact, in the C-Lead method, you alternate between people and task orientations as you work through the sequence of eight styles.

Each of the people-oriented styles has an odd number in the sequence (1, 3, 5, and 7), reflecting their emphasis on the "irrational" or "soft" side of your leadership personality. And each of the task-oriented styles has an even number in the sequence (2, 4, 6, and 8), reflecting their emphasis on the "logical" or "hard" side of your leadership personality.

> All you need to do is raise the levels of commitment and competence in your people in order to produce great performances.

Taking People Through the Full Sequence

To fully develop both commitment and competence, assuming they start with none of either, you simply use each of the C-Lead styles in turn:

1. *Reassure.* The leader helps followers cope with the stresses and challenges of work life by being supportive.
2. *Challenge.* The leader pushes the follower to "wake up" and get more involved in critical issues and concerns.
3. *Empathize.* The leader listens to follower's side, understands how follower feels, and works with follower to choose appealing goals.
4. *Inform.* The leader provides information about the circumstances and big picture plans that guide follower's work.
5. *Explain.* The leader explains clearly what followers must do and why, then provides informative feedback on how well the followers do it.
6. *Direct.* The leader oversees followers in whole units of work, telling them what to do and supervising and correcting as they do it.
7. *Guide.* The leader guides development by helping followers pursue stretch goals and try new things to improve skills.
8. *Delegate.* The leader trusts followers to take on full responsibility for meaningful tasks.

> You need to *build* both employee commitment and competence before you can delegate anything.

By the end of this sequence, you should have people who are high in both task commitment and task competence. They know their jobs and want to do them well. That's why the sequence ends with delegating the tasks to them. But note that it never begins with delegating the work. That's what many managers do, but it shortcuts the leadership sequence. It makes people responsible for tasks that they do not fully believe in and that they are not fully prepared to perform.

The sequence of styles builds commitment and competence (generally in that order) in a natural, comfortable manner. This development process is illustrated in Figure 2-2. In the next two sessions, we'll see exactly how this development process works.

Do you really have to use all eight styles in order each time you give someone a new task or want to improve their performance of an old task? No. It's rarely that complicated because you rarely start with a clean slate. Usually there is some commitment and some competence to work with. You just have to figure out what's missing and use the style or styles that fill the gap.

So let's get started! First, we'll do a session on how you use the commitment-oriented C-Lead styles to fill in any gaps in commitment. Then we'll finish up with a session on how you build competence using the rest of the C-Lead styles as your guide.

> Figure out what's missing and use the style or styles that fill the gap

FIGURE 2-2. THE LEADERSHIP PROCESS IN COMMITMENT-BASED LEADERSHIP.

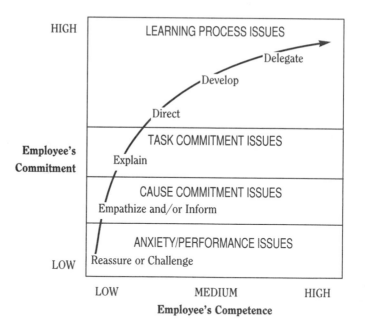

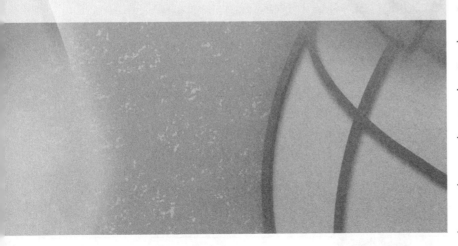

Leading to Build Commitment

Most managers recognize the inherent value of committed and competent employees. And they may even put considerable effort into these two areas. Yet, in general, they focus on competence first. In the C-Lead method, you need to reverse this traditional sequence because it just doesn't work. You need to build commitment before you worry about how competent your people are.

Start with commitment. Don't worry about how competent or capable they are until you know you've nailed the commitment issue. Why? The reason for this is simple common sense (even if it isn't well known). People do great work only when they feel committed to their work. Until you get them 100 percent on board and eager to perform, you can't lead them to higher levels of performance.

Why Do We Always Get It Wrong?

By the way, people often ask me why we as a society tend to emphasize competence instead of commitment. If that's a mistake, why is it so widely done? How come most managers don't see the error in this habit? I think it's because we traditionally teach students that way, and all managers spend many long years as students first.

Think about how school works. Do the teachers first convince students that algebra is a really great thing to know? Certainly not! They couldn't care less what the students think about the subject. In fact, I've never heard of an algebra class that starts by talking about the applications of algebra and "selling" the idea that it is an incredibly important thing to learn.

Instead, teachers use their positional power to force students to spend many long months of their lives learning how to do algebra without ever telling them why. Competence before commitment. And you know what? Most students don't learn algebra well or fast as a result. They just couldn't care less. They only do it to pass the tests.

This example is especially compelling to me, because I got all the way through school and college without really mastering mathematics. Sure, I passed all my required courses, but I just did it to pass my required courses. It wasn't until I decided to go to graduate

> Do the teachers first convince students that algebra is a really great thing to know?

school that I realized I needed to know algebra and statistics a lot better than I did.

But once I was really motivated, I was able to relearn these subjects quite quickly, with nothing more to help me than a few cheap math review books. In fact, I was amazed to discover that it wasn't really that difficult. With my newfound commitment to learn, I was able to master the needed math in just a few weeks of studying. I probably doubled my competence level in less than a month. Compare that to the twelve years of schooling it took to develop the first half of my competence in basic math! That's the difference between a committed learner and an uncommitted learner.

Yet managers universally focus on the *whats* before the *whys*. They overlook the need to build commitment. They struggle to build competence, forgetting that competent performances are built on a firm foundation of commitment.

So, the thing you want to think about and work on first when you focus on your people is their commitment to their work. How?

Building the First Level of Commitment

First, you have to check their level of participation commitment. Participation commitment is enthusiasm for participating in the work. Ask yourself if they really want to "be there." Do they find the sorts of challenges and opportunities in their workplace appealing? Or do they act overly bored—or perhaps overly anxious or fearful?

The biggest driver of participation commitment is the level of challenge people feel in their work. The right level of challenge produces high participation commitment. The wrong level destroys participation commitment.

You often find the wrong level of participation commitment. When anxiety levels are too low *or* too high, you have to work on participation commitment.

Imagine for a moment that you are managing a game, not a workplace, and that to get people to play hard you have to make that game appealing. The first thing you'd have to do is get the level of challenge right. Not too easy—that's boring. Not too hard—that makes failure too likely.

> Competent performances are built on a firm foundation of commitment.

If work is either too challenging or not challenging enough, you get the same psychological response—a loss of commitment. In either case, the problem comes down to control. People need to feel they can, by trying hard, take charge of events in their lives and make good things happen. So their effort needs to produce results.

$$Effort \rightarrow Results$$

Mess with either side of this effort-results formula and you mess up commitment. When things are too predictable, easy and boring, you take the effort part away. People get the same results whether they try or not, which means *they don't matter*. They don't control results through their own efforts. Results happen with or without their commitment. So why be committed?

Same with excessively hard or challenging situations. Even a big effort often fails to produce good results. So high levels of challenge hurt the results side of the effort-results formula.

High levels of stress and anxiety are good indicators that the situation is too challenging. And when people are overly pessimistic and negative, that's also a sign of excessive levels of challenge.

Fixing Participation Commitment Through Leadership

The reassure and challenge styles of leadership adjust the level of challenge and make sure there is an appropriate level of performance anxiety. Your goal is anxiety in moderation. Performance commitment is high if and only if employees feel slightly anxious about succeeding.

With this background understanding, you can see why the reassure and challenge styles are necessary. Let's review these approaches to leadership:

> Reassure: Help employees cope with the stresses and challenges of work life.

> Challenge: Push employees by raising the level of challenge.

Once you realize how important it is to manage levels of challenge, it is easy to provide appropriate leadership. You can set the

---

Your goal is anxiety in moderation.

---

stage for great performance by raising performance commitment in your people. And, once performance commitment is high, you can go on to the next level of commitment.

Do They Know Where You Are Going?

Let's say you are an old-time captain of a sailing ship, and you have rounded up a great crew and assigned them tasks on your ship that give each of them just the right levels of challenge. They are eager to get to work. They have high participation commitment.

There's just one thing they don't know, however. That is that you have decided to try to sail all the way around the world without stopping in any port. This will be a really long trip and you want to try to break the record for doing it. But the crew assumes it is a normal trip, just going from one port to another. After a few weeks at sea, they start to grumble. "Where are we going?" they ask, and "What's with this captain? Why doesn't he tell us where we're headed?" If you continue to keep your goal secret, the crew's performance will continue to deteriorate. And in time, you can even be pretty sure they'll consider a mutiny, all because you've failed to build another essential type of commitment. Participation commitment is a good start, but it is just the first layer. Really committed, gung-ho employees also are supportive of your goals and plans. We call this *cause commitment* in commitment-based leadership.

A cause is something to strive for, a direction in which to move. It can be a compelling mission or challenging goal. Whether it's solving a problem, beating a competitor out of a sale, increasing productivity, or saving enough to afford upgraded equipment, the cause needs to be important to your employees. It gives them a purpose, a reason for working beyond the simple economic need to work. It makes work exciting and meaningful.

> In time, you can even be pretty sure they'll consider a mutiny.

Why Not Be the Best?

How do you as a leader create significant cause commitment? First, and most obviously, you need to articulate a cause or purpose for your people. If you can't think of anything else, just make it your goal to be the *best* at whatever you do. It's surprising how few managers and businesses make this their goal. And it's also surprising how those who *are* the best in any area got that way. It starts with the simple realization that someone is going to be the best, and it might as well be us! A goal such as this is very empowering.

Building Cause Commitment Through Your Leadership

To build cause commitment, you need to "sell" your goal or cause in two ways: logically and emotionally. You do this by giving sensible reasons why the goal is appropriate—you show why it could work. And you also do this by building emotional support for the goal—you get people excited about it, which requires you to share your feelings of excitement and anticipation.

Your double focus on the rational and emotional sides of cause commitment is necessary because nobody really throws themselves into any cause unless they are both emotionally and rationally involved in it. Both sides of the brain need to be engaged. Or, another way to think of it is to say you must win both their hearts and their minds.

With this background on cause commitment, you can see why the empathize and inform styles are necessary:

> Empathize: Listen to employees, understand how they feel, and work with them to select appealing goals.

> Inform: Explain why a particular direction or goal makes sense and how it relates to their work.

Once you realize how important it is to involve your employees in a meaningful goal or cause, it's natural to focus on building cause commitment. And as soon as you begin to use goals to inspire performances, you'll find it easy to increase your use of the empathize and inform styles.

> You must win both their hearts and their minds.

Do They Want to Do THEIR Part?

Even when employees are eager to participate and believe in the cause, they may not want to do the specific tasks you assign them. So you have to build one more layer of commitment: task commitment.

It is one thing to support a general cause or direction, and another to commit to specific tasks. For example, most people agree that city streets should be kept clean of litter. But few of us are eager to volunteer for a day of cleanup!

Employees can have high participation and cause commitment but still not want to perform a *specific* task.

Fixing Task Commitment Through Leadership

Task commitment is often the problem when an employee performs some tasks well but others poorly. The manager may assume this irregular performance reflects a lack of competence in some areas. But often, the employee simply does not feel that all of the tasks are important enough to deserve his or her best work!

Do All Tasks Deserve Maximum Effort?

In theory, every task that has to be performed in any organization is part of a bigger process. Each is a building block. Each adds efficiently and effectively to a whole. Therefore, everyone has but to perform their own specific tasks well, and the whole process will work at peak efficiency.

But in practice, businesses are rarely that well designed. They are simply too complex and too changeable. There's no way every single individual's assignments can be rationalized to fully support and fit into the whole. There are always some jobs that don't fit in very well, don't really make as much sense as they could, and are either inefficient or, worse, counterproductive.

If you as a leader expect your people to give their best effort to each task, you had better be sure each task *deserves* their best effort. If they suspect they are wasting their time, their effort levels

> Be sure each task *deserves* their best effort.

will understandably fall. And you may not be able to revive them for other, more important tasks.

So keep a little corner of your mind open to the possibility that specific tasks don't make enough sense. Stop to ask yourself and your employees *why* a specific job needs to be done and *whether* it could be done in a better way. This reality-checking behavior is a healthy and necessary part of any high-performance workplace.

To create high task commitment–commitment to specific tasks, you need to make each task important and compelling. You can do this by helping your employees answer three important questions about each task: the what, why, and how questions. And you know what? It's not at all hard to train your people to take an interest in these three questions. They are questions we all naturally feel an urge to ask when given an assignment. The traditional workplace stifles the employee's urge to ask these questions, but it isn't hard to revive this healthy instinct to understand the task.

Here are the questions you want your employees to ask, and how you can help them answer the questions:

1. "What should I do?" Define each task clearly and accurately. Often, employees simply don't understand exactly what's expected of them.
2. "Why should I do it?" Make sure each task is important, and explain why it is important so the employee has a clear line of sight from the specific task to the overall goal or cause.
3. "How well am I doing it?" Surprisingly, most employees feel that their managers don't give them enough feedback. They aren't sure whether they are doing a good or bad job. Giving employees more frequent and accurate feedback helps build their task commitment.

When you become aware of the importance of task commitment and make an effort to answer the what, why, and how questions, you find it natural to use the explain style:

Explain: Tell employees what to do and why it must be done, and give useful feedback about how they perform.

> Everyone has a natural urge to know more about their tasks.

Good work! Now you've built high commitment on several levels, from the most general to the most specific. By attending to commitment issues, you are able to develop higher commitment levels in your employees. That's a great foundation for high performance levels, but it isn't the whole structure. You've got to build one more layer before you're through. Commitment without competence is of little value, so now you need to add the finishing touch—you need to make sure your people are competent to perform their tasks well.

Incentives that *Lead*

Approximately 26 percent of U.S. businesses use some form of incentives to boost performance, according to a survey by the Incentive Foundation. That's a small figure considering that rewards and incentives generally have a significant effect on attitudes and performances. But even worse, most incentive programs ignore the principles of good leadership and therefore tend to provide inappropriate leadership. Yet incentives are seen by employees as part of their boss's leadership style, which means organizations can design incentives to help provide needed leadership!

Most executives favor cash incentives. Like Robert Sbarra, CEO of Sbarra and Co. Inc., they say, "I think my employees can intelligently decide what they want to do with their money." This is a classic application of the delegate style to incentives. Give employees the money and let them design their *own* programs. And, since the delegate style is grossly overused by managers, it is no wonder that cash incentives don't seem to work as well as hoped, according to most studies!

Travelscape.com uses a better designed program for the average employee. Each month, employees elect a winner from among their peers based on performance excellence.

This peer review process gets employees thinking about what they should be doing, why, and how. In other words, it employs the explain style of leadership.

The winner in Travelscape.com's contest is recognized and rewarded with a trip. This special treatment sends a supportive, posi-

> Incentives are seen by employees as part of their boss's leadership style.

tive message to employees that boosts morale. In other words, it employs the reassure style of leadership too.

The winner in Travelscape.com's contest goes on a trip to Las Vegas, which is a top destination for this travel company's customers. So, according to the company's COO, Tom Breitling, "They get to visit hotels, see the shows, visit the restaurants, and be a part of our number one area destination sold." The benefit to the company? "It enhances employees' product knowledge." In other words, it employs both the inform and guide styles of leadership to build commitment—unlike many incentive programs, which risk leading to discouragement and a loss of all that great commitment you've worked so hard to build.

Do your incentives and rewards help or hurt employee commitment?

Leading to Build Competence

Trying hard is great, but it only works when combined with working smart. Commitment without competence produces friction. Heat without light, you might say. And in the end, getting people to work hard at something they aren't qualified to do is setting them up for failure.

So in this session we'll review leadership styles that allow you to lead your people to higher levels of competence. Your goal is to help them work smarter. Too often, people simply do not know as much as they need to about their own jobs. In fact, most employees are doing tasks for which they are not fully qualified, no matter what their resumes might say.

How can that be? How could the average employee be under-qualified for his or her work?

There are several reasons. First, work is changing faster right now than it ever has before. The rate of change in organizations and industries is accelerating over time. So that means everyone must cope with new challenges—for which they may not be fully prepared. Basically, we all have to learn new tricks at an increasing rate.

Second, because the average employee lacks detailed, continuous feedback about his or her performance, performances are often worse than employees realize. People just don't have sufficient information to know the difference between a mediocre, good, or great performance. And if you don't know how you are doing, it makes sense that you can't achieve mastery. Imagine trying to learn to play the piano with ear plugs in your ears. How much better could you become if you removed them?

Third, most managers do not provide much structure and organization for employees' work. When I say this in a live workshop, managers generally object, at least at first. They argue that they certainly do provide structure. But then it turns out that the kind of structure they provide isn't the same kind of structure I'm talking about.

If you provide controlling structures, you aren't structuring the tasks. You're structuring the people. So rules and regulations about where and when people do or don't do things are not helping to clarify their work.

Here's a simple metaphor to explain this concept. Imagine that you want to train a dog to do tricks. You set up some hoops in your

> Getting people to work hard at something they aren't qualified to do is setting them up for failure.

back yard and tell the dog to jump through them. She doesn't. Instead, she runs away and hides in the neighbor's yard. So next you build a fence to keep her in your yard. Okay, now she'll stay in your yard because of the controlling structure you built. But will she learn the trick any better? Certainly not! You could keep her fenced in the yard all her life and she wouldn't become a trained circus dog.

Instead, you need to create task structures. If you want a dog to jump through a hoop, you need to create incentives and rewards for her. You need to show her what to do, reward her when she does it, and withhold rewards when she doesn't. That's the essence of animal training, and it represents the most simplistic approach to structuring tasks.

And note that if you use these simple training techniques, you should be able to train your dog perfectly well, with or without a fence. The structures designed to control your dog have nothing to do with the dog's learning or performance. They just control the dog. They don't create a learning and performance environment.

If you take this metaphor too literally, you might think you can train employees just as you train pets. It won't work, not at least if you want to train them to be independent performers. And you do. You want them to pitch the tent, sell the tickets, and put on the circus without you. So you need to develop a lot more initiative and many more competencies in your people than simple animal training techniques can produce. I'll show you how to build competence in employees in a second, but first, let's make sure we agree on the key point from that metaphor of a circus dog. The point that carries over to human experience is the distinction between structuring people (or animals) and structuring performances to build competence. You need to structure the work, not the people. Okay?

Building Competence with Your Leadership

Competence is the knowledge and experience needed to perform a specific task. Your goal as a leader is to build your employees' competence. However, before you work on this goal, you need to decide what knowledge and experience each specific task requires.

> You need to structure the work, not the people.

The first step toward analyzing any task is to break it down into its component parts or activities. For instance, a sales job might be described as "selling." But that's not a detailed enough picture of the task for you to use in leading an employee to high levels of competence as a salesperson. So you have to take a minute to analyze the sales task and decide what specifically it involves. It might involve some or all of the following:

- Planning sales presentations
- Identifying prospects
- Telephoning to set up meetings with prospects
- Demonstrating the product
- Answering technical questions/solving customer problems
- Developing personal relationships with buyers
- Making sure orders are fulfilled properly
- Keeping accurate written records

As a leader, you'll make the most progress by focusing on one or two of these more narrowly defined tasks at a time. Telling someone that they need to become a better salesperson is too vague. Telling them that you think they could do a better job of selling if they got better at identifying prospects and setting up meetings with them is a lot more specific and actionable.

Success Is Attitude Followed by *Action*

The whole point of taking a narrow approach to defining specific tasks is to help you and your people convert good, highly committed attitudes into specific, helpful actions. Success is a lot more than high commitment. It's attitude turned into action. And that takes a narrow focus on developing competence in the specific actions needed for peak performance.

Studies of athletes show conclusively that you don't get better just by playing. You have to practice specific parts of your game. The soccer player practices dribbling, defending, attacking, shooting, corner kicks, penalty kicks, and so forth. Similarly, a golfer goes to the driving range to work on drives or sets up a place to practice putting

> Studies of athletes show conclusively that you don't get better just by playing. You have to practice specific parts of your game.

on a carpet or in the back yard. We know this is true, and we naturally isolate and practice essential skills in order to master any sport. Yet the technique is applied far less often to work than to sports.

So when you start thinking about employee competence, make sure you focus on specific, well-defined actions—one at a time. Pick one part of one task that seems important for the individual and the job. Understand it. Practice it. Improve it. That's how champions are made, whether on the playing fields or in the workplace.

Using Your Leadership Styles to Build Competence

When you narrow your focus to specific tasks, you can then begin to work on raising competence in these narrow areas. But how you help employees improve depends to a large extent on their existing level of competence. If they are beginners, they need a different style of leadership than if they are intermediate performers. And if they are already quite expert, they need yet another style. Let's look at each of these styles.

Working with beginners

Remember, beginners are those who are not currently competent in a specific, narrowly defined task. Never mind that they may be good at lots of other things. If they don't know how to do the thing you are concerned with right now, treat them like beginners.

For beginners, you need to use the direct style of leadership. In it, you give employees clear directions as they perform. You show and tell them what to do. This style of leadership requires very close supervision on your part. It's your job to talk and walk them through it so that they catch on quickly and don't fail.

The direct style involves the following strategies:

- Show and tell
- Simplify
- Teach in steps
- Supervise!

When you take the time and care to direct someone's efforts, they will get the idea quickly and soon move on to an intermediate level.

> You need to treat beginners, intermediates, and experts quite differently.

Working with intermediates

When an employee has some knowledge and experience already, then you should not direct his or her every move. Instead, you need to give these employees more control over their efforts. That's the only way they can learn to perform better. Remember, the ultimate goal is for them to perform well without your help, so you have to begin to let go.

But because they are not yet expert, you still need to provide structure and support as they perform. Keep an eye on them, and step in to make suggestions or offer informative feedback—positive or negative. This approach employs the guide style of leadership, in which you help employees grow by encouraging them to try new things and improve their skills.

It is called the guide style because your role is like that of a guide on an expedition. Your knowledge and information helps the members of the expedition find the path and make progress. And when problems arise, they can appeal to you for guidance. But it is their expedition, not yours.

In leadership, as in expeditions, guides have to know their place. If they take over, they strip their employees of their initiative. The only way to become an expert is to take charge of your own learning experience. Guides help their employees make this transition.

If you have heard or read about coaching as a style of management, then what you've heard may apply here. The guide style is similar to a good coach's approach. But it isn't like bad coaching, so be careful whom you model your behavior on. What do I mean? I mean that coaches need to know they are not players. They can't run a game. They can only run the practices. The players have to run the game, with the advice and support of the coach.

Same with leaders. They can't be on the playing field when intermediate-level employees perform. They need to be watching from the sidelines, developing strategies, offering advice, and planning the next practice session. A lot of managers are poor coaches because they try to take charge of everyone's performance. Don't fall into this trap, no matter how loud those overpaid professional basketball and football coaches shout. Okay!

> Your role is like that of a guide on an expedition.

Leading experts

If you successfully guide your intermediate employees toward increased knowledge and experience in their jobs, you will gradually find that your people are becoming quite expert in what they do. Now it's time to move on to the culminating leadership style, the one we've all been waiting for! It's time to delegate.

The delegate style requires the leader to trust the employee to perform well out of the leader's sight. It is essential that you truly let go and trust the employee. This means you can't always be sneaking around, checking up on them. That sends the signal that you don't trust them. If they are truly ready—high commitment and high competence—then all you need to do is ask them to tell you how they are doing. They'll know. You don't need to check.

But even though you trust them to supervise their own performances, you still need to make sure they know what they are supposed to be doing and that they get good feedback about how they do. Even experts can get confused or lose their focus, so don't ignore them. Talk with them (or e-mail with them) regularly to discuss what they are doing and how it's going.

When They Reach the Top, Pick a New Mountain

Oh, and one more thing. Remember that neither work nor employees can stay the same for very long. Competitive forces demand that work changes. Improvements and innovations are always important. And human nature demands that employees continue to stretch by learning new or improved skills.

So the experts whom you delegate work to need to be reconsidered periodically. At least once a month, stop and think of ways to increase their level of challenge slightly. Ask them if they can increase their productivity or quality even more. Or ask them if they can learn to do something new and different. That way you keep them vital and involved, and you keep your top performers on the cutting edge.

> Human nature demands that employees continue to stretch by learning new or improved skills.

Session 7

Putting It All Together

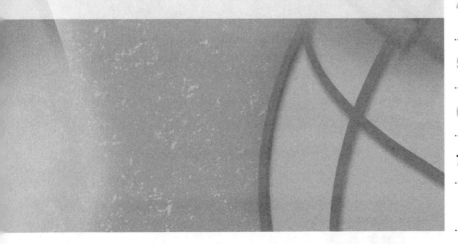

You've already reviewed the need for task and people orientations and the importance of building commitment and competence in your people. And in the previous sessions, you've seen how each of the eight C-Lead styles can be used in sequence to build three layers of commitment and then move people from beginning to intermediate and, ultimately, expert levels of competence.

If you actually have to vary your behavior as a manager through the entire eight-style sequence, you clearly will have to exhibit quite a bit of flexibility. And it is possible to do so, but not very easy. In fact, however, managers rarely need to make use of more than a few styles in any leadership situation. Often only one is needed to get an employee on track.

So the final step in mastering commitment-based leadership is to learn how to diagnose each situation in order to identify the specific style or styles needed. Here's how.

Check Commitment First

Start diagnosing your employees' leadership needs by asking yourself if you think they are fully committed. Do they genuinely want to do what you need done? If you have any concern about their commitment, stop and ask yourself the following questions:

> *Are they too worried or stressed*? If so, then they need you to use the reassure style. If not, go on to the next question.

> *Are they too complacent and content*? If so, then they need you to use the challenge style. If not, go on to the next question.

> *Are they emotionally involved in and supportive of your goal or plan*? If not, then you need to use the empathize style. If so, go on to the next question.

> *Do they agree rationally with your goal or plan*? If not, then you need to use the inform style. If so, go on to the next question.

> Do they genuinely want to do what you need done?

Do they understand exactly what their part is, why it is important, and how their performance will be evaluated? If not, then you need to use the explain style. If so, go on to the next question, which concerns their competence level.

Next Check Competence

With the above questions, you have evaluated all the key components of commitment and have identified which of the five commitment-oriented leadership styles you need to use, if any. Once you can answer each of these above questions so as to "pass through them" without having to employ any of the commitment-oriented leadership styles, you are ready to work on competence. To do so, you need to answer one more question:

Are they beginners, intermediates, or experts at the specific task you have in mind for them? If beginners, you need to use the direct style. If intermediates, you need to use the guide style. If experts, you need to use the delegate style.

Trying Your Hand: A Leadership Case

Now let's see how well the C-Lead method of leadership works in a simulated management situation.

Imagine you are the manager of a radio station. You are concerned because the staff plays music and produces talk and news programs much as it has for many years, and as a result, the audience is smaller and older each year. To sell advertising at a good rate, you need to attract a younger and larger listening audience. In fact, the owners of the station have warned you that you and your entire staff will be replaced at the end of a year if you don't double the station's audience.

So the writing is on the wall. It's a case of modernize or die. You don't want to lose your job and your employees certainly don't want to lose theirs. So you expected them to be ready and willing to help you change the radio station's programming in order to attract more listeners.

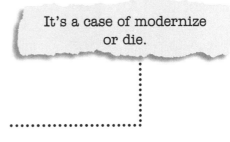

It's a case of modernize or die.

Instead, your initial suggestions and instructions fell on deaf ears. It's been three weeks since you announced in a staff meeting that major changes had to happen. So far, nothing has happened. You are naturally feeling frustrated with your staff. Your instinct is to threaten them unless they do what you want immediately. "No more Mr. Nice Guy," you said to yourself when you looked in the mirror this morning.

But on the drive to work, you remembered something you'd learned in a leadership workshop: you need to diagnose any situation before choosing a style. The style you feel like using is the challenge style. Your instinct is to tell them in no uncertain terms to wake up and smell the coffee, or maybe the smoke of their own jobs burning! Yet you have not diagnosed the situation fully, so you decide to marshal the facts. Here is what you need to know about your employees' state of mind:

1. They are definitely aware of the dangers facing them. You've kept them informed about the problem, and they know the owners are on the verge of taking drastic action.
2. They seem to be highly anxious and concerned. You have overheard lots of worried conversations around the station. In fact, they seem too worried to think clearly about what to do next.
3. They don't seem to "get" the need to change programming in order to appeal to a younger audience. Maybe they don't realize that this is where the listeners—and the advertisers—are. Maybe they don't realize they can't only provide programming for people who are just like them. And even those who understand intellectually the need to change the station's appeal don't seem to be excited or enthusiastic about this transition. They simply feel attached to the old ways.
4. You have talked with several of them about their lack of progress, and they all admitted that they had not yet begun to change in the necessary ways. One of the talk show hosts said, "I know I could be inviting younger, more trendy visitors onto the show, but I just haven't got around to it." From comments like this, you figure they understand perfectly well what their tasks are. They just don't seem to have the energy and enthusiasm to get started.

> You are naturally feeling frustrated with you staff.

5. They are very competent in all aspects of running a radio station. Your staff is among the most experienced in the area. You figure that if they ever got on board and started working on your plan, they could execute it with ease.

Okay, So What Style(s) Do They Need?

Reviewing your notes, you decide that the radio station staff needs you to lead in the _____ style, followed by the _____ and _____ styles. These three styles should fix the obvious _____ problem, after which you can easily _____ the work to your employees.

(Yes, YOU need to fill in these blanks. You're the manager, after all, not me! If you aren't sure, reread the list of facts above and check their commitment and competence levels. What's missing that you need to provide through your leadership? You can use the questions under the previous two headers to find out. See Check Commitment First and Next Check Competence for the series of questions that guide you to specific leadership styles.)

Want to Check Your Answers?

Now that you've diagnosed this leadership situation, let's see whether you agree with my view of it.

It is clear from the first point that the radio station employees are well aware of the dangers and challenges facing them. Therefore they do NOT need you to increase their level of anxiety using the challenge style. So your first instinct, to get mad and start giving them ultimatums, was definitely wrong.

It is clear from the second point that they are in fact overly anxious already. This means their participation commitment is naturally going to be low. To raise their commitment, you have to use the reassure style. You need to help them handle the unusually high levels of stress they feel right now. You need to be supportive and kind, not tough. Try doing something nice for them. Order them pizzas for lunch. Have a massage therapist come in and give everyone back rubs in their chairs. Give them some simple, easy first steps that you

> If they ever got on board and started working on your plan, they could execute it with ease.

> Some of your staff does not fully understand the facts of the situation.

know will result in immediate success, whatever you think will help them adjust to the new challenges and regain their confidence.

It is clear from the third point that your staff does not fully support your goal of attracting a larger, younger audience to the radio station. They all lack emotional commitment, so the empathize style is necessary. Listen to them carefully, trying to understand how they feel. This will help you present your plans in ways that feel good to them. It will help you understand any emotional attachments to the "old ways" so that you can bring about the transition in a sensitive, understanding manner. Major changes such as you have in mind require a period of mourning and adjustment.

It is also clear from the third point that some of your staff does not fully understand the facts of the situation. They may not know that you and the owners have chosen the most logical and likely-to-succeed plan. You need to share your information about the market with them by using the inform style as well as the empathize style. Together, these two styles will build the cause commitment that is so obviously lacking.

Finally, it is clear from the fourth and fifth points that these people are pros who understand their own tasks and have a high level of competence. You probably don't need to worry about task commitment. Once they sign onto the cause, they'll know what tasks they need to perform in order to accomplish it. So don't worry about using the explain style right now. And their extensive experience means that you won't need to direct or guide their work as they develop new programming either. Once you fix your commitment problem, you should be able to delegate the work to this able team of employees.

Reviewing your notes, you decide that the radio station staff needs you to lead in the *reassure* style, followed by the *empathize* and *inform* styles. These three styles should fix the obvious commitment problem, after which you can easily *delegate* the work to your employees.

In sum, your analysis of the leadership situation tells you that you need to use the reassure style, followed by the empathize and inform styles. These three styles will address the problems in participation commitment and cause commitment. When you fix those foundational attitudes, your people should begin to perform the way you want them to!

Why True Leadership is Impossible in a "Corporate Ladder" Environment

Scaling the corporate ladder is a sign of one's trustworthiness; not necessarily of one's inherent productivity. Subservience and sycophancy are rewarded; initiative, which by definition demonstrates a lack of dependence on senior staff, is not. Initiative, after all, carries with it the risk of showing up more senior staff which causes them to lose 'face;' therefore, it is disloyal, and thus not encouraged . . . Senior managers are always right even if they are wrong, and junior employees should not express their opinions before seniors do.

–MICHAEL BACKMAN
(OF THE *ASIAN WALL STREET JOURNAL*,
QUOTE FROM *ASIAN ECLIPSE*, WILEY, 1999, P. 72)

As this quote points out, the traditional corporate hierarchy deafens senior managers and strikes juniors dumb. Nobody is willing to see, hear, or speak "evil," even if it is the simple truth.

If you lead in a highly directive, authoritarian style, you will create this corporate ladder mentality in your people. Then they won't be of much use to you or your organization. Be careful to diagnose each situation and adapt your style to the needs of your people. Otherwise, they'll adapt their style to what they think you need, which is not likely to be healthy for them or you.

> If you lead in a highly directive, authoritarian style, you will create this corporate ladder mentality in your people.

The Employee Motivation Course

Overview of Course III

In this chapter you will learn how to generate unusually high levels of motivation in your employees. You will do this not by using what many people have come to term "jelly-bean motivation," in which tacky contests and awards are offered to cynical employees, making most of them more cynical and less motivated. Instead, you will learn to "turn on" your people by aligning the right tasks and feedback and by relating to them in appropriate ways.

The employee motivation course gives you powerful new ways to think about your task as a manager and a variety of useful, hands-on strategies you can use in one-on-one or group interactions with employees. This course covers quite a bit of ground and consists of the following sessions:

Session 1: Building Employee Motivation

Session 2: The Motivation Process

Session 3: Challenge and Motivation

Session 4: Feelings and Motivation

Session 5: How to Use Recognition and Rewards

But before we dive into the specifics covered in these sessions, let's take a moment to think about the role motivation can play in the success or failure of an organization.

When you set high standards and believe in your heart that people can achieve those standards, and when you recognize achievement publicly, you are going to get higher levels of performance.

—JAMES M. KOUZES AND BARRY Z. POSNER, *Encouraging the Heart*

Session 1

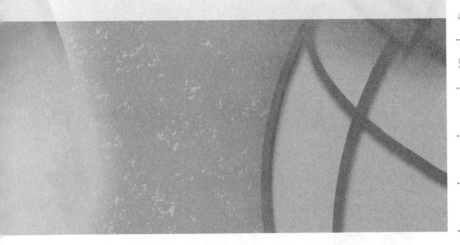

Building Employee Motivation

Introduction

In the small town of Amherst, Massachusetts, two rival copy shops competed for many years. One was a Kinko's store, part of a successful nationwide chain. The other was a small undercapitalized shop organized as a collective and run by a group of young people dedicated to creating a better work experience for themselves and a better alternative for customers. This upstart called itself Collective Copies and operated out of an inexpensive second-floor space, in contrast to the prominent ground-floor retail store occupied by Kinko's Copies. And Collective Copies always seemed to have old and inefficient machines compared to the modern technology showcased at Kinko's. When I first saw the two stores, I was pretty confident the local upstart would be gone within a few years. I'd seen that story played out too many times to expect a miracle.

I was wrong. Somehow Collective Copies kept winning more customers. It gradually improved its equipment and bootstrapped its way into a better ground-floor space. And, over time, Kinko's seemed to lose momentum until one day its windows were papered over and its machines gone.

The local upstart had won. The major chain store had been forced to close. What happened?

A financial analysis doesn't explain the result. Kinko's had distinct cost advantages. It hired minimum-wage employees, whereas the owner-operators of Collective Copies expected to pay themselves reasonable wages. And the chain presumably could negotiate better deals with equipment and paper suppliers because of its size. All else being equal, big chain stores always eat local competitors for lunch.

But all else wasn't equal. The employees of Collective Copies seemed to be more motivated and enthusiastic. Year after year, they kept trying new ideas, offering new services, and winning new accounts. They had a can-do attitude that made it easy to work with them. They made sure customers got what they needed when they needed it. In short, they seemed to be more motivated to succeed than their better-financed competitor. And in the long run, motivation made all the difference. It always does.

> The local upstart had won. The major chain store had been forced to close. What happened?

In this course, we'll look at the hidden power of employee motivation and learn how to harness it to make your people perform better and to improve your bottom line. But before we go on to the first session of the course, I want to warn you that this course is not a standard of MBA programs. In fact, there is no course on employee motivation in the core curriculum of any business school as far as I have been able to determine. And that is a very interesting thing. If motivation can make all the difference, why isn't it a main focus of study for future managers and entrepreneurs? Well, it's because of our tradition of rational management.

To date, employee motivation hasn't been easily reducible to formulas you can crunch on your pocket calculator. It's the "soft stuff" that successful executives and entrepreneurs learn or know instinctively but that business schools have not yet bottled up very successfully. That's okay, of course. Sometimes we have to go well beyond the business school campus to learn what we need to know about how to succeed in business! And fortunately, employee motivation is an area in which I have done quite a bit of work as a consultant, trainer, and writer in the past. I've learned a lot about the subject by observing exceptional managers, by reading in psychology and other fields, and by seeing how other trainers and consultants get great results.

In the following sessions, I'll lead you through a practical, real world approach in which you raise employee motivation levels through a simple four-step process. Each session corresponds to one of the steps in the motivation process. And if you want to get and keep high motivation levels, you simply need to work with this process on a regular basis. Now on to the first session!

> It's the "soft stuff" that successful executives and entrepreneurs learn or know instinctively.

It's surprisingly important to work on employee motivation. I say surprisingly because most managers are unaware of how strong a link there is from employee motivation to bottom-line performance. As a result, most managers treat employee motivation as a secondary issue. They think about it occasionally and devote no more than five to ten percent of their time to it.

When you measure employee motivation levels, you find that the vast majority of employees in the vast majority of businesses are not very motivated. They are operating at medium to low motivation levels. They aren't really excited or fired up about their work. They don't mind doing it, most of them, and sometimes they enjoy it. But work isn't as meaningful and exciting as it would need to be in order for them to be highly motivated most of the time.

Motivation and Meaning

What happens when people are not highly motivated? Their performance is as mediocre as their motivation. They rarely rise to their potential. Think about an athlete competing in a sport, say a player in a tennis tournament. If her motivation were not high, how would she do? Would you expect her to place in the top three? Obviously not. It takes more than skill and fitness to win a tournament. It takes effort, enthusiasm, and drive. Unless the player is focused on and caught up in the game, believes she can win, and really wants to win, she won't.

It's the same for employees, except that we don't really expect our employees to win any tournaments. We don't ask for or receive exceptional efforts and superlative performances. The whole system works on the assumption that people will do a decent day's work, rather than a great day's work. And that's a reasonable assumption when you don't put a lot of thought or effort into motivating people.

But employees and managers alike are not that happy with the status quo. Managers often complain that their people make silly mistakes and don't care, and that their people are always trying to get away with doing less instead of more. And employees often grumble about their work and say they wish they could do something more meaningful. So operating a workplace at medium to low motivation levels is not very rewarding for the people involved. It creates

> The whole system works on the assumption that people will do a decent day's work, rather than a great day's work.

ongoing friction and frustrations that the occasional special event or award program cannot possibly erase. That's why the majority of people don't really enjoy their work experiences most of the time.

As a result of these problems, operating a business in which employee motivation is medium or low imposes human costs that are hard to see because we are accustomed to the current system. But the costs are very real nonetheless.

Motivation and Profits

The greatest and most direct costs of operating with a poorly motivated work force are felt on the bottom line. Employees who are not really fired up do not produce and perform at as high levels as they are capable of. So it should be no surprise that their organizations don't either.

Yet most managers are unaware of the magnitude of the impact attitudes have on profits. It is interesting that this linkage is poorly understood and, in fact, rarely taught on business school campuses or in basic supervisory trainings. Yet it is one of the most obvious and important formulas in all of management. It can be expressed most simply as follows:

Management behavior→Employee motivation→Business performance

How strong is this causal relationship linking management behavior to employee motivation to bottom line performance? It is stronger than most people expect. I cite some helpful statistics in another book I wrote, *Motivating and Rewarding Employees: New and Better Ways to Inspire Your People*:

- In one large-scale study I performed with more than a hundred companies, increases in employee satisfaction explained 39 percent of increases in profits. That's a pretty big handle managers hold in their hands.
- In another study by the consulting firm Surcon International based on interviews with millions of employ-

> Most managers are unaware of the magnitude of the impact attitudes have on profits.

ees, employee attitude measures predicted between 40 and 50 percent of changes in corporate profitability, depending upon the company.

As these two studies indicate, the range of influence is basically from 40 to 50 percent. Depending upon the circumstances in any specific case, better attitudes drive about half of all changes in profit levels.

So next time you think you need to focus on the bottom line, keep in mind that your employees' attitudes and feelings are directly linked to your organization's bottom line!

Motivation Vs. Satisfaction

In my treatment of motivation's impact on profitability, I have deviated from the party line taught at most business schools and believed by most managers (see Fiction and Fact sidebar). There is an ongoing debate at business schools as to whether job satisfaction is important to job performance, and many studies have wrestled with the question over the years.

Do satisfied employees perform significantly better? In some studies, yes, in others, no. But the current consensus is that there is not a strong link between satisfaction of employees and bottom-line profitability. I'm not surprised. Satisfaction is too vague and general a measure. If you survey employees to find out if they are satisfied with their jobs, you may or may not be measuring motivation. Highly motivated employees are satisfied because their work is engaging and challenging, and they enjoy the opportunities for accomplishment it provides. But people can be satisfied for other reasons, too. If they aren't used to being challenged, people may be satisfied because their work does *not* challenge them to excel. So employee satisfaction alone is not sufficient to produce high performance. The moral? Worry about the motivation. Improved performance and satisfaction in a job well done is bound to follow.

> A man can succeed at almost anything for which he has unlimited enthusiasm.
>
> —CHARLES SCHWAB

Motivation Is the Cornerstone of Management

Managing people should be all about motivating them. As a manager, you need to ask yourself routinely if your people are performing near their peak potential, or not. Usually they are not. Lots of things can go wrong to shut down motivation and move performance toward the mediocre routine. But managers are in the people business. Their job is to get things done through other people. If they aren't constantly trying new ways to do that job better, they aren't doing their job.

Sometimes you will encounter employees who simply aren't doing their job and clearly don't want to. They are just seeing what they can get away with. With hard work, you might turn such negative employees around. On the other hand, it might be more productive to simply replace them with people who do want to work. Managers don't have to motivate people who don't want to work.

Employees Want to Be Motivated

Unlike teachers and parents, who also have a motivation challenge, managers do not have to work with whoever who shows up. Employees are carefully screened before hiring to ensure they have relevant skills and are compatible with the organization. And they can be fired if there is a well-documented pattern of failing to perform according to clear instructions and policies. So managers have the luxury of a special selection of people to work with, people who are reasonably well suited to their work, chose to apply for the work, and are therefore ready and willing to get motivated. That's the best possible scenario under which to pursue motivation.

It should be easy to motivate employees. And it is, in theory at least. However, easy does not mean quick or simple. It is a full-time job to create and maintain an environment in which employees are inspired to perform well. To do so, you need to think about motivation regularly, at least daily. And you need to think about the link-

Fiction and Fact

Fiction: Employee attitudes have a minor impact on secondary factors like turnover, absenteeism, and health, but do not have a significant impact on bottom-line returns.

This belief is justified in part by a general inability of academic researchers to document clear links from employee satisfaction to employee performance. Managers might well have learned this fiction from textbook quotes such as the following one from a leading business school text: "So why are positive job attitudes important if they are not related to bottom-line indicators of performance?" (Craig C. Pinder, *Work Motivation in Organizational Behavior*, Prentice Hall, 1998, p. 257.)

Fact: While general satisfaction is not significant, specific attitudes can and do produce superior individual and bottom-line performances. These attitudes generally take the form of commitment to the organization, desire to work, and satisfaction with the job. Raise employee scores on these motivation-oriented attitude scales, and you have highly motivated employees who will help the company be more profitable.

ages between a wide variety of factors and the motivation levels of your employees. For example, the way in which you share information with employees can have a profound impact on motivation levels. And the way in which you structure their tasks and give them feedback affects how they perform those tasks.

Lots of things relate to motivation, which makes it complex. On the other hand, the fact that lots of things relate to motivation means there are lots of things you can do to *work* on motivation levels. So complex is good. It means you have lots of options. I'd rather tackle a construction job with a full toolbox than a single hammer, even though the full toolbox makes the job more complex. Same with motivation. And so I'm going to present the process and approach that forms the basis of a full-blown corporate training course or seminar on the subject of motivation. I'm going to let you get your hands on as many tools and plans as possible. In the next session, we'll roll up our sleeves and begin working on employee motivation through the four-step employee motivation process.

> I'd rather tackle a construction job with a full toolbox than a single hammer, even though the full toolbox makes the job more complex. Same with motivation.

Session 2

Closing the Feedback Loop

In this session of the employee motivation course, I'm going to begin a four-step method for boosting the motivation of your employees. It is based on several simple principles, which I'll explain where they apply. The four steps are as follows:

1. Make the results of their work more visible
2. Adjust their jobs so that they have an appropriate level of challenge
3. Boost their morale to maximize optimism and hopefulness
4. Check the accuracy of feedback to give them a greater sense of control over results

When you've spent a little time on each of these steps, trying out some changes at each step, then you should see an increase in motivation and a resulting increase in both individual and organizational performance.

When you make it through the sequence, you will have made some lasting improvements. But on the other hand, some of the changes will cease if your efforts cease. So the smart thing to do is to simply go back to step one and repeat the process. In fact, managers should probably be cycling through this process continually. That is a practical way to make working on motivation a priority.

Now I'll give you some specifics to keep in mind when working on the first of these steps. We'll take up subsequent steps in later sessions of the Employee Motivation Course.

> In old adventure movies, sometimes the heroes get lost and find themselves on the edge of a steep cliff or hole whose depth they cannot judge because of the darkness.

Step 1: How Do You Make the Results of Their Work More Visible?

In old adventure movies, sometimes the heroes get lost and find themselves on the edge of a steep cliff or hole whose depth they cannot judge because of the darkness. To test the depth, they always dropped a rock over the edge and listened for it to crash into the ground or splash into water at the bottom. And, if the movie was an especially scary one, the rock would never hit bottom. No sound at all.

Well, many of the things employees do are analogous. Their work disappears into the bottomless pit of their organization. They never hear what happened or receive any direct feedback about the quality of their work. They are performing no-splash tasks.

Another metaphor is also useful to illustrate this problem. Imagine that instead of managing employees you are running some kind of competitive game—basketball or something like that. Except that in this game there are no scoreboards, the rules are vague and changeable, and nobody is very clear about how points are made. So the players are never certain whether they are doing the right thing or who's ahead. The obvious thing to improve the quality of play is to post the scores so that everyone has a clearer understanding of the results of their actions.

Most managers have some difficulty seeing this problem. They don't recognize that employees are lacking in feedback. And they don't quite see at first what to do in order to make progress toward the goal of better knowledge of results.

Are you providing enough feedback?

The way to see this lack-of-feedback problem clearly is to look at or think about a specific employee doing a specific job. Visualize that employee coming into work and going through his or her routine. What tasks are performed? In what order? How many things are done in a day? Now, stop and think about the feedback that employee receives from each of the tasks performed in the day.

Is there some feedback from you, the manager? Do you sometimes correct the employee if you notice a mistake or praise the employee if you see everything is going fine? Probably, but how often? Most managers simply don't feel they have the time to "hover over" an employee and provide constant feedback. As a result, employees generally perform dozens to hundreds of tasks before their manager comes around and says anything about their work. Most of the time, most employees work beyond the immediate supervision of their supervisors. So they don't get regular feedback from their managers, only intermittent feedback. Some employees say that they only get specific feedback about how their boss thinks they are doing once or twice a year, when the formal performance review must be done.

Another common problem is inaccurate feedback. If an employee does something poorly, will negative feedback result? If the answer is

> Employees generally perform dozens to hundreds of tasks before their manager comes around and says anything about their work.

sometimes but not always, then the feedback may be inaccurate. Similarly, if employees sometimes get negative feedback when they do the right thing well, then there is an accuracy problem. And accuracy problems are a lot more common than most managers realize.

For example, let's say a team of employees is responsible for supporting a major corporate client for a company that sells computer services to other companies. And perhaps one employee on the team doesn't follow through, letting the others do more than their share. If this employee gets away with it, then the message to all members of the team is clear: there is not an accurate link between your performance and your results. There is a disconnect somewhere. And that's highly demotivating! Similarly, let's say that some of the employees on that team do a really good job. They make an extra effort. But because of factors beyond their control, the client switches to a competitor. They will not be praised for their good work in all likelihood. But they should be, or they'll see another one of those disconnects between performance and results that are so bad for motivation.

Do they understand the whys?

As a manager, you can boost motivation by looking for ways to improve the speed and accuracy of feedback and to make the *purpose* of the game more visible, too. Tell employees the rules as often and accurately as you can. Don't ever take it for granted that they know why they are here and why the work is important. It only takes a moment to mention the purpose of a task or the impact a task has on product quality, customer perceptions, cost control, or whatever. Tell them why they are doing specific tasks. If you don't know, figure it out. One of your most important jobs as a manager is to know why.

When the why question is clear to you and your employees, then it's easier to create those scoreboards they need to stay motivated by the game. You might not see this relationship between telling them why they are doing and telling how they are doing at first, but it is a powerful one. The answers to the why question actually drive the answers to the how question.

Watch out for disconnects between performance and results!

For example, let's say you run the front desk of a hotel. You teach your employees that they need to make sure customers feel good about their interactions with the staff. That way, customers will feel good about their stay and will come back and also refer new customers. So you start the motivation process by explaining the game. Why are we here? In part, to make sure that customers feel better as a result of their interactions with us, not worse.

When employees understand the why, then the how is clearer. For example, when they answer customer telephone calls from guests of the hotel, they should be friendly, cheerful, and helpful in order to try to *improve the guest's mood*. And it makes perfect sense to evaluate their telephone behavior according to this goal. As a supervisor, you can listen to the tone of those conversations and tell them if you think they are sufficiently upbeat and empathetic to accomplish the goal. You could also do periodic customer surveys to get customer feedback on the same question. By focusing on specific performance goals, sharing those goals with employees, and giving feedback relevant to those goals, you can greatly increase the employees' knowledge of results. You can help them see how they are doing more clearly.

Can you put employees in charge of their own feedback?

At some point you will max out. You will, for example, not be able to monitor every single telephone call between the employees and guests of a hotel, not unless you want to do nothing else in a day. When you reach the limits of your own ability to provide feedback, then you need to teach employees to provide more and better feedback for themselves. (In fact, the feedback employees give themselves is the most motivating kind!) For example, you might create a simple checklist or form that an employee at the front desk of a hotel could use to track each phone call. It could be as simple as the form in Figure 3-1.

> The manager's most important job is to know *why*.

FIGURE 3-1 SELF-FEEDBACK FOR TELEPHONE CONVERSATIONS WITH HOTEL GUESTS

Date : _____   Employee : _____

Rate each telephone conversation you have with a customer:

Did I help caller feel better about his or her stay?	No = 1 2 3 4 5 6 7 = Yes
Did I help caller feel better about his or her stay?	No = 1 2 3 4 5 6 7 = Yes
Did I help caller feel better about his or her stay?	No = 1 2 3 4 5 6 7 = Yes
Did I help caller feel better about his or her stay?	No = 1 2 3 4 5 6 7 = Yes
Did I help caller feel better about his or her stay?	No = 1 2 3 4 5 6 7 = Yes
Did I help caller feel better about his or her stay?	No = 1 2 3 4 5 6 7 = Yes
Did I help caller feel better about his or her stay?	No = 1 2 3 4 5 6 7 = Yes
Did I help caller feel better about his or her stay?	No = 1 2 3 4 5 6 7 = Yes
Did I help caller feel better about his or her stay?	No = 1 2 3 4 5 6 7 = Yes
Did I help caller feel better about his or her stay?	No = 1 2 3 4 5 6 7 = Yes
Did I help caller feel better about his or her stay?	No = 1 2 3 4 5 6 7 = Yes
Did I help caller feel better about his or her stay?	No = 1 2 3 4 5 6 7 = Yes
Did I help caller feel better about his or her stay?	No = 1 2 3 4 5 6 7 = Yes
Did I help caller feel better about his or her stay?	No = 1 2 3 4 5 6 7 = Yes

It takes only a second to check or circle the numbers on the scale in Figure 3-1 after each call. And when employees do it, they are scoring themselves. That way, they get immediate feedback whether you are there to supervise them or not. To encourage employees to use such a form, you might offer a small reward at the end of the day for all who have remembered to self-rate their phone calls. But I'd let them keep the forms, as they may want to follow their own performance over time using them.

"But they won't be accurate," complain most managers. "Why won't they just lie and say they rate a 7 on each call?"

Accuracy is not really the point. Don't use this system to punish or reward, just to inform. And remember, the point is to inform employees about their purpose, to give them "how" feedback about the important "whys" of their work. So you don't need to collect and examine such self-feedback sheets at the end of the day, or to compare one employee's sheet with another. You just need to require that they use the sheet and explain to them that by using it they will be able to keep the key performance objective in mind. If they were practicing their serve in tennis, they'd no doubt make a mental note of whether each practice serve was in or out. This is the same sort of thing. You can't improve without keeping track of performance. You need to know your score.

When you combine more and quicker feedback from you, the manger, with new ways for employees to keep their own scores, you can do a great deal to improve employees' knowledge of their results. You can make their performances more visible to them. They will be able to see how they are doing. And that's the first step to higher motivation.

Principle: Inform vs. Control

Managers often end up telling employees what to do or how they are doing. That's good for motivation, or bad; it depends on whether you are playing a controlling or informative role. If the employee sees it as having to do something to please you or comply with company rules, that's controlling. If the employee sees it as learning more about how to do a good job or how well he or she is

> Accuracy is not really the point. Don't use this system to punish or reward, just to inform.

> Don't let employees become dependent on your views of what is good or bad.

doing, then that's informative. Scoreboard-style feedback is informative. It tells you how you are doing. Saying, "I see that your productivity rate is going up. Good work," is drawing attention to an informative measure of performance. Saying "That's good" or "that's bad" is more controlling as it makes the employee dependent upon your view of what's good or bad. Check your feedback to make sure it is informative if you want to increase employee motivation.

Session 3

Challenge and Motivation

As you may recall from the previous session of this employee motivation course, managers can use a simple four-step process to boost employee motivation. It is as follows:

1. Make the results of their work more visible
2. Adjust their jobs so that they have an appropriate level of challenge
3. Boost their morale to maximize optimism and hopefulness
4. Check the accuracy of feedback to give them a greater sense of control over results

We reviewed ways of making the results of work more visible and saw how this approach can help boost motivation in your employees. Now we will look at the second step in the motivation process, in which there are also powerful links between what you do as a manager and how motivated your people will be.

Step 2: Adjust Their Jobs So That They Have an Appropriate Level of Challenge

In step one you worked on providing more and better feedback so that employees know exactly how they are performing. When you get good feedback, you know when you are doing well. You also know when you are doing poorly. And if you are doing poorly, it's easy to get discouraged. So when managers try to boost motivation or improve performance, they often end up discouraging their employees instead of motivating them.

For example, take the case of a company that performs customer surveys for other companies. As it grew, it added more offices and more employees to handle the greater number of projects. In one new office, the manager was frustrated that employees did not seem to be able to write clear, professional reports to the customers. Every project ends in a report, so report writing is a core part of the work. But the employees this manager was assigned made lots of careless errors in the reports.

These mistakes made the company look unprofessional and called the accuracy of the conclusions into doubt. Yet when the man-

> If you are doing poorly, it's easy to get discouraged.

ager started insisting on reviewing each report before delivery, the employees became disgruntled. They complained that the manager was too picky. They complained that they were having to work extra hours on rewriting reports. They said the work was more difficult than they had been led to believe when they were hired and that they ought to be paid more. And they kept making mistakes so the manager felt she was putting in far too much time correcting their work. Everyone was unhappy and job motivation levels were falling. What to do?

Employees are not going to be motivated unless there is an appropriate level of challenge. They need tasks that are not too easy and not too hard. They need just the right amount of challenge to require them to stretch and grow a little. When work is too easy, it is boring and employees fall into a feeling of entitlement. They no longer feel like they need to pull their weight. When work is too hard, however, employees lose motivation for other reasons. They feel too anxious. They get discouraged. Either way, their enthusiasm for participating in the game of work falls when the challenge is not appropriate to their current level of skill.

In the case I described a moment ago, where employees are writing poor reports, the problem is that the task is too difficult. It is not easy to learn to write well. Employees who don't write well aren't going to learn to write well overnight. To keep requiring them to write good reports guarantees that they will fail repeatedly. And that is not going to do their motivation any good!

If employees continue to do a poor job, even when they are getting clear feedback and know their performance is unacceptable, then you should try to adjust the level of challenge. You don't want them to be receiving negative feedback too often. You want them to receive more positive than negative feedback. In fact, most employees need positive results more than half the time, and many need positive results at least three-quarters of the time. People aren't as thick-skinned as you might think. They don't enjoy failing, and they don't like criticism. The right level of challenge for them is one in which they feel pretty confident they can do at least a decent job and only need to be corrected or to correct themselves occasionally.

So it's not good for an individual's motivation to fail too often. If they aren't doing a good job, then they probably need an easier

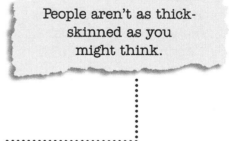

People aren't as thick-skinned as you might think.

task to perform for now. And you know what else? It's definitely not good for the organization to have people doing tasks that seem to be too much of a challenge for them. From the organization's point of view, messing up even one in fifty times might be too much. Certainly a situation like the case I described earlier is unacceptable, in which employees routinely make errors in their written reports to clients. What will the clients think?

So the solution to that problem is to readjust the task so as to bring down the level of challenge to one which is appropriate to the employees. If they aren't good writers, then asking them to write reports is not realistic. And unrealistic expectations are highly demotivating. So the manager in this case needs to ask herself how she can redesign the report writing task so that it is a realistic challenge for the people she has to work with.

How do you redesign a task?

It's difficult to redesign tasks. Tasks often exist because they make sense in and of themselves. A driver needs to drive a truck, for example. It's hard to imagine a redesign of that task appropriate to poor drivers. You could have drivers drive a toy truck around the parking lot until they got good enough to go on the road, but that's stupid. The company wouldn't make any money that way. Same with writing those client reports. If you permitted employees to write grade school-style reports, the task would be easier, but the company wouldn't be able to keep its clients. So the task requirements often end up determining the level of challenge, and most managers take a *task perspective* when designing and supervising jobs.

However, there is always another perspective if you are willing to think creatively about the work. It is the employee perspective, and it involves looking at the task from the perspective of what support the employee needs in order to do the task well. You can add more support if the challenge is too high, or reduce the support if the challenge is too low for optimal motivation.

Increasing the level of support

Support is anything that makes the job easier to do. Anything. Open your mind to the possibilities. Here, for example, are some of

> You can add more support if the challenge is too high, or reduce the support if the challenge is too low for optimal motivation.

the kinds of support you could use to make the job of writing client reports an easier one. This is simply a creative listing of any and all ideas, which is the first step toward finding the *right* idea:

- Require employees to use the spelling and grammar checkers of a word processing program.
- Create paragraph templates for commonly used points and let employees cut and paste these into their reports.
- Hire a professional editor to edit each report.
- Give employees examples of excellent reports that they can use as starting points, rewriting to fit their specifics.
- Create a computer program with hundreds of template paragraphs and fill-in-the-blank sentences so that employees don't have to write a report from scratch.
- Have employees fill in a questionnaire or form and use it as the basic reporting format instead of a text-based report.
- Have employees report the results on a cassette tape and then have a writer turn them into written reports.
- Change the format of reports so that they are shorter and easier to write.
- Change the format of reports to include more graphs and tables and fewer words. Use a computer program that creates good graphs and tables automatically.
- Team up employees, pairing worse writers with better writers, and require them to write and edit reports together.
- Require all employees to submit reports to you two days before they are due to the client so that you can mark up and return them for improvements.
- Break up the job by creating a specialized report writing position. Reassign the one employee who writes the best reports to doing it full time. Others can take up the slack left from reassigning this person since they will not have to write their own reports any more.
- Offer internships to English majors from nearby colleges to give them a chance to learn business writing—by editing your client reports!

There are always creative ways to provide more support.

I don't know how many of these possibilities would work in specific situations, but I do know that when you start viewing tasks from the employee perspective, you can always think of many possible ways to offer more support. And when you develop a long list of alternatives, you are well on the way to a solution. You can try one or a few of the alternatives that seem most likely to work. If they don't work well, you can modify them or try some of the other alternatives.

In many cases, employees seem to be unable or unwilling to improve. They keep doing a poor job. If they know it, if the scoreboards are appropriate and visible, then the problem isn't a lack of good feedback. So telling them they are messing up isn't going to fix the problem. Fix the task instead by adding more support so that the level of challenge is more appropriate for your people. It's amazing how a minor adjustment in the level of challenge can eliminate persistent performance problems and boost employee motivation!

Principle: Get the Level of Challenge Right

Have you ever played horseshoes? You toss a U-shaped horseshoe at an iron stake in the ground. If the shoe lands around the base of the stake, you get a point. If it misses, you don't. Now, this game is only fun if you get the distance between yourself and the stake just right. A beginner needs to stand closer, an expert farther away. Everybody has to stand just far enough to make it tough to get a point, but not impossible. If you are too far away, the game is discouraging and you'll quit. If you are too close, the game is trivial and you'll quit. So the game of horseshoes illustrates the importance of a reasonable level of challenge. Get the level of challenge just right and any game or task can be engaging and motivating. Get it wrong, and people will want to quit.

> Our team is well balanced. We have problems everywhere.
>
> —TOMMY PROTHRO, AMERICAN FOOTBALL COACH

Session 4

Feelings and Motivation

I n this session, we will complete our tour of the employee motivation process by examining the many things you can do to boost employees' performance in the last two steps of the motivation process. We'll focus specifically on steps three and four. As you will recall, the process involves the following four steps:

1. Make the results of their work more visible
2. Adjust their jobs so that they have an appropriate level of challenge
3. Boost their morale to maximize optimism and hopefulness
4. Check the accuracy of feedback to give them a greater sense of control over results

We've already explored some powerful ways of boosting employee motivation and building bottom-line performance in previous sessions. Now let's look at the third step in the process, in which you use the tools and techniques of emotional motivation. Haven't heard of that? Well, neither have a lot of managers, but it is one of the most powerful management methods available to you. Let's take a look.

Step 3: Boost Their Morale to Maximize Optimism and Hopefulness

In the first two steps of the motivation process, the manager focuses on giving employees better knowledge of the results of their performances and on adjusting their tasks so that the employees have an appropriate level of challenge. These steps should help build employee motivation. But they won't necessarily create peak motivation and performance levels on their own. Unless employees are feeling good about their work, they will not reach peak motivation levels. An employee's emotional state is the hidden foundation of motivation.

This third step in the process focuses on employees' frames of mind. You'll learn how to appreciate and improve upon your employees' emotional states. And you'll learn to create a positive, optimistic attitude toward work. Why? Because of the fundamental principle that:

It takes a positive frame of mind to get motivated!

Like a building's foundation, which we never actually see, there is a vital emotional foundation to motivation. And it turns out nobody looks at it very often or has much of an idea what it's made of. It's just down there somewhere. Or is it?
—*STREETWISE MOTIVATING AND REWARDING EMPLOYEES* (P. 100)

That seems like nothing more than simple common sense. It is. Yet it is difficult to apply in the average workplace because it is not a part of the traditional management role to create positive employee attitudes. Feelings aren't supposed to have anything to do with work. But they do. Of course they do.

So much writing and theorizing about organizations operating under "norms of rationality" has affected not only the academic study of work and motivation but the very practice of management. To be rational has been the vogue; to be emotional or to be seen as emotional has not been in vogue for many decades.
–PROFESSOR CRAIG C. PINDER, *WORK MOTIVATION IN ORGANIZATIONAL BEHAVIOR* (PRENTICE HALL, 1998, P. 93.)

Which path are employees on?

To get a handle on employee feelings as they relate to motivation, ask yourself whether employees are feeling resistant or motivated right now. Motivated people feel good about a task or goal. They can't wait to pursue it. Their positive feelings toward their work make them optimistic and enthusiastic. They see problems as opportunities. I call this perspective the motivation path, and it leads to exceptional performances.

In contrast, resistant people feel bad about any task or goal they are given. They don't look forward to pursuing it. Their negative feelings toward their work make them pessimistic and dispirited. They see opportunities as problems. I call this perspective the resistance path, and it leads to variable performances at best.

Figure 3-3 illustrates these two options and the feelings axis that separates them. If you take the time to figure out whether your people are feeling up or down, and shift them toward up if necessary, you will find it much easier to create and sustain high motivation levels.

> To get a handle on employee feelings as they relate to motivation, ask yourself whether employees are feeling resistant or motivated right now.

FIGURE 3-3

How Feelings Drive Performance

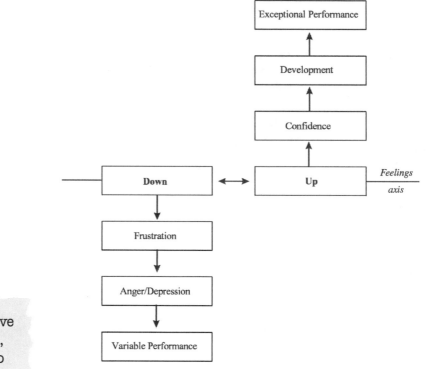

Reproduced by permission of Alexander Hiam & Associates

Employees with a positive outlook feel in control, confident, and eager to perform.

In addition, people with a positive frame of mind, those on the motivation path, feel more in control of their lives. They don't react as victims when they have a setback. They cheerfully regroup and try again. Their positive attitude prepares them to take charge of their own work. They are confident they can do better. They look within themselves for the answers. They are easy to motivate because you can tap into their own internal, or intrinsic, motivation.

But people with a negative frame of mind feel like bad things happen to them. They feel helpless instead of in control. Minor setbacks knock them off course for long periods of time. And they do not respond well to appeals to their internal motivation. They require large doses of external pressure from their managers to keep them going. And that's no fun for managers. You don't want to have to push your people uphill. You want them to pull you uphill. So it's vital to build the right emotional foundations for motivation by getting your people into a positive frame of mind.

Encouraging the heart

James M. Kouzes and Barry Z. Posner believe that managers should do specific things to try to make their employees feel good. They call this encouraging the heart. Here are some of their recommendations:

- Get a small annual calendar and use it to record the birthdays of your employees. Also record the anniversary dates of when they were hired. Send each a note or card or stop by for a visit on those dates. (And I'll add to their suggestion that employees always appreciate a small birthday present!)
- Create a Hall of Fame—an area for small plaques, thank-you notes, and other praises and recognition for employees.
- Find out what it's like to walk in another's shoes by volunteering to do an employee's job for a day.
- Write at least three thank-you notes each day. Kouzes and Posner explain that "We've never heard anyone complain about being thanked too much, but we've all heard lots of complaints about being thanked too little!"

> When was the last time you *thanked* an employee or associate?

Are you empathetic and considerate to employees?

Empathy is a powerful and easy-to-use tool in motivating employees. If you are aware of and interested in how they feel, they will tend to feel better about their work. It's really quite a simple formula. By raising your awareness of their feelings, you help them feel better. You don't have to do anything to change their feelings. Simply be more aware of them and they will change themselves.

Managers who make an effort to be conscious of how their people feel generally inspire more positive feelings in their people, and better performances too. Some things are pretty simple in management and this is one of them, a real no-brainer, but it runs against our tradition of rational management so managers rarely try the trick.

How do I know that most managers don't try being empathetic and considerate? Because I've surveyed employees from more than a hundred organizations to find out how empathetic they felt their supervisors were. And the result was a negative rating. On average, employees say their bosses are quite the opposite of empathetic, whatever exactly that is. Inconsiderate is probably the best word for how managers are seen by their employees.

And if your employees see you as inconsiderate, their motivation will be limited and their performances stunted. You will never see what they are truly capable of until they view you as empathetic and considerate of their needs and feelings. So how can you show them you care?

Are you empathizing with employees?

Empathizing means sensing how someone feels. You know how to be empathetic. You are probably very good at empathizing with people in some circumstances. For example, you may be very empathetic toward children, babies, or pets. Or you may pick up on it right away when a good friend or family member is sad or stressed out. But do you apply your empathy skills to your employees? Few managers do. They don't realize it's part of their job to create the right emotional foundations for motivation, so they don't know that their employees' feelings are important.

But once you know that employee feelings matter, it is easy to start attending to them more carefully. For example, when you greet an employee in the morning or during the work day, you will naturally take a greater interest in finding out how they feel than if you didn't know their feelings were important. So instead of a passing "Hello," you will stop for a moment and check in with them. You might ask them if everything is okay, or how they are feeling. And

The greatest motivational act one person can do for another is to listen.
—ROY E. MOODY,
PRESIDENT,
ROY MOODY AND ASSOCIATES

when you ask them these questions, your natural empathy will help you stop and listen to them. Really focus on what they say and what they don't say. If you make it a point to figure out exactly how they are feeling, you will be surprised at how easily you can pick up on their attitude. Then you can acknowledge their feeling respectfully, showing them you know and care.

For example, let's say you bump into one of your people in the middle of the afternoon as you pass each other in a corridor. Stopping, you say, "So, how's everything going?" And, because you have reminded yourself you want to figure out how they are feeling, you stop and watch them attentively. So they stop too and say something noncommittal, like, "Oh, fine, How about you?" But you have an idea they aren't very happy. The answer isn't very convincing, their tone fell off instead of rising. And they look troubled or distracted.

So instead of answering their question directly, you try to learn more about how they are feeling. Maybe you say, while smiling to let them know you aren't being critical, "I'm not convinced yet. Are you sure nothing's bothering you?" And then maybe they say, "No, not really, it's just . . . " And now you are getting somewhere. You've poked them just enough to let them know you really want to know how they are feeling. Now all you have to do is listen and nod encouragingly, and maybe ask a further question or two to find out what's troubling them. Then you can end the conversation by saying something like, "Well, I'm glad to know how you are feeling, and I hope things look up soon."

Notice that all you've done in this example is uncover and acknowledge some negative feelings. You have not taken on the responsibility of fixing the problem. You don't have to do anything for your empathy to begin helping the employee's mood improve. If there is obviously something you can do, and it makes good sense to do it, then go ahead. But don't feel that you have an obligation to jump through hoops to keep anything bad or stressful from ever happening to your employees. Life, and work, are not like that. They are full of downs as well as ups. You might smooth out some of the bumps, but you can't remove them all. Your employees need to cope with their problems and rise above them. Your empathy and concern helps them respond in a more resilient fashion.

> Acknowledge your employees' feelings respectfully to show them that you care how they feel.

If they thought you cared, they wouldn't think you were unfair

Most employees believe that their employers treat them unfairly. They nurse grudges. They feel helpless in the face of unjust treatment. And that keeps them from moving up the motivation path toward peak performances. By being more empathetic and considerate, you can beat this unfairness rap. But you've got to be more considerate than the average manager, or your people will fall prey to the same attitudes that characterize a majority of employees according to a Towers Perrin survey:

PERCENT OF EMPLOYEES BELIEVING THAT

Promotions are unfair	65%
Companies don't consider employees' interests in decisions affecting them	69%
Job opening aren't filled with the most qualified candidates	51%
Top performers aren't rewarded with higher pay	66%

Opportunities to achieve make employees feel great

Opportunities are motivating because they tap into the feel-good power of personal achievement. You feel good about yourself when you accomplish something important. Achievement and appropriate recognition for that achievement ranked at the top of the list of employee motivators in the classic studies by Frederick Herzberg, studies which every MBA student must read but which few ever try to apply in their own work. Instead, people continue to try to motivate with the factors that Herzberg says have low to medium impact on motivation, such as salary, work conditions, and status.

Now we'll take a brief look at the final step of the motivation process, in which you revisit the feedback employees receive to make sure it is as accurate as possible. You will probably be surprised to learn that most employees do not get very accurate feedback about the quality of their own performances!

> People continue to try to motivate with the factors that Herzberg says have low to medium impact on motivation, such as salary, work conditions, and status.

Step 4: Check the Accuracy of Feedback to Give Them a Greater Sense of Control Over Results

I already talked briefly about the importance of accurate feedback in the first step of this motivation process. As the last step, you need to take another hard look at the accuracy of feedback. Inaccurate feedback is commonplace and always hurts motivation.

Here are some of the more common ways in which employee feedback is biased or confused, creating inaccurate or hard-to-see links between performance and results. Try to avoid or fix these problems if you see any of them:

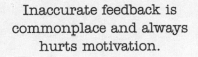

Inaccurate feedback is commonplace and always hurts motivation.

- When your own mood biases your feedback. Often, managers give out rewards and praise when they are in a good mood and are grumpy, critical, and strict when they are in a bad mood. That means vital feedback is determined by how the manager feels, not by how the employee performs. To avoid this problem, complain only about how you feel when you don't feel good. Avoid complaining about how employees are performing if that's not the root of your bad mood.
- When the results of employee performances are long term. If employees are working on a long-term project, like trying to design a new product or land a new client or implement a new program, then they do not get much feedback in the short term. Even if they eventually succeed, this positive feedback was not available during the project and so did not aid their motivation or boost their performance. To solve this problem, you need to create short-term benchmarks for them to pursue.
- When feedback is on the group level, not the individual level. If employees cannot see how their own specific performances affect the feedback, then they aren't getting accurate personal feedback. This is a very common situation. For example, take a factory in which the main goals have to do with overall quality and productivity goals for each shift. Whether the shift accomplishes its goals or not is only a partial indicator of how each individual performed. Some days the goals

will be met with ease even though some individuals are feeling bad and don't try very hard. To avoid this problem, make sure you have good measures of individual performance as well as group performance.

- When performance measures are inappropriate or inaccurate. Companies often have institutionalized measures of performance that aren't very accurate or relevant. For example, some doctors working in HMOs are measured and compensated in part by how many outside referrals they make, with the assumption being that more referrals to specialists is bad and fewer is good. This measure is designed to control costs. But instead, it destroys motivation and produces resistant attitudes. Why? It is inaccurate as an indicator of the quality of a doctor's work. Perhaps some doctors make unnecessary referrals, but many more make appropriate referrals. If they stopped making referrals, doctors would often be withholding needed care. They know this is too blunt a measure and they resent the feedback it produces.

To avoid these kinds of problems, review feedback and measures of performance regularly, checking to make sure that they are accurate and appropriate and focus on the key indicators of performance quality.

It All Comes Down to Curiosity

As you work on and think about motivation in each of these four steps, be sure to encourage employees to be inquisitive about their own work. Anyone who performs a job with curiosity will test different strategies and methods. They will explore the relationships between how you do the work and what results you achieve. They will therefore be able to learn from feedback. But when people just keep their heads down and do their job the same way every day, no amount of feedback in the world can improve their performance. Employees aren't open to feedback and able to use it productively unless they are interested in how to improve.

> With so many ways to reward people, you may ask, 'How do I decide how to reward each person?' The answer is simple: Ask them.
>
> —MICHAEL LEBOEUF, THE GREATEST MANAGEMENT PRINCIPLE IN THE WORLD

If your people don't seem very interested in improving, make a point of asking them for their ideas about how to improve things. Let them know you want them thinking. And when they do have ideas, listen to them respectfully and praise them for their interest. Even if their ideas seem worthless to you, they are valuable to the employees. People who are thinking about their work are motivated and ready to make improvements. Encourage this healthy frame of mind.

Many managers say they want more employee motivation, then fail to recognize and encourage it when they see it. Here's what motivation looks like. It looks like employees who are interested in how to do their work and want to do it better. If you see anything of that sort, jump on it. Fan the flames. It's true motivation, and it is rare enough in businesses that few managers recognize it when they see it!

> Be sure to encourage employees to be inquisitive about their own work.

How to Use Recognition and Rewards

Session 5

If you've already gone through the first four sessions of this course, you will know that there is a four-step process through which you can build employee motivation. It aligns employee goals with those of the organization, takes care of the essential emotional foundations of motivation, and insures appropriate feedback and constructive interpersonal relations in order to boost job motivation levels. Do all that and you've taken care of the essential fundamentals of motivation.

Now you can have some fun!

If you wish, you may now layer some exciting or inspiring or just plain funny recognition and reward programs on top of that solid motivation foundation you built. I often refer to recognition and reward programs as the frosting on the cake. If you've baked a good cake, a good frosting will make it special. But too often, managers forget about the cake and just slather thick frosting over an old, dry biscuit. When they still don't get a big response, they add decorative icing, fancy frosting flowers, and the like. But nothing they do seems to stimulate employees' appetites, because down under all that frosting something is old and rotten. That's why the average employee reward program is a dud, no matter how exciting the rewards. And that's why I've left this module on rewards until the end of your course. I know everyone and their uncle tries to sell you on fancy rewards and contests up front, before you've even looked at cake recipes, but we are going to do it right.

What's at Stake: Your Credibility!

Why do it right? Why not just order up a fancy reward program and get back to work? Because if you don't do the preparatory work in the first four sessions, that program will fall flat on its face. Or, to be more precise, it will land in *your* face. You'll have frosting all over you. You will look like a fool to your people, and it will take you a long time to rebuild your credibility. Your leadership is at stake here. Don't mess it up!

When managers throw a reward program at demotivated employees, the employees react with cynicism, resistance, and withdrawal. They sense the disconnect between the talk and the walk. It

> When managers throw a reward program at demotivated employees, the employees react with cynicism, resistance, and withdrawal. They sense the disconnect between the talk and the walk.

pisses them off, and sometimes it even drives them off. Reward systems that look like two-dimensional movie sets don't work and employees don't like them. Here are some comments from employees who didn't like their employers' reward programs:

> "They treat us like kids."

> "It's stupid, but we all go along with it. What else can we do?"

> "Once a month, they feed us well and give us prizes and awards. The rest of the time, they treat us like dogs."

> "Do they really think I'm going to work extra hours every day all year for a one in a thousand chance of going to Hawaii for the weekend?"

> "For every idea that gets a reward, thousands of suggestions are ignored. Is that supposed to motivate me?"

> "Right. Like I'm going to work harder for play-money coupons when I haven't had a proper raise in three years."

> "My boss used to leave me alone except when he wanted to chew me out. But ever since that training he keeps coming around and bugging me to 'catch me doing something right.' I don't want an insincere pat on the back from him. He doesn't know the difference between good and bad work anyway."

In each of these cases, managers have skipped over the four-step process of building motivation and have tried to frost an old cake with fancy new programs. The responses are predictable. They always range from neutral to negative when you apply rewards without building the foundations of motivation first. Rewards are symbols of effective motivational management and the sincerely excellent efforts it generates. On their own, symbols are meaningless at best, and at worst can connote the opposite meaning from what you intend. Be careful when you work with rewards!

On their own, symbols are meaningless at best, and at worst can connote the opposite meaning from what you intend. Be careful when you work with rewards!

Successful Rewards: The High Involvement Approach

Rewards work well when they stimulate high involvement on the part of employees. You don't get high involvement unless you've taken care of the basics first. When you do, then rewards work very well indeed.

What does high involvement mean?

Specifically, employees need to be engaged with the reward or recognition system on two dimensions: rational and emotional. Only when you have high involvement on both levels do you get a motivational bang for your reward buck, as the High Involvement Approach to Motivation (H. I. A. M.) grid portrays. If you've done your homework as described in earlier sessions, it should be fairly easy to find a reward or recognition method that generates high involvement. But if not, no amount of creative effort now will produce the involvement you need to make a program succeed.

> Employees need to be engaged with the reward or recognition system on two dimensions: rational and emotional. Only when you have high involvement on both levels do you get a motivational bang for your reward buck.

FIGURE 3-4

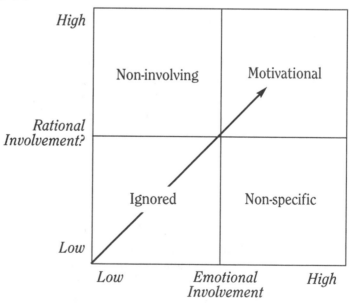

Recognition and rewards are ineffective, even counterproductive, unless they generate both rational and emotional involvement for employees. Rational involvement comes from tight links to employee performance. Emotional involvement comes from genuine positive feelings.

As the grid shows, reward and recognition methods that do not win employee involvement on either the rational or emotional dimensions will not get any attention. They will tend to be ignored. But it could be, and often is, worse! If you generate involvement on only one of the two dimensions, you will get some attention, but it won't add up to a positive response. You are likely, in fact, to see inappropriate or even negative responses to the rewards. They won't have the desired effect, but they may have other less desired affects.

If a reward gets lots of emotional involvement but little rational involvement, you will get employees' attention. But the effect will not be specific to the behaviors you wished to stimulate and reward. That's potentially dangerous, because you will have aroused their emotions in a nonspecific and uncontrolled manner.

Take the example of a company that decided to do something about slipping sales quotas by offering a very expensive and attractive two-week trip to the Caribbean for two to the salesperson who sold the most in the next six months. This prize was highly coveted. Everyone wanted it. Everyone's spouses or significant others wanted them to win it too. So there was plenty of emotional involvement.

But despite this high emotional involvement, the contest hurt motivation and generated negative attitudes in the sales force. Why? Because the rational side wasn't well thought out. Salespeople faced many new competitors, and the company didn't give them tools or strategies to improve their sales so they felt unclear about how to win the prize. In addition, there were fairness issues because some territories had more sales potential than others and the contest didn't take this into account. Finally, some of the salespeople worked in teams and were not sure how their individual efforts might or might not be counted in the contest. These problems made the salespeople question the contest on rational grounds and spoiled the motivational impact of it. Even the person who won the trip didn't feel that good about it because she worried that the contest had been arbitrary and unfair.

When you take care of the rational side and work out rules and methods that are fair, accurate, and obey all the rules of good feedback, then you can build the kind of rational involvement needed to make a reward motivational. But again, you have to take care of the

> Even the person who won the trip didn't feel that good about it because she worried that the contest had been arbitrary and unfair.

other dimension too. A rational, well-designed sales contest with an emotionally boring and unappealing prize won't work either. People will say they know they ought to get up for it and try their best, but they just don't seem to feel like it. They will lack the inspiration that emotional involvement provides.

Testing a Reward or Recognition System

How do you know if a reward or other recognition method will work? Easy. Just find out whether employees view it as both rationally and emotionally involving! If they do, then you know your reward takes the high involvement approach to motivation and will rise to the motivational quadrant of the H. I. A. M Grid. Here's a simple instrument with which to test employee involvement in a reward or recognition program. This version is designed to be filled out by you, the manager or supervisor, but similar questions can also be asked of employees to check that they see the reward the same way you do:

Interpreting Your Score to Increase the Reward's Impact

Will a particular reward work? Will it be received with enthusiasm and will it boost employee motivation—or will it generate cynicism or lack of interest and fail to increase motivation and performance levels significantly? It depends upon your scores on the two sets of questions on the opposite page.

Here are the score ranges. Use them to help interpret your scores by converting them from numbers to levels:

NUMBER OF YES ANSWERS OUT OF 12:	LEVEL:
1–4	Low
5–8	Medium
9–12	High

Using this scale, interpret your results from each of the two sets of questions.

> Here's a simple instrument with which to test employee involvement in a reward or recognition program.

Circle yes or no

yes no 1. Do employees know exactly what behaviors the reward is supposed to encourage?

yes no 2. Do employees believe that they can control the results upon which the reward is based?

yes no 3. Is the reward given quickly enough for employees to remember what it is all about?

yes no 4. Does the reward encourage behaviors that are also encouraged by managers on a daily basis?

yes no 5. Does the reward encourage behaviors that are also encouraged by the organization's rules and systems?

yes no 6. Does the reward encourage behaviors that are also encouraged by employee compensation systems?

yes no 7. Does the reward encourage behaviors that are also encouraged by formal performance review systems?

yes no 8. Is the reward consistent with other reward and recognition programs?

yes no 9. Is the reward consistent with the ways in which employees are trained?

yes no 10. Is the reward consistent with the ways in which employees are managed?

yes no 11. Is the reward consistent with the organization's top-priority development goals?

yes no 12. Is the reward consistent with employees' personal development paths and goals?

Now stop and tally your scores for the first dozen questions. How many yes answers did you circle?

_____ = **Rational Involvement Score**

Good work. Now lets complete the instrument by answering the next set of questions:

yes no 13. Is the reward fun in employees' eyes?

yes no 14. Is the reward exciting to employees?

yes no 15. Is the reward highly desirable to employees?

yes no 16. Do employees feel positive about their work in general?

yes no 17. Do employees feel in control of their performance results?

yes no 18. Do employees receive more positive than negative feedback in general?

yes no 19. Do employees feel very little or no fear about their work situations?

yes no 20. Do employees feel that the reward symbolizes good personal opportunities for growth and development at work?

yes no 21. Do employees feel that there is open, honest communication between managers and employees?

yes no 22. Do employees feel confident of their ability to do the rewarded things well?

yes no 23. Do employees feel optimistic about their work?

yes no 24. Do you feel good about the employees this program rewards?

Finally, please tally your scores for the second dozen questions (numbers 13 through 24). How many yes answers did you circle? _____ = **Emotional Involvement Score**

Set 1 (Questions 1–12) Rational Involvement Score is _____.

Set 2 (Questions 13–24) Emotional Involvement Score is_____.

Use the questions in the instrument to help you target specific problem areas.

If a current or planned reward or other recognition program scores *high* on both rational and emotional involvement, you've got a winner! But most do not, at least at first. If you score medium or low on rational involvement, review the feedback mechanisms to make sure the reward and other feedback is clear, accurate, and timely. Check to see that there are clear paths between employee behavior and results. Also check for consistency with organizational goals, other rewards, and employee requirements and instructions. Use the questions in the instrument to help you target specific problem areas. Work on these areas in order to create a context in which high rational involvement in the reward is likely.

If you score medium or low on emotional involvement, then employees are not likely to become emotionally engaged with the reward in question. You need to check the many contributors to emotional involvement, including the baseline emotional state of employees, the emotional appeal of the reward itself, and other factors which the second set of questions will help you identify. Basically, any no answer on either set of questions signals a very specific problem area that may sabotage your reward.

Need Reward Ideas?

Now you know how to evaluate rewards to make sure they are effective. You can use the grid and instrument to make sure that any existing reward programs create high involvement. And you can also evaluate candidates for new rewards in the same way. You are now in the position to have some serious fun by focusing on creative reward concepts. And you will find that a creative approach to rewards is helpful because over time the same old rewards begin to become boring and lose some of their emotional appeal. So something new can add excitement and build emotional involvement.

But what new ideas for rewards should you consider? One way to tackle this creative task is to look at examples or benchmarks for inspiration. Lots of other managers are struggling with the same question. Some of the reward concepts they've come up with might inspire you to improve upon your own ideas. Here is a selection to get your thinking started.

Cisco Systems and Microsoft Corp. are trying out a new program in which employees earn "ClickRewards" for improved customer service or other performance goals. The rewards are good for a wide variety of merchandise accessible to employees on a Web site, where they can also check in to see how many points they have. (The software is provided by Netincentives of San Francisco; see www.net-incentives.com for details of their system.)

Quite a few companies are discovering the "secret" of resort/workshop destinations as incentives and rewards. Instead of offering a traditional trip to top salespeople, for example, why not offer a retreat at a fabulous resort that includes fun and educational activities? That's what Terra Noble in Puerta Vallarta on the West coast of Mexico offers. You can cue up meditation, art therapy, massage, kayaking, whale watching and other activities. And you can even have a team of employees do developmental exercises that build confidence, creativity, and rapport. Or you could try something a little closer to home, like the Wyndham Peachtree Conference Center in Peachtree, Georgia, where there is a 19 acre corporate training facility offering forest adventures. Why not let your incentives and rewards strengthen your people, not just entertain them?

Spotlight hidden contributors with an attractive desk lamp, complete with an engraved plate on its base thanking the employee by name. That's what one manager decided to do at Chevron, where they have since adopted the practice and call it the Spotlight Award. It's given periodically to someone who routinely makes an extra effort to help out and get things done—and who may well feel that his or her efforts have gone unnoticed.

Install a miniature golf course in the office. And encourage employees to leave their cubicles and play together. Am I serious? Absolutely! And so is Illinois-based Lipschultz, Levin & Gray, a successful accounting firm that recently renovated its offices—with a miniature golf course in the middle. Why? Well, nobody was talking to each other. Everybody was hunched over their own piles of work.

Here's a selection of creative reward programs to get you started!

The idea was to get people talking and cooperating more. And to introduce an element of fun. Does it work? According to company representatives, revenues are way up and employees are more enthusiastic about their work. And about golf, too.

Recognize talented performances with your own version of Academy Awards. That's what Viacom's Human Resources department does, starting with a peer nomination process and culminating in an elaborate award ceremony in which nominees and winners are given star treatment, from a cocktail reception and dinner through a real on-stage award ceremony complete with crystal trophies. Oh, and don't forget the employees who submitted nominations. At Viacom, they receive thank-you notes. And of course every employee participates in the event and is aware of the buzz created by posters, announcements and preliminary events leading up to it as well.

Why not try something really silly, like awarding top performers a chance to listen to a "motivational speaker" that turns out to be, well, a set of high-quality stereo speakers? That's a suggestion from Bose, the speaker manufacturers, and I kind of like it. Most motivational speakers are a lot more boring than the ones Bose offers, after all!

> Reward employees with a great work environment.

Reward employees with a great work environment. According to David Russo, VP of human resources at SAS Institute, "Recognition can come from more than just a name on a plaque. It can come through the environment you give your employees. The environment is in itself part of the reward employees get for working here." That includes nicely designed and maintained office space and a great many family-friendly benefits, like on-site child care—one of the most popular rewards among SAS employees with children.

Don't forget the lowly T-shirt! It's easy and inexpensive to have T-shirts silk-screened with custom -designed art and messages to commemorate any special event. Some companies create T-shirts for events like a fun run or community service day. Others create T-shirts emblazoned with the names of project teams. Or how about a SURVIVOR shirt with a clip-art picture of a sinking ship for those special employees who worked extra hours to put on a special event, handle a seasonal rush, or deal with a major initiative like a move into a new facility? Check your phone directory for silk-screeners near you. Many have creative types on staff who'll help you with a design for a minor fee.

It's a dog's life, working for pet food maker The Iams Co. At least it certainly is for the pets who accompany their masters to work. This company permits employees to bring their dogs to work. A similar policy helps retain employees at Advent Software Inc., where marketing manager Leslie Kranz explains that "The job market is so competitive here in California that pet policies are used to attract employees." Wow. Or should I say bow wow?

One Last Thing: Please Don't Do It Backwards!

Notice that the four-step motivation process ends with rewards and recognition for exceptional performance. That's not the beginning of the process. It's the end. Yet most of us look first to rewards and recognition programs for solutions to motivation and performance problems. As a result, most supervisors and managers are disappointed with the results of rewards and recognition. Remember to create the right performance context first. Worry about rewards later, when you've built the foundations for good performance and you know there will be exceptional behaviors to reward!

> Pet policies are used to attract employees.

Thirty Ways to Motivate Employees in Thirty Days

Want to make some quick, simple improvements that boost motivation in your workplace? Try any of these thirty ideas. One or two are bound to catch your eye!

1. *Recognize that motivation really does drive bottom-line performance.* Highly motivated employees really do perform better. And organizations with better performing employees really do perform better. On average, changes in employee attitude drive as much as half of the changes in corporate profitability. Take advantage of hidden links that give managers new and better levers with which to boost bottom-line performance.

Make a commitment to do something about employee motivation every day.

How? Make a commitment to do something about employee motivation every day. This will naturally lead you to treat employee motivation as a core issue, not a peripheral one. You will begin to manage interpersonal relationships, build the emotional foundations of motivation, and create motivating work environments.

2. *Stop using motivation methods that don't work.* When you keep telling employees what to do and they keep messing up, who's being stupid? Some might say doing the same thing over and over, when it obviously doesn't work, isn't too sharp. Yet we often do just that, trying the same supervisory behaviors over and over and getting more and more frustrated when they don't work.

   How? If a method doesn't seem to produce the commitment or competence you need, then stop and ask yourself why. Try to learn from the experience. And make a point of trying another approach next time. If you keep experimenting, eventually you'll find a better approach.

3. *Acknowledge that employees may be motivated by things beyond their work.* Dynamic employees with significant growth potential generally are passionate about a hobby, sport, or cause beyond the workplace. These outside interests need not compete with their work. Their pursuit of mastery in their outside activities can be used to stimulate growth and motivation on the job as well.

   How? Acknowledge that they are real people with their own interests. Find out what turns them on. Encourage and recognize their outside accomplishments. (Give them time off to run a race, organize an event, do a volunteer job or climb a mountain. Announce and praise their accomplishments.) The positive attitudes these outside accomplishments generate will carry over to their work. With your management support, it's a win-win situation: The more employees accomplish outside of work, the more they'll accomplish in their jobs as well.

4. *Recalibrate your motivation scale.* We routinely accept mediocre motivation at work, forgetting that everyone is capable of high motivation levels. By looking at nontradi-

tional benchmarks, we can recalibrate our sense of what truly high motivation is. Sharing this realization throughout the organization helps create a vision of motivation for everyone to pursue.

How? Ask employees and managers for examples of exceptional motivation. Seek out and share stories of exceptionally motivated explorers, athletes, musicians, artists, volunteers, inventors, and entrepreneurs. Find out what activities or pursuits have created maximum motivation in the past for employees. Encourage people to discuss these incidents and think about why they evoked such high motivation.

5. *Teach employees to measure their own success.* Employees who keep track of their performances are able to notice and document their development. They create their own scoreboards and are able to track their wins more effectively than any manager.

How? Every performance goal can be reduced to a simple, easy-to-track measurement. If the goal is not inherently quantitative, create a judgment scale to rate performance against. Today, only employees operating machinery in quality-oriented factories track their own performances routinely. Tomorrow, every employee should be measuring his or her own success.

6. *Measure and track motivation levels. How can you manage something you don't measure?* Yet most organizations and managers have no idea how motivated their people really are. The typical employee satisfaction poll does not measure motivation. If you start to measure motivation, you can realistically expect to learn how to manage it. Without good measures, you'll never get any better at managing motivation.

How? Use a simple, repeatable instrument such as the Job Motivation Level (JML) Inventory. Take periodic measures of overall employee motivation. And encourage supervisors to track motivation within their own spans of control on a routine basis.

7. *Ask employees what they want.* Employees are motivated by what motivates them! Different employees have different

> Today, only employees operating machinery in quality-oriented factories track their own performances routinely. Tomorrow, every employee should be measuring his or her own success.

goals and desires, and therefore need different performance and development opportunities. You can't motivate individuals with generic programs. To maximize motivation, ask each employee what turns his or her on.

How? One way is to do participative goal setting whenever you assign a task or project. Another is to have employees prepare personal strategic goals and plans, as they do at DELTA Dallas Staffing.

8. *Learn to recognize and eliminate threats.* Employees often feel that their managers use threats to try to motivate them, yet managers routinely deny it. They don't mean to threaten employees, but if that's how it feels to the employees, then it is a threat and it's damaging to motivation levels. So managers need to learn to recognize the things that employees see as threats and work on eliminating or reframing them. Opportunity is an effective motivator. Fear is not.

How? Identify situations in which employees feel that rewards or resources are withheld for inadequate performances. Examples: The performance review that is seen as controlling access to raises and promotions. Rewards and bonuses that are seen as arbitrary based on management judgment or preference. Unreasonable work requests (such as working all weekend) that are backed up with an implied or felt threat such as job loss. Reframe each of these situations to make it clear that rewards may be given based on superior performance, but that rights will not be withheld for normal levels of performance. If uncertain as to whether something is seen as a reward or a threat, ask yourself what the most cynical employee might think. What would a Dilbert say?

9. *Stop distracting employees.* Most employees want nothing more than to focus on doing their jobs better. But from their perspective, critical incidents distract them, leading to worries about communication, security, fairness, respect, and other key job criteria that managers rarely recognize. If you first take care of employees' most fundamental intangible requirements, you can then shift the focus from their concerns to your motivation and performance agenda.

> If uncertain as to whether something is seen as a reward or a threat, ask yourself what the most cynical employee might think. What would a Dilbert say?

How? Ask employees what bothers or worries them about their work and workplace. Or refer to the many employee surveys that cover issues like open communication, security, management commitment to a course of action, fairness, respect and trust, and the presence of development opportunities. It is easy to give employees the free intangibles they require, but most managers don't realize they are withholding these employee essentials.

10. *Communicate!* Open communication is most employees' number one priority. And the majority of employees say their managers don't communicate openly with them. But a majority of managers say they do. Who's right? Wrong question. If employees feel you are withholding information they need about their work or workplace, they will lose motivation and develop resistance to your management. Then it's time to communicate more openly.

   How? Since employees and managers generally see this issue differently, the simplest fix is to ask employees what they want to know. Ask them one-on-one, by e-mail, in meetings. Give employees at least one chance a week to ask you for information. And then give them the information, unless it is truly vital to keep it secret. It rarely is. Usually the information is not secret. It's just kept secret because nobody thought to tell employees.

11. *Ask employees for information about their performance.* This method turns on the power of informative feedback, which is information about how you are doing. The more information, the more intrinsic motivation. So good managers try to offer informative feedback. But do you always know the details? Probably not. So instead of telling them, ask them for information about their performance.

   How? Ask questions designed to encourage the employee to think about and report on performance in specific ways. Questions like "What results did your team get yesterday?" and "How many callers have you been able to handle in the last hour?" stimulate employees to develop their own informative feedback. And informative feedback boosts intrinsic motivation.

> Give employees at least one chance a week to ask you for information.

12. *Explain your reward systems.* Arbitrary rewards generate cynicism, not motivation. Employees feel their managers don't respect them when a new program is announced out of the blue. They complain that the company treats them like children. Show you respect employees and appreciate their need to know by informing them fully about any new rewards.

   How? To avoid this problem, explain any new reward or award in detail, making sure you describe what it is and why. Also address their specific concerns about how it will affect them and their jobs by providing clear answers to their personal impact questions.

13. *Increase overlap.* In many organizations, employees and their managers are simply too busy to see much of each other. And if they rarely have opportunities to interact, managers aren't able to apply their interpersonal skills and management abilities to the task of motivating employees. Find ways to increase the overlaps between employees and managers.

   How? Schedule shifts and events so as to insure that managers and employees will be in the same places at the same times. Also manage space so as to increase overlaps. For example, reassign offices or reconfigure layouts, doors, and corridors so that employees and managers will naturally bump into each other more often in the workday. You can't motivate anyone you don't interact with regularly!

14. *Carry an idea notebook.* What do employees think? Do they have any good ideas? Who cares! At least that's the attitude many employees assume their managers take. Yet most managers wish employees would share more of their ideas and insights; they just aren't very good at asking. They tend to interrupt or overrule ideas without really meaning to, accidentally discouraging the very behaviors they desire.

   How? A simple way to overcome this common problem is to carry a blank notebook reserved for recording employee ideas. Managers who make a practice of collecting at least a page of ideas each day become great listeners overnight, and their employees suddenly seem to be full of ideas.

> Find ways to increase the overlaps between employees and managers.

15. *Motivate with knowledge.* The pursuit of mastery in any one area tends to lead to excellence in every area. Employees who get excited about learning are more likely to grow and develop in their work. That's just simple common sense. So why not use knowledge and learning as a reward and motivator?

    How? There are many ways. Link tuition support, conferences, and training events to performance goals or recognition by peers. And offer knowledge as a perk for all to encourage employees to pursue learning. Offer employees subscriptions of their choice from a list of educational publications. Give out books and self-study tapes as rewards or presents. Knowledge is a powerful motivator, and it's remarkably inexpensive in relation to its value!

16. *Offer "sticky praise."* It's hard to find time to mention and recognize good performances. But your employees want you to notice. The positive recognition helps keep them motivated. Quick, simple handwritten notes are an easy way to make your "praise quota" for the week.

    How? Select a seldom-used or distinctive color of small or midsize sticky notes. Call it your Praise Pad. Only use it to leave brief, personal thank-you notes and good-work notes where employees will see them.

17. *Show off their skills.* At the Lunt Design Center in Greenfield, Massachusetts, an old silverware factory has been opened up to visitors. Viewing paths lead past employee workstations so that visitors can learn how a set of tableware or a Revere bowl are made. It's a fascinating show. The craftsmanship traditionally hidden within dingy factories and taken for granted by customer and manager alike is revealed as a special set of skills. The positive feedback provided by admiring visitors is a far more powerful motivator than anything the managers could do or say.

    How? Are there special skills and techniques within your work force? Is expertise acknowledged or is it taken for granted? Think about ways of showing off employee skills. For example, a different employee could be interviewed and photographed each month, providing content for a display in

> Quick, simple handwritten notes are an easy way to make your "praise quota" for the week.

a prominent lobby or an ad in a trade magazine. There are always ways to show off employee skills. And no company is without some skilled employees worthy of showing off.

18. *Reward individuals for group contributions.* In this era of teamwork, individuals often feel like their personal contributions are overlooked. One recent survey found a "deep, profound dissatisfaction" with the way performance is evaluated and rewarded among U.S. employees. Companies are getting better at recognizing team accomplishments. But the individuals on those teams need regular recognition in order to keep their motivation high.

How? Assign team leaders the task of reporting the best thing each team member does each week. Use the reports to post a list of the results or write thank-you notes to the employees each week. Also encourage supervisors and peers to recognize individuals' contributions informally, as they occur. And consider a peer recognition program in which individuals are given prize points to hand out to each other.

19. *Encourage positive peer-to-peer feedback.* Managers are busier than ever. Asking them to provide frequent, personal, positive feedback about employee performance can be unrealistic in many organizations. Yet the evidence is clear that positive feedback motivates. So where will it come from? Try peers. Programs and cultures that encourage peers to praise and encourage each other end-run the problem and can be highly effective at boosting motivation and performance.

How? One way to create a peer recognition culture is to train employees in how to recognize and praise good performances. Why should this vital skill be confined to managers? Another is to create a reward program in which employees receive recognition certificates they can hand out to their peers. The certificates can be redeemable for prizes, points, trips, gourmet coffees, or whatever you want to offer to make the program appealing to all. When peers begin to recognize and reward each other, the impact on motivation can be quite dramatic.

> One way to create a peer recognition culture is to train employees in how to recognize and praise good performances.

20. *Check the job*. Motivating people to do a job that's not right for them simply will not work. Yet we tend to focus on the person, not the job, when the person isn't motivated. Sometimes it's the job instead. That's why adjusting the job parameters can lead to a big boost in motivation.

    How? Check that the assignment reflects the person's competency levels realistically. If not, break down the job into smaller but still meaningful units, or provide more instruction or support. Jobs often need to be modified in minor ways to match them to the people before you can get high motivation or superior performances.

21. *Ask for self-motivated people*. When companies hire employees, they are more likely to screen for competencies than attitudes. Yet attitudes drive motivation, and motivation drives on-the-job learning and performance. Why not screen for employees who fit the profile of highly self-motivated performers to start with? It is a lot easier to train a motivated employee than to motivate a trained employee!

    How? Seek employees who have demonstrated high levels of optimism, enthusiasm, job motivation, and achievement motive in the recent past. Use personal interviews and job references to seek these attitudes. Also encourage self-motivated individuals to apply for jobs by emphasizing the value of these attitudes in recruiting materials or job ads. And advertise performance incentives, not just salaries and benefits, when you describe new openings. You find what you seek, so make sure you look for motivated people!

22. *Help employees feel good*. It's easy to forget that motivation is a feeling, a positive feeling, to be specific. Employees won't feel motivated if they are feeling down instead of up. The manager's first job is to help create a positive emotional foundation on which to build motivation.

    How? The first step is simply to become aware of two powerful links: The link between your employees' feelings and their motivation levels, and the link between how you behave and how your employees feel. If you try to be up and enthusiastic, and if you try to focus on your people's strengths

> Why not screen for employees who fit the profile of highly self-motivated performers to start with? It is a lot easier to train a motivated employee than to motivate a trained employee!

instead of their weaknesses, then you will help them feel more positive when at work. And that leads quite naturally to a higher state of motivation, which in turn produces more rapid learning and better performances. The important part of cheerleading is the leading part, not the cheer part. Adopt the positive attitude of a cheerleader, and you will lead your people to higher motivation levels with ease.

23. *Create simple opportunities to succeed.* According to *Streetwise Motivating* (Adams, 1999), "The emotional foundation of the motivation path is really a habit of thought. Get people feeling good about anything—even something as goofy as putting on a good Friday afternoon barbecue for the office—and you help them develop a habit of thought that will carry over to their work and boost their motivation and performance in all they do."

    How? Encourage employees to become more optimistic and hopeful by boosting their sense of self-efficacy—their feeling that they have mastery over the events in their lives and can meet challenges effectively. Do so by giving them fun challenges you're sure they can master. For example, next time you schedule a team work session, assign team members jobs such as planning and bringing refreshments or preparing a list of thinking points. And when time permits, ask employees to plan and put on a motivational event or reward party. Opportunities to do volunteer work for the community also boost self-confidence and build job motivation.

24. *Give smaller, more frequent rewards.* It is common to give out fancy awards or valuable rewards at the end of a program, quarter, or year. These infrequent opportunities to recognize star performances lend themselves to ceremony and generate a lot of attention. But they are not generally as motivating as more frequent, smaller rewards.

    How? Shift your reward budget to emphasize more frequent recognition and rewards. Use many small rewards to keep the links between performance and results clearly visible and give employees more opportunities to succeed. If you do use a grand prize-style reward, build up to it through a

> Get people feeling good about anything—even something as goofy as putting on a good Friday afternoon barbecue for the office—and you help them develop a habit of thought that will carry over to their work and boost their motivation and performance in all they do.

series of smaller rewards and events to keep the focus clearly on improving individual performances.

25. *Be empathetic.* In surveys, employees say that their managers are not at all empathetic or considerate. They see their direct supervisors as using directive leadership and delegation, not empathy or consideration. Yet an empathetic approach leads to more motivated and committed employees. When managers remember to think about the people dimension of management as well as the task dimension, they generate far more motivation.

How? To be more empathetic in employees' eyes, make a point of listening and trying to understand how they feel. Remember that empathy is different from sympathy. You don't have to necessarily agree with someone to empathize with them. You just have to sense how they are feeling and thinking. That simple effort makes a significant difference in how they relate to you and how they feel about their job.

26. *Motivate with control.* Managers assume control is their job. But in truth, control is motivating so employees should be given as much as is possible. The idea is to hand them personal control of anything that you don't have to control centrally, such as what kind and how much lighting they work under. (What's the difference in cost between a dimmer and an ordinary switch? And did you know that many employees will gladly supply their own desk lamps if given the option?)

How? Let them control their immediate work environment by identifying any variables that are not of consequence to safety or company image and giving employees freedom to control them personally. If necessary, set some parameters, but make sure there is significant freedom within the parameters. Employees at an Amazon.com shipping center are permitted to wear headphones and listen to the music or books of their choice as they sort inventories and pack orders. Employees at some computer companies are permitted to bring their pets to work. And many employees are permitted to decorate their workspaces—but the majority are not. Why not? What's to be gained by taking even this most

> Managers assume control is their job. But in truth, control is motivating so employees should be given as much as is possible.

fundamental personal control away compared to the motivation that might be gain by giving more control?

27. *Demonstrate commitment to your own initiatives.* If employees encountered a squirrel in the road with as much intelligence as they attribute to their CEO, many of them would feel no compunction about running it down. From the employee perspective, managers often seem to be as indecisive as a squirrel caught in the headlights. First they jump one way, then they dart another. What's important one week is forgotten the next. How can employees get motivated to do your bidding when they don't think you are committed to it? If you pick and stick to a durable goal, making a point to communicate it regularly and relate short-term initiatives to it, they will see you as more committed and their commitment will rise too.

   How? First, don't pretend to a more certain knowledge of the future than you have. If you claim certainty, then have to change direction, your credibility is damaged. Managers who openly share their thinking processes generate more employee commitment. Second, avoid the "program of the month" approach to management. Take time to select a theme and approach that you can stick with for a year or more. Third, don't make overly narrow or specific goals your major purpose in life. For example, ISO certification is great, but not as an organization's overarching purpose. If it's purpose is to improve its quality and value in customers' eyes, then employees can commit to an ISO process and many other possibilities without thinking management can't make up its mind.

28. *Tell them why their work is important.* Employees find that the opportunity to achieve something important makes their work meaningful. And that is the most motivating thing of all.

   Accomplishment and achievement are powerful motivators, yet we seldom put them to work as much as we could. Managers generally focus on getting employees to do their work well, but that does not automatically lead to a sense of accomplishment. If you do your work well, you feel proud of

> Pick and stick to a durable goal.

your performance. But you must also believe that your work is important for that to lead to a sense of accomplishment. Is it? Not unless its importance is made clear in some way.

How? Managers need to be clear themselves about why specific employee tasks and assignments are important and how they fit into the big picture. Then they need to communicate these reasons. The trick is to remember to tell employees what and why—not just what to do, but why it's important. Adopt the verbal habit of incorporating why references into feedback and instructions. For example, you can say, "By preventing typos from slipping past, you will do a lot to maintain our valuable relationships with clients. Little things can make a big impression."

29. *Market the work, not the company.* Employees are painfully familiar with your company's identity. No point pushing it down their throats with logoed hats, pens, pads, T-shirts, pins, and posters. Use those to build customer awareness, since that's the main point of brand advertising. But employees do respond to the marketing of their work.

How? Put your designers on the job of giving each important team, plan, or project its own visual identity. Make it exciting and attractive. Give only those working on it access to the mugs, pens, caps, or whatever you put the project identity on. Let them control distribution of a box of caps, for example. Their enthusiasm for their project will naturally grow as a result of your helping them give it an identity they can be proud of.

30. *Ask open-ended questions.* In survey research, close-ended questions are more common because they are easy to code. People have to say yes or no, or some such set of defined choices. But in general conversation, questions that limit the possible answers are often seen as rude and overly controlling. They signal a lack of interest in or respect for what the other person has to say. Yet managers routinely use close-ended questions instead of open-ended ones when speaking to employees. A simple shift toward greater use of open-

Market employees' projects to them!

ended questions invites employee involvement, signals respect, and builds motivation.

How? Try framing questions using open-question building blocks such as "Why?" "How?" "Tell me about . . . ," "What do you mean by . . . , " "Do you see any alternatives I haven't considered?" and "How do you feel?" Then don't forget to listen to the answer!

If there happen to be thirty-one days in the month, here's one more idea you can use to boost motivation and maximize performance!

31. *Increase the task clarity.* What's that? Task clarity is when you are clear what you are doing, why you are doing it, and how well you are doing it. Studies have found that task clarity is a better predictor of salesperson motivation and performance than experience or size of commission. And the principle applies to other job categories as well.

How? Increase task clarity by helping employees see that they can have a personal impact on results and by making sure they get fast and accurate feedback about their performances.

> Tight feedback loops maximize employee feelings of responsibility and control.

The Organization Course

Overview of Course IV

Let's get organized! Organization is a common thread running through effective management. Whether it's organizing your own time and work, getting a team to function better through organization, or keeping an entire business well organized, your organization skills do make a difference—a big difference.

I'm not an advocate of excessive organization. My view, based on the growing need for flexible, innovative approaches, is that the right organization is generally a minimal organization. Provide enough structure, but not too much. Too much structure confines you. It can take the fun out of business, and it certainly saps initiative and is the enemy of creativity.

On the other hand, it's also dangerous to have too little organization. The right balance is essential. Stay on the verge of chaos, or perhaps the verge of rigidity. Somewhere between those two precipices is a ridge that you can climb as far as you wish to go.

How? There are people who spend six years getting Ph.D.s in organizational behavior, so I'm not going to cover the entire field. Nor am I going to confine myself to this field—there are other, more practical approaches to organization you also need to know. I strongly recommend you become an active benchmarker when it comes to methods of organization. Peak into other people's and businesses' systems. Borrow a page from someone else's appointment book. Try a team planning method that worked elsewhere. Organization is part science, part art—the best part of each, where people are innovating, inventing, pushing the envelope to try new things. Get into that action and you will become an active, creative, inquisitive organizer, which will lead you to ways in which your organization can help you out-compete others. New solutions—to old problems or new—are the major source of competitive advantage in business. See if you can become a source of new solutions to the many organizational problems you'll run into in business!

Session 1: Organizing for Flexibility

Session 2: Organizing People for Flexible Productivity

Session 3: Developing a Collaborative Team

Session 4: Expanding Your Personal Capacity

Each of the following sessions is a potential source of new ideas and approaches to the many problems of organizing work effectively:

British general Harold Alexander's assistant once asked Alexander the reason for his habit of tipping into his "out" tray any letters remaining in his "in" tray at the end of the working day. "It saves time," explained Alexander. "You'd be surprised how little of it comes back."

Organizing for Flexibility

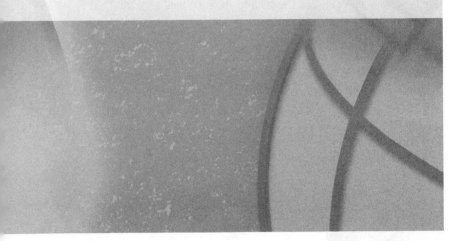

Session 1

The manager is often called upon to organize. There are people and projects, budgets and schedules, and there is always space—floor plans, work spaces, storage spaces, selling space, and so forth. There is a science of organizing, in fact, several sciences. Organizational design specialists focus on how best to organize people—who should work with and report to whom, how they should communicate, who should take responsibility. The manager of people in the real world also thinks about organizing, but not always in terms of the science of management. The organization chart with its definitions of reporting structures—who reports to whom—is still the premier tool of the manager because it makes clear essentials such as who is in charge of whom and who is responsible for what functions or areas.

In this lesson we are going to explore organizing in all its many forms. But I'm going to start by thinking about how to organize space instead of people. Then I'll go on to people in the following sessions. I know that's a bit unconventional, but I'm convinced that when you have a well-organized workspace, you are 90 percent of the way toward having well-organized work.

> I'm convinced that when you have a well-organized workspace, you are 90 percent of the way toward having well-organized work.

Organizing Space to Fit the People and Tasks

Most MBA courses teach organization from a people perspective, ignoring issues concerning the layout of space, for the simple reason that managers organize people often and space rarely. In general, they work with the office or production space layout they inherit, and they rarely even fiddle with location of equipment or furniture. The space is viewed as fixed, and the people are supposed to adapt to it.

I think that's foolish, and I'm sure that in the future MBA programs will shift focus toward adapting the space to the needs of the people instead of the other way around. There really is no choice if you want the most from your people, because, as researchers and practitioners are now learning, the space has a huge impact on the way people perform. In the future, the most successful managers will probably be much more sensitive to issues of space and physical design than most managers are today.

In addition, there are some interesting lessons to be learned from designers that we can apply to organizing people as well as space. Perhaps the most powerful one is the principle of tight-fit versus loose-fit design.

If it is true that we cannot predict accurately how many pieces of technology will be in the office (or briefcase) or what size configuration they will be, then the least effective office design is what we could call "tight-fit" design. This is the kind of design in which, for example, an overhead projector is fitted precisely into a hole in a conference table so that it can be dropped from sight when not in use. Sounds great, and it is—until the projector size becomes one inch larger, or smaller, or has a different shape. Then the table becomes useless.

—FRANKLIN BECKER AND FRITZ STEELE, *WORKPLACE BY DESIGN*

In tight-fit design, physical space is configured to fit specific purposes and plans. Almost every workplace and workspace is at least a moderate example of tight-fit design. But there is a gradual trend away from tight-fit approaches. Here are a few examples of this trend:

- The shift away from built-in office spaces and toward open areas with modular cubicles made of partitions that can be broken down and moved around.
- The shift away from so-called computer tables and back to flat-topped desks that allow you to set up or remove any computer equipment you wish to work with.
- The growing popularity of folding tables and chairs, which are often used to set up customized configurations for training sessions and meetings.

> There is a gradual trend away from tight-fit approaches.

In each of these examples, the basic building blocks of the work environment are made more flexible so that they can support multiple uses and permit changes in the way people work. The shift is from tight-fit design to loose-fit design.

In loose-fit design, the workspace—and the fittings, furniture, and equipment within it—are designed and configured to accommodate as many changes as possible. For example, the architects who designed a new headquarters office building for Union Carbide worked out a basic office module that is designed to fit either one or two workstations or a conference table. The room is set up, wired, and lit to accommodate these multiple configurations.

In most office buildings, especially the more prestigious and "modern" ones, the architects fail to provide that much flexibility. There are rooms that really only work as conference rooms because of their size and fittings. Other rooms are dedicated as single-person offices because of their built-in fixtures and furniture. Still other rooms can only support layouts featuring interlocked cubicles.

Specialized businesses create many tight-fit room designs, too. The telemarketing or telephone service center is usually hard-wired (literally) to support a bank of workstations, all in a line, with sound-proof barriers between them. If you want to try other configurations, you are out of luck. So nobody thinks about other configurations. The assumption is that rows and rows of individual employees will sit side by side, trying not to be distracted by the hum of people around them as they perform their sales or service duties by phone.

But is this the best way to set up the work? It depends. I'd like to have lots of other options to try out if I managed a call center. What if I made a circular arrangement of desks, facing out, with the people in the middle? Then the angle to their nearest neighbor is more oblique and neighbors are less likely to see and be distracted by each other. Or what if I staggered each desk to create a diagonal zigzag layout? This maximizes the physical distance between each person, so it should reduce the background noise. Or what if I wanted to redesign those jobs so that people collaborated somehow on teams? Then I'd want to put the workstations in cells within the bigger room.

The point is, unless I have freestanding desks and chairs with long, unfixed telephone and power lines to them, I can't explore alternative arrangements and work concepts at all. And newer business values emphasize exploration instead of compliance, as you know. Without the ability to modify the workspace easily and quickly, you and your people cannot explore or even imagine many options that are available when the workspace is flexible.

> The assumption is that rows and rows of individual employees will sit side by side, trying not to be distracted by the hum of people around them.

In a rapidly changing business environment in which the advantage goes to those who innovate and respond rapidly, tight-fit design is a disadvantage. It maximizes efficiency *so long as things remain the same*. But as soon as things change, a tight-fit design gets in the way and efficiency falls again. Even worse, the tight-fit design prevents you from changing your approach, from questioning your assumptions, from being a creative explorer of new options and approaches. In other words, tight-fit design prevents you from being a successful manager in many cases.

In contrast, loose-fit design permits and encourages experimentation and change. It gives you flexible building-block spaces, fixtures, and equipment instead of dedicated ones. And it never nails anything down. In the ideal loose-fit design, the people working within the design can actually pick up and move everything whenever they want to. It should be easy and fun to "remodel" your workspace.

Building-Block Offices?

Until recently, I leased a suite of offices in an old brick building overlooking the expansive, parklike common of an old New England town. I didn't design the building, of course, but the rooms I rented were generously sized and didn't restrict me to any specific floor plan. I have a hard and fast rule for my own office space: I must be able to pick up and move anything in it by myself. I make only one exception to this rule—an antique desk that has been in my family for generations and that I need a partner to handle. But everything else is flexible. Even my conference table breaks down into top and base, and I can (and have) move it from room to room and place to place within my rooms. My big work tables, including the workstation on which I keep the computer equipment I'm using for my writing at the moment, are all made up of identical old student desks of oak, which I can use as building blocks to make up varied shapes and configurations. I only buy two-drawer file cabinets for the same reason. If I want to stack them and make a big four-drawer unit I can, but they can also be used to form a long counter or as table bases.

I'm going into this example because I can say from my own experience that it works. I have reconfigured my own workspace

Also consider the aesthetics of work space. Recent research shows that people are much more effective and committed in work places they *like*.

many times to accommodate a new project or approach. When I need someone to work closely with me for a while on a big project, I can easily configure a workstation to fit his or her needs within my own flexible area. When I need to find room to accommodate the books and papers of a new research topic, I can easily make a home for the project using file cabinets, bookshelves, and a desk. If I want to accommodate a large group for a meeting, I can clear the floor of one of the rooms in a hurry and bring my extra chairs and tables in for the event. There are also many ways to support a meeting or work session. I have portable folding easels to hang large chart pads on instead of a fixed whiteboard on the wall, but I've also discovered I can hang a row of huge pads from several of my six-foot-high pine bookcases and create the temporary equivalent of a wall covered with whiteboard. I use oriental rugs on the old oak floors instead of wall-to-wall carpeting because it is easy to move rugs around or even pull them out in order to suit the latest configuration of furniture. There is a lightweight TV/VCR combination that can be set up wherever we need it to view training films. I've even had a video crew in here to do some filming, which necessitated moving everything around in order to get lighting and background right.

Now, I'd love to tell you I was incredibly smart for having adopted that portability rule back when I first set up my business. But in truth, it was just dumb luck! At first my business, like many new ones, was a fly-by-night operation. I rented office space by the month and moved whenever I needed a little more room. And I certainly didn't have the income to justify fancy office furnishings or the moving company needed to relocate them. So I simply acquired lightweight, practical, modular furnishings with the vague intention of replacing them with "real" fixtures later on.

But after more than a decade of use, I've learned that modular and flexible is a great advantage. If I had a big, expensive executive desk set, I'd have to sit at it. I'd have to make room for it. I'd have to set up my office so as to support only one workstation—a big polished-wood desk with one executive chair behind it and a couple padded visitor chairs in front of it. Then I could work in one of two ways. I could sit at my desk and look through the files my executive secretary brought me, or I could sit at my desk and talk to the one

> If I had a big, expensive executive desk set, I'd have to sit at it.

or two visitors who my secretary scheduled to keep those seats on the other side of the desk warm. As it is, I am able to roam freely through a much more varied and interesting environment. I have many places and spaces for work, including lots of interesting project piles. And I can change my workspace to suit the latest idea or project. I know I could never have done half the things I've been able to do without the loose-fit design I fortuitously adopted.

Why It's Cheapest to Have the Best Furniture

As a manager, you too can adopt a loose-fit approach, even if you don't have the opportunity to select or remodel the basic floor plan itself or if you've inherited big old metal desks with bolt-on side units or other office dinosaurs. By the way, do you know why most secretary's desks have those irritating L-shaped add-ons that only attach to one side? Those were designed to fit the standard IBM Selectric typewriter of thirty years ago. Too bad they don't fit a modern personal computer and printer, huh?

One of the easiest ways to make your office space more flexible is to trade in "high status" office furniture for "low status" furniture. Because loose-fit design principles aren't widely appreciated, you will find that almost everyone actually wants big, ungainly, hard-to-move office furniture. Bigger desks are valued over smaller desks. Desks with bolt-on attachments that dramatically reduce their flexibility are even more valued than regular desks. And hellishly heavy four-drawer metal file cabinets are much more highly valued than cheap, lightweight two-drawer cabinets. So if you currently have furniture that does not permit you to take a building-block approach to layouts, you should be able to solve the problem without spending any money. If you are in a big organization, someone will probably trade with you. If you aren't, locate the nearest big office furniture supplier that handles used equipment, and they'll help you trade down to more, smaller, and lighter pieces of furniture.

I recommend the same approach in light manufacturing and service facilities. Try to avoid dedicated equipment. Favor more and smaller units that can be combined in many ways over fewer and heavier units that restrict your ability to redesign. You never know what business you'll be in next year, after all.

> One of the easiest ways to make your office space more flexible is to trade in "high status" office furniture for "low status" furniture.

If you can exercise any control over the floor plan itself, then do your best to use that influence to win as much flexibility as possible. In particular, do your best to increase the *amount* of space available to you, and to get more *open* space rather than space that is partitioned already.

Sometimes you can use the same trading down strategy that works for furniture, since in many organizations the most flexible space is the least prestigious. For instance, I know a manager who was able to move into a cavernous floor in the old building of his firm by giving another department his smaller space in a prestigious set of rooms in the new executive suite.

Conventional wisdom favors the new over the old and says you should be as near the center of power in your business as possible. I disagree, for the simple reason that you have to trade so much flexibility in order to follow these brownnosing rules. The manager who moved into the unwanted old office space was able to do all sorts of things with team-oriented arrangements of people that the other managers could not do, and I don't think it was a coincidence that he got much better results too.

Inspiration: Weekend Moving Party!

One nonprofit organization I know holds periodic weekend moving parties at its headquarters suite of offices. Employees who want to rearrange their space come in voluntarily on Saturday morning. They line up a technician to help them reconfigure the computer network if need be, and they order some pizza or other refreshments to keep up their strength. Then they start moving everything around.

Does this sound like fun? Who'd want to move furniture at the office over the weekend? But people do, for the simple reason that they are able to *control their own workspaces* as a result of this practice. In general, the entire staff participates. And there is considerable discussion in the weeks preceding one of these moves so that everyone has thought about what the constraints and concerns are. There is usually a general idea or strategy agreed to in advance as well, but no specific plan because it's hard to anticipate exactly what the best new configuration will be. Options present themselves when you start moving the furniture around. Ideas come up. And when the dust settles, the office is reconfigured to better meet current needs. People may have traded offices or furniture. Those who are working together right now have moved their desks nearer each other. The new person who gets distracted by background noise has moved into one of the back rooms. The computer workstations are relocated to accommodate new requirements. It's all about change. And change is good!

The Solar System Business Model

If you are one of the many small business owners or executives who actually make the decisions about what space to rent or lease, then you can do a great deal more to maximize the flexibility of your space. The key rule of thumb is to *negotiate hard for short-term leases*. One-, two- and three-year leases are considered short term by the real-estate industry, but a year or two can be an eternity in most businesses today, so don't even think about anything longer than a few years. Also consider a core space that you really dig into, supplemented with shorter-term leases of satellite space for project-oriented staff or temporary housing of teams or temporary workers. The business that rents one ten-thousand-square-foot facility is a lot less flexible than the business that rents five two-thousand-square-foot facilities, even though both have the same amount of space.

But, the experts will say, if you rent just one dedicated space you achieve greater efficiencies. People don't have to walk or drive between facilities to meet. It's easier to keep control of your people if they are all in the same place. And you might get a little cheaper rent by renting one big place because that gives you more leverage in the negotiation with that single landlord.

Hogwash. Don't believe them for a minute.

If you know exactly what the future holds—what kind of work your business will be doing, how many people you will need to do it, and how they should be configured to do that work—then go ahead and rent one big space. But if there is any chance that these variables will change, avoid an all-or-nothing approach to your space!!! You want to remain effective, and to do so you have to be ready to change. Once again, we need to remember that being efficient is of no use at all if you are doing the wrong thing well. The business that survives surprises is the one that can do many things reasonably well instead of only one thing superlatively. Apply the loose-fit principle to the way you organize and configure your workspaces and you will maintain that vital flexibility.

> Being efficient is of no use at all if you are doing the wrong thing well.

Organizing People for Flexible Productivity

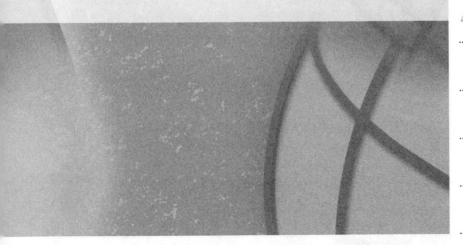

The traditional approach to organizing people is perhaps best summed up by three words: responsibility, authority, and accountability.

Responsibility is an obligation to perform specific tasks or accomplish specific goals. You can give someone responsibility for something. That makes it his or her job to see that specific something gets done. When you organize people, one of the first things you need to think about is who will have responsibility for what. And when you think about how to hand out responsibility, please think of it in two ways:

- who's responsible?
- what tasks are they responsible for?

As in all things to do with good management, you need to think about the people and task dimensions. Pick the right people. Make sure they have the skills and attitudes needed for the task. Also pick the right task. If you make someone responsible for a meaningless, impossible, or vague job, he or she won't accomplish anything of use to you or him or herself. (Please read Chapter 3, The Employee Motivation Course, too!)

Authority is power to act. It can involve direct action—doing specific tasks— or it can involve decisions about what to do and how to do it. Either way, authority is part and parcel of any management position. You need to have enough authority to do your job effectively, and so do your people. Someone who is responsible for handling customer complaints but has no authority to make exceptions to the rules will not be able to do his or her job well. Sometimes the right thing is to give the customer something to make up for a problem. But without authority, it won't happen.

So in a sense, authority and responsibility need to be properly coupled in order to empower employees with the authority to execute their responsibilities. It's a common fault of managers to give out more responsibility than authority. That undermines employees. Please don't make the same mistake when you hand out assignments. Thanks!

What's Accountability?

Accountability is generally distinguished from responsibility by saying that managers can delegate accountability but not responsibility. The idea is that you can make someone accountable by saying he or she is in

> Someone who is responsible for handling customer complaints but has no authority to make exceptions to the rules will not be able to do his or her

charge of a task and needs to be answerable for the task. When you want to know how the task is coming, you just ask the person who's accountable and he or she will account for it. In management theory at least, this is different from responsibility. But I find the difference remarkably hard to appreciate. And I notice that dictionary definitions of accountability generally use the word responsibility and vice versa. So you know what? I don't think you need to struggle over this distinction.

In fact, I urge you not to separate accountability and responsibility, even if you can figure out how. If someone is to do a job well, that person needs to be fully responsible and accountable for it. And if he or she works for you, face it, you are also fully responsible and accountable for that person's work. Neither of you can or should shirk the full range of responsibility for getting the job done.

So let's not worry too much about semantics. Let's just think hard about the key issues of responsibility and authority. When organizing people or defining their jobs, make sure you think through what they should be doing and what authority they need in order to do it well.

For example, make sure that your people:

- have the authority to get and use any equipment and materials necessary to their work;
- have the authority to collect and respond to feedback about the efficiency and effectiveness of their work;
- have the authority to make decisions necessary to routine execution of their work; and
- know exactly what the definitions of their responsibility and authority are.

Job descriptions generally focus on responsibilities, not authorities. For example, a job description for a sales manager might say that the employee "is responsible for managing the sales force and making sure sales reach or achieve the targets for each territory based on the annual plan." Well, that's a lot of responsibility, and it's going to take some authority. For instance, should this same sales manager have any authority for setting territory sales targets? For hiring and firing salespeople? For setting up territories? For managing lead generation systems? There are many things that a sales manager might need to be able to do in order to execute the responsibility for achieving sales quotas.

> Job descriptions generally focus on responsibilities, not authorities.

There are some things over which you might want to give only partial authority—do you want your sales manager setting artificially low sales quotas in order to insure that they are easy to achieve? In general, you want to bundle as much authority as is reasonably possible with that responsibility, otherwise you risk undermining the employee. Employees who don't control the key variables affecting their performance lack task clarity. They become discouraged. They are at risk of acquiring learned helplessness. These are losing attitudes, and they virtually guarantee that no one will make a success of the job.

When you hand out responsibility without sufficient authority, you set the stage for negative attitudes. Poor performance is the ultimate result. So be very careful to organize and structure jobs and tasks so as to insure healthy attitudes in those who do them. Keep authority and responsibility in balance.

In practical terms, *if you don't trust someone to take on full authority for a job, then don't give them responsibility for it*!

Most Jobs Are Heavy on Responsibility and Light on Authority

If you ask people what they are responsible for, you generally get a pretty long list. Ask them how much authority they have in their organizations, and you'll get a long pause, or a short list at best. That's because managers routinely assign people to work that they think the people are not really able to handle.

If, for example, you put someone on the floor of a retail store to handle customer questions, make sales, and keep the shelves attractively and appropriately stocked, then you really need to give that person considerable authority. I don't know about you, but I'd want authority to fiddle around with store layout and stocking in response to what I hear my customers complain about or ask for. I'd want lots of authority when it came to how the store treats customers. For example, I'd want to be able to offer to special order something, or to give them a deal on something in stock because I could tell they would walk away unless I sweetened the pot. I'd want to be able to build relationships with major, long-term customers, which might mean sending them a personal note when a sale is coming up or when a new product I think they'd like is about to come into stock.

> When you hand out responsibility without sufficient authority, you set the stage for negative attitudes.

There are lots of things a really effective retail salesperson might want to do in order to perform his or her job really well and maximize sales and profits. But almost all retail salespeople are given extremely limited authority. In fact, many have no authority at all. They even have to ask their supervisor for permission to go to the bathroom. If they are not to be trusted with a basic decision like when to go to the bathroom, why should they be trusted with the store's two most important assets—its stock and its customers?

Well, in truth, many retail sales clerks should not be trusted with the stock or the customers. They are simply untrained, minimum-wage employees who are not expected to care about their work or to stick with the company for more than a few months. That's why they aren't given any authority. They'd make a mess of it for sure! But my point is that means they are also not fit for the responsibility of their position. If you can't trust them, don't trust them to handle your customers.

> If you don't trust employees with your other assets, why do you trust them with your customers?

I picked the example of the retail sales clerk in part because I know, based on extensive data collected by Surcon International (Chicago), that supervision of retail salespeople is a key limiting factor in many companies. If you want to increase profits in retail, the most effective thing you can do in general is to improve the quality of supervisory management. And I think one of the reasons is that people are hired into jobs in which responsibility is out of balance with authority.

The finding holds true in general for all sorts of companies and jobs, too. Employees whose jobs are not well structured and organized perform below their potential, and so do their companies. This issue is worthy of careful attention no matter what kind of positions you supervise. In all likelihood, your people are given too many responsibilities, or too much authority; one or the other. It's up to you to decide which. If you think the job is simply too big as currently defined, then you want to scale back the responsibilities until they are in balance with the more modest level of authority that position has. Alternatively, if you think an employee is able to handle his or her current levels of responsibility, then you need to give that person more authority in order to bring it into balance with his or her responsibility.

> If you can't trust them, don't trust them to handle your customers.

> Most people pass their days following the strictures of some absurdly narrow job description. Boxed in. It's time to break the box.
> —TOM PETERS, THE TOM PETERS SEMINAR: CRAZY TIMES CALL FOR CRAZY ORGANIZATIONS

But whether you reduce responsibility or increase authority, make sure that you recalibrate all jobs so that the two are appropriately balanced. That is a central and vital principle of organizing people, and one that managers have traditionally gotten wrong a lot more than they've gotten it right.

Managing for the New World of Business

What it really comes down to is that you are organizing yourself and your people based on yesterday's practices but for tomorrow's markets. That's fine when things are static; not so smart when things change. And here is how they are changing. Then you needed to be efficient; now you need to be effective, creative, and flexible. (See Shifting Values table for details.) So how does that affect the way you organize people and their work?

Think about that fundamental shift and it will liberate your thinking about organization. In the coming years, business leaders and leading businesses will rewrite the book on organization. I want you to write the first chapter, not the final appendix.

SHIFTING VALUES

Old Business Values	New Business Values
Realism	Optimism
Efficiency	Effectiveness
Control	Creativity
Uniformity	Optimality
Standardization	Change
Compliance	Development
Planning	Exploration
Tight-fit design	Loose-fit design

Developing a Collaborative Team

One of the new and difficult challenges managers face is how to organize work teams. Teams are everywhere, and for good reason. They bring together the right people for a short-term project or need. They help organizations be flexible and adaptive. But only if they work.

And many teams spend all their time talking, planning, fighting, or avoiding meetings. In this session, we'll focus on how to organize teams that really work.

The Challenge of Teamwork

Teamwork is great when everyone pulls in the same direction. But sometimes you have the sense that people aren't pulling very hard. Their commitment seems low. They are more interested in their "other" work and don't give the team their full attention. Other times you have an even worse problem: team members are pulling all right, but in opposite directions!

As a manager, you *will* have to worry about teams, formal and informal, every day of your working life. You will use teams frequently to get projects done. You will sometimes lend one or more of your people to cross-functional teams, which threatens your control of and access to your people. And you will often have to serve on teams of various sorts: committees, project teams, planning groups, and the like. Your work life will be infused with the requirement for teamwork, but will it be infused with team spirit?

A good team is a wonderful thing to manage or serve on as a member. It rises above petty disputes and individual requirements. It brings out the best in its members, helping them become more than they could possibly be on their own. Behind most breakthroughs in business you will find a good team. But on the other hand, good teams are surprisingly hard to find. Mediocre teams, however, are everywhere.

The managers and employees I've talked to over the years are all working with teams. Managers generally run at least a few, and most employees are on at least one team. When you look more closely at project structures and production processes, you also discover that there are many collaborative working situations that,

> Many teams spend all their time talking, planning, fighting, avoiding meetings, or not working.

while not formally called teams, still require close teamwork from their participants. As a result, it is fair to say that the work of business is by and large accomplished by teams.

Why Teams Suck

So teams are a daily reality of work life. Managers have to make teams work in order to get their own work accomplished, which means you need to know how to make a team click, how to get everyone up to speed and contributing productively. Otherwise, your teams will fall prey to these widespread problems, problems that make the large majority of teams inefficient and frustrating to work on or manage:

- Members do not fully buy into the team's mandate
- People "coat-tail" on the work of others
- Members defend their turf instead of cooperating
- Meetings are dull and nothing seems to get accomplished
- The team's purpose seems vague or irrelevant
- Members feel that the team is inefficient and a waste of their time

Most people who serve on teams in business report that they don't feel the teams are as productive as they should be. It is simply hard to get psyched about the team meetings. A "Why are we here?" mentality takes over, and little good comes out of the experience. In fact, the majority of people who are assigned to teams end up regretting or resenting it!

The standard answer, provided by the majority of corporate training courses and teamwork consultants, is that teams go through several development phases before achieving a productive maturity in which everything really works. This answer, derived from observations of teams, is accurately descriptive of many long-term teams. They do indeed seem to go through several relatively dysfunctional stages before being able to perform effectively. Here is the team development model most experts use:

Managers have to make teams work in order to get their own work accomplished.

1. Forming. The focus in this stage is on bringing the people together and establishing the team's purpose. It can take some time to get the group defined and brought up to speed.
2. Storming. The focus in this stage is typically on defining the basic ground rules and debating the team's purpose and approach. Personalities clash, problems surface, and differing views of the project are argued over. In theory at least, this period of discord is helpful as it brings everything to a boil. The alternative is for people to just shrug their shoulders and say, "Yeah, whatever," which means they are not really very involved with the team or concerned about the work.
3. Norming. In this stage, things finally begin to click and the team members learn how to work productively with each other. Teams often develop their own social customs and styles of work to accommodate the requirements of their members and the task itself. Who does what, when, and where, and how meetings and discussions are conducted—all those little details of cooperative relationships have to be worked out so that the team can communicate well and share work effectively.
4. Performing. In this final stage, the team is, in theory, well ordered and cohesive and ready to move forward and perform at or near its potential. But note that the team had to go through a kind of "trial by fire" development process in order to get here. The key point of this model is that you cannot expect teams to perform well upon formation. It takes additional work and time to bring them up to speed and turn them into real teams.

The standard model says teams go through four stages: forming, storming, norming, and, finally, performing.

The Team Collaboration Model

I don't have any particular objection to the team development model. It often fits the actual development process of a team fairly well, and it does remind us that team-building is the only way to get to a high-performing team. Teams don't just happen. They have to grow and develop since they depend upon a high order of collaboration. So this model reminds us that as managers we need to nurture teams, not just establish them. But, beyond that, I don't find the model very helpful. It doesn't really tell me what to do to fix inefficient teams or make sure a new team learns to work together quickly and efficiently. How can you beat the odds and avoid a long, unproductive, and probably unpleasant development cycle for a team?

To answer that question, I prefer to apply that most fundamental of managerial models, the task/people matrix (which is at the heart of my approaches to motivation and leadership as well).

The way I like to apply that supervisory model to teams is to define the two dimensions as:

- Team members' focus on each other, and
- Team members' focus on the team's work.

When you have a group of people who are highly involved in their interpersonal relationships—each other—and are highly involved in their project or assignment—the team's work—then you can be confident they will find ways to perform effectively and efficiently. They will, in other words, be self-organizing.

And when you create a self-organizing team, you really lick the organization problem because *the team has the capacity to reconfigure itself as it goes in order to stay well-organized for whatever challenges it may face.*

Great teams are characterized by members who are involved with each other and with the team's project. When everyone is at this level of involvement, true collaboration and teamwork is not only possible but inevitable. In fact, you can define good teamwork as the collaboration that arises when all the team's members are highly involved in the team and its work.

When you plot the two dimensions of this team collaboration model, you get a grid that looks like Figure 4-1.

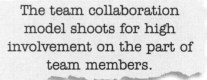

The team collaboration model shoots for high involvement on the part of team members.

FIGURE 4-1 TEAM COLLABORATION MODEL.

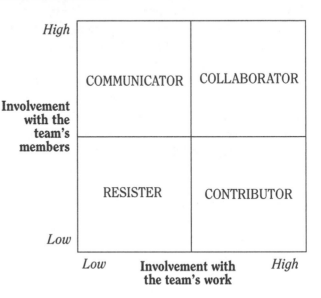

Reproduced by permission of Alexander Hiam & Associates.

> As a manager, your task is to get everyone involved in the team at a high level as soon as possible.

Teams generally start out with relatively low involvement. Members are not that engaged with each other or with the team's work to start with. But to be effective, they need to move upward on both dimensions in a hurry. *As a manager, your task is to get everyone involved in the team at a high level as soon as possible.* That's how you create the conditions in which collaborative teamwork flourishes. So this grid gives you a simple way of thinking about the task of making teams productive.

Specifically, you build teamwork in any group by working on the members' involvement in their group and/or their task. You work on the people dimension or the task dimension. It's pretty simple, really. And the guiding principle to keep in mind as you work on these dimensions is to build involvement. Get them focused on and engaged with their team members and the team's purpose or project. If you can get them fully engaged, they will develop their own ways to collaborate effectively. They will become a team. So just stick to building that essential involvement in the team and its work. The rest will follow.

By the way, you can also use the team collaboration model to focus your efforts as a manager. Sometimes teams are having trouble because of the people side of the equation, and sometimes it's the task side. It isn't always low involvement across both dimensions–especially if the team has been around for a while. And when only one dimension is a problem, it's easier to fix the team because you only need intervene in that one area. You either build task or people involvement, but not both.

Here's how to diagnose each of these possible problem areas.

Low involvement with the team members
Signs of this problem include:

- Members spend little time together
- Members don't know very much about each other
- Members rarely communicate outside of formal team sessions
- Members communicate largely through formal channels
- Members do not think about each other very much
- The team chooses to meet infrequently
- The team does not get together informally for work or play
- Team meetings/discussions are formal and structured

If you see symptoms such as these, you probably have a group of people who are not very involved with each other on a personal level. That will keep them from becoming effective collaborators. You need to think of ways to boost their personal involvement.

I want you to look for these sorts of symptoms, but I also want you to notice what *isn't* in that list. A lot of things that we often assume are essential to good team relations are left out.

For instance, you don't see anything about getting along, not arguing, or agreeing. That's because people who are highly involved with each other and their group will not automatically get along. In fact, discord is often a sign of involvement, because it means people care!

> Discord is often a sign of involvement, because it means people care!

Nor do people have to respect or like all their team members, or even believe that the team is composed of the right people. As long as they get personally involved, they will *become* the right team over time. Almost any group of employees can find a way to work together effectively, if they are sufficiently involved in that quest.

So all you need is involvement at this point. Interpersonal issues are acceptable and, to be honest, quite probable. It's hard to match people so that they get along perfectly. Heck, half of U.S. marriages end in divorce! You can't expect to "marry" a group of five or ten people and have it work out perfectly. So shoot for a realistic goal—just get and keep them involved with each other and they'll find ways to collaborate over time.

Low involvement with the team's work
Signs of this problem include:

- Team members tend to do their own work before the work of the team
- Members do not seem to have a detailed knowledge of the team's work
- The team does not seem to be very active
- The team does not generate many results in the course of a week
- Some members are waiting for others to complete tasks
- Members often look to their leader for instructions
- Members wait for assignments rather than working independently
- The team is following a simple plan without exploring at all
- Team members do not seem particularly interested in the work of the team
- Members question the importance of the team's work

> Debate about what to do is a healthy sign of involvement.

Also note what's left off this list. There are many things people frequently assume are necessary for teamwork that are probably not worth worrying about, such as agreement within the team concerning what to do, how to do it, or who should do what. Let them argue about the plans and goals! That's their problem, and they will generally solve it as long as they are engaged enough with the work of the team to understand the issues and take them to heart.

Similarly, I don't include expertise. Sure, you want to try to put people with appropriate expertise onto the team, but on the other hand, too often that's not fully practical. You have to make do with the people available. Many teams lack some of the knowledge needed to make their work easy. In which case, there are two likely outcomes. First, the team might fail. It could easily mess up. Or second, it could learn. It could acquire the expertise needed to succeed. And the latter is much more likely if the team is highly engaged in its work. It takes high involvement in the task to get into learning mode. So you really just need to manage involvement in the work and the team will then tend to manage its own learning.

As you can see, this is a startlingly simple model for how to organize and manage teams. It's certainly simpler than any other serious model I've seen in business. But it is also more effective and powerful than other approaches I've seen because involvement in the people and the work of the team really does drive team performance. All the manager has to do is worry about these two simple factors and the team will worry about the rest.

Building Team Involvement

Here are some examples of ways managers can build involvement levels in order to boost teamwork and move a group toward true collaboration.

To work on personal involvement, you need to find ways to throw the people together and encourage them to get to know and care for each other. Find or make up activities that require them to trust each other. Encourage them to spend time together, and if they won't, send them on retreats, outings, a shopping trip, or anything at all that brings them together personally. It does not have to be work related, because the goal is to build *personal* involvement. In the long run, you will find that personal involvement is actually very work related!

Also encourage and stimulate sharing, as in sharing information about their lives or sharing favorite ideas, things, music, recipes,

> Find ways to throw the people together and encourage them to get to know and care for each other.

etc. Especially encourage sharing of aspirations and successes. Ask people what they do for hobbies, what they do on vacation, if they've done anything for a charity lately, been on any neat trips, and so forth. Have their children won any awards or games? Overcome any problems or illnesses? Personal involvement is a natural process that can be encouraged by encouraging team members to open up and share their lives with each other. The more you know about someone, the more you will collaborate with and help out that person.

And I also recommend that you attend very carefully to a simple measure I call overlap. Overlap is the extent to which people are together in time and space in contexts in which meaningful, genuine communication can take place. Sounds like a rarity in business, doesn't it? And it is. Most people do not overlap very much with other people in their work, and this lack of natural, meaningful overlap prevents many teams from coming together and forming cohesive groups.

You can increase overlap simply by organizing people, schedules, space, and agendas so as to create more overlap. It's very simple really. Just find ways to throw those team members together in the same time and space, without excessive structure, so that they have the opportunity to come together as human beings, not just team members. Then you will find that involvement in the essential human dimension of the team will build quickly and naturally.

One clear indicator that personal involvement is building is that team members will start taking care of each other. They will act in supportive, considerate, empathetic ways. When you see that happening, then you know you're on the road to a team with exceptionally high personal involvement—and thus with exceptionally high performance potential!

What about building involvement in the team's *work*? Well, the biggest problems keeping people from being interested in and excited about work are:

- lack of detailed information about the work and its context
- lack of a "line of sight" from the work to its higher purpose or meaning
- work that seems either too boring or too difficult
- lack of clear, informative feedback about the quality of the work

> Just find ways to throw those team members together in the same time and space, without excessive structure, so that they have the opportunity to come together as human beings, not just team members.

To overcome these problems, you simply need to apply the principles of good management to the team's work, as described for example in the courses on leadership and motivation.

Specifically, make sure your team members know all about the team's project. Share all the *information* you can get your hands on, even if it seems boring, irrelevant, or too high level. It's not! Not for those who have to commit to the team's work for a significant period of time. Employees want and need much more information than they usually get.

Also make sure your team members see why the team's work is important. Infuse it with *meaning,* with purpose. Show how it fits into the big picture. Give them that essential line of sight from their daily tasks to the goals and purpose the work serves. (If you don't know why their work is important, then maybe the work isn't worth doing!)

Next, check the level of challenge. People are motivated by a reasonable level of challenge, one that stretches them but doesn't tear or break them. It's just like training an athlete. You don't ask them to stretch a muscle twice as far or run twice as far today as yesterday. That is too much and will kill their motivation and enthusiasm. You've got to give them a reasonable level of challenge. Put on your coaching hat when managing teams, and make sure there is an exciting, but reasonable, challenge for them to pursue.

Oh, but also watch out for work that seems too boring and easy to do. Too little challenge is just as demotivating as too much. A coach wouldn't ask an athlete to run around a track all day at half speed. What a bore! What a waste of talent! Yet we often cue up jobs that seem dull and lifeless to team members. If the work the team needs to do seems trivial and overly simple to them, they won't feel any personal sense of challenge. So your job as a manager is to raise the level of challenge. You can do this in many ways once you start thinking about it. Add some additional requirements. Shorten the time frame. Increase the quality standards. Like the other team problems I've covered, a lack of challenge is not a hard problem to fix—once you know to look for it!

The final factor I want you to consider in building the team's involvement in its work is whether team members are getting the right kind of feedback. To learn a lot more about feedback, go back

> Put on your coaching hat when managing teams, and make sure there is an exciting, but reasonable, challenge for them to pursue.

over the employee motivation course in Chapter 3. But right now, I can give you some very simple but powerful principles to follow:

Principles of Great Team Feedback

1. Team members should know how to measure their performance
2. Team members should always track their own performance
3. Team projects and/or support should be designed to make it easy for the team to perform above "C" grade level on whatever its performance measures might be (or else the team is working at too high a level of challenge and will receive too much negative and not enough positive feedback)
4. Teams need feedback that informs them about how they are doing, not feedback that tells them what to do (this has to do with shifting from controlling to informative feedback—a powerful way to increase motivation and involvement in work!)

If you follow these simple rules of team feedback, you will build teams that have high involvement in their work. They will think about it, care about it, and be excited by their accomplishments. And that, combined with their high involvement with the people of the team, will insure exceptional performance.

> Teams need great feedback in order to produce great performances.

Expanding Your Personal Capacity

Why organize? The answers to that question are many and varied, but they generally come down to one of two things. Either people are seeking efficiency or they are seeking effectiveness.

Now, efficiency is a great goal. It's when you want to do something more easily, quickly, and cheaply. Organizing a production line makes work more efficient. Creating set policies and having everything in its place makes work more efficient. Breaking down big jobs—like building something—into little jobs—like assembling just one part of the something—makes work more efficient. But these organization strategies do not necessarily make work more *effective*.

Effectiveness is when you do the right thing. That's different from efficiency, in which you do something well. When you shift your focus and update your activities, that's increasing your effectiveness. When you get at the root cause of a problem or error and eliminate it, that increases effectiveness. When you learn to do something better—or teach your people to do it better—that's effectiveness at its best. So doing the right thing—effectiveness—is also a great goal as you organize people, work, space, time, and anything else you can find to play around with.

In fact, you can argue that success in business or life is simply a matter of combining efficiency and effectiveness. In other words, doing the right things well. If so, then all you ever need to think about in organizing is efficiency and effectiveness. And that is in fact a pretty good approach.

But I want to take you even further now by combining efficiency and effectiveness with a third organizational issue—one that is often overlooked: growth.

You can also organize to *grow*. Growth and development—for you as an individual, for the individuals you supervise, and for the organizations in which you live and work—is a reasonable and meaningful goal, too. And I believe that when you pursue all three of these goals—efficiency, effectiveness, and growth—then you will truly be on the road to mastering organization and will be able to benefit most fully from your organization skills.

> Success is simply a matter of doing the right things well.

What does organization have to do with personal and business growth? Growth is in fact the best reason to organize. And to turn that around, organizing is one of the best ways to grow.

When it comes right down to it, simple organizational issues generally stand between us and our goals. To grow anything—our expertise, our incomes, our businesses, even our families—takes resources. Time, money, effort, passion, and many other inputs must be marshaled and applied to that growth goal, whatever it might be for you personally.

And to do that well, you need to organize well. Disorganization prevents you from pursuing your growth goals efficiently and effectively. In fact, I guarantee that you are not currently as well-organized to pursue your growth goals as you could be. In fact, I'll bet you could grow at least twice as fast if you simply got organized to support your growth.

For the majority of individuals and businesses, new and better approaches to organizing can produce more growth and development than anything else they could do, including obtaining investment capital!

Yup, you heard me. I think you'll find that organizing to pursue your personal growth goals will get you farther right now than money would.

Organizing to Expand Your Capacity

The trick to organizing in order to grow your business, income, or anything else is to organize in ways that expand your capacity to do the things needed for growth. For example, if you are in sales, you can only line up so many prospects and make so many sales calls a day. When you run out of time, you run out of growth potential.

So does that mean you can only make so much in that sales position and no more? Certainly not! At least not if you are willing to examine the capacity constraints that limit your growth potential. As soon as you start looking hard at the things that limit your ability to line up prospects and make sales pitches, then you can begin to expand your upper limits. You can find creative ways to widen those bottlenecks.

> You will never "find" time for anything. If you want time you must make it.
> —CHARLES BUXTON
>
> • • •
>
> Take all the swift advantage of the hours.
> —SHAKESPEARE

To stick with the example of a salesperson for a minute, because it is an easy one to follow, let's imagine some of the ways this salesperson might get around the limitations on how many calls one can make in a day. Here are some organizational ideas that widen the bottleneck:

- Target areas in which prospects are more densely located (if they are near each other, then travel time is minimized)
- Find ways to bring prospects together, for example, by giving sales seminars, workshops, speeches, and the like
- Offload other activities that clog your schedule so you can spend all your time in sales meetings
- Experiment with mass media to bring prospects further along (telemarket them, for example) and reduce the personal time needed to close each sale
- Bring in low-level assistants or interns and have them do some of the prospecting work and perhaps even call on lower-quality leads for you
- Consider building a sales organization in which you run a group of expert salespeople instead of doing the sales yourself
- Change the way you sell so as to make it quicker and easier to close a sale, allowing you to make more sales each day
- Focus only on people who are really ready to buy (many sales calls are to people who aren't yet ready and thus waste a lot of selling time). To do this, you probably need to contact many more potential prospects and select out those who have an urgent need to see you.
- Find some way of enticing prospects to come to your office or a central location to meet you, saving you the drive time.

Before you say, "Hey, those sound like great theories, but in reality, they'd all be hard to implement," I want to tell you that each and every one of these strategies has been used effectively by many salespeople in many different industries. I've collected these strategies by talking to the exceptional salespeople who seem to break the rules and achieve far higher levels of success than their compatriots. So I know these strategies can work.

> Every one of these strategies has been used effectively by many salespeople in many different industries.

I also know *why* they work. They work because they expand the person's capacity to do what they are best at and what they make the most money doing. They get you working on the efficiency and effectiveness of *processes that limit your growth*.

Tom LeDuc, a successful entrepreneur, likes to ask people how valuable their time is when they are doing whatever they make the most money doing. At some point in time, just about anyone in business has put in at least a few hours in which they were worth hundreds, thousands, even hundreds of thousands of dollars. But most of the time, they aren't earning anything like that peak level.

So he asks them why not. And, of course, the answer is because they aren't doing whatever it is that makes the most money most of the time. They are doing other things instead.

So the basic idea is simple. Stop doing things that limit your growth potential. Do a lot more of the things that maximize your potential. And to do so, I highly recommend you start by figuring out where you are wasting time and effort. Then you can reorganize to focus on the things that matter most and are most likely to help you achieve your personal goals.

Using the Capacity Expansion Worksheet

Here is a little activity you can use to put these powerful ideas into action in your own work. It's called the Capacity Expansion Worksheet, and I developed it with an associate named Charles Schewe. I've tried it in some of the trainings and workshops I've given, and I can tell you people find it pretty helpful. It works. But I have yet to publish it as a commercial product, so this is the first time it's appeared in print.

To use it, simply follow the instructions. Then think about the results.

Good luck! Although in truth, if you learn to organize sufficiently well, you won't need good luck to accomplish your goals!!

Great opportunities come to all, but many do not know they have met them. The only preparation to take advantage of them, is simple fidelity to what each day brings.

—A. E. DUNNING

Capacity Expansion Path Worksheet

Instructions

You should be doing things that:

    a) you are particularly good at (they match your skills and intelligence)

    b) you make the most money from doing

Yet you probably do a lot of things in the average workday that don't meet one or both of these criteria.

One reason you, like most of us, don't use your time efficiently is that you probably don't keep track of how you use your time. You can't learn without measuring. So start by keeping track of what you do in a typical workday. Use your daily planner or a pocket notebook to "study yourself." Every hour on the hour, make a note of what you are doing.

If you have to, set a wrist alarm watch or carry an old-fashioned kitchen timer with you to make sure you write a note every hour.

Keep doing this exercise for as many days as you can stand. At least two or three. Three days times eight hours is twenty-four notes about what you do. That's a good sample.

Now you are ready to answer the question of what you do and whether it meets the two criteria above.

Analyzing the Results

Look over your list of activities. First, highlight any that rate a total of five or six. In other words, that you gave ratings of 3 and 3 or 2 and 3. These are things that you need to be doing. In fact, you probably need to do more of them. But do you have the time? Are you capacity-constrained from doing the things you do well and make money from? Most of us are.

To increase your capacity to do these important things, think about ways of cutting back on all the other activities that take up your time. The list probably includes lots of things that you aren't uniquely good at and/or that don't make you very much money.

> **Goal:** Do only the things that you are best at—and that others value the most.

Worksheet

Use the following worksheet to find out what things you currently spend time on that you ought to hand off to someone else in order to make more time for the things you are good at and that make you money.

Enter your own list of activities if you've done some research, or use our generic descriptions of what typical businesspeople do with their time.

Activity	How Good at it Are You? 1 = not good 2 = in between 3 = good			How Much Money Do You Make from It? 1 = not much 2 = in between 3 = lots		
Opening mail	1	2	3	1	2	3
Paying bills	1	2	3	1	2	3
Answering the phone	1	2	3	1	2	3
Writing letters	1	2	3	1	2	3
Handling customer complaints	1	2	3	1	2	3
Shopping for supplies	1	2	3	1	2	3
Making cold calls	1	2	3	1	2	3
Scheduling sales calls	1	2	3	1	2	3
Making sales presentations	1	2	3	1	2	3
Putting together marketing materials	1	2	3	1	2	3
Cleaning the office	1	2	3	1	2	3
Driving to meetings	1	2	3	1	2	3
Filling customer orders	1	2	3	1	2	3
Writing up customer orders/contracts	1	2	3	1	2	3
Looking up prospect addresses/numbers	1	2	3	1	2	3
Filing	1	2	3	1	2	3
Accounting	1	2	3	1	2	3
Going to the post office	1	2	3	1	2	3
Writing reports	1	2	3	1	2	3
Keeping your journal	1	2	3	1	2	3
Developing a database	1	2	3	1	2	3
Developing business plans	1	2	3	1	2	3
Going to the bank	1	2	3	1	2	3

Scheduling personal appointments	1	2	3		1	2	3
Meeting with associates/staff	1	2	3		1	2	3
Entertaining clients	1	2	3		1	2	3
Entertaining prospects	1	2	3		1	2	3
Entertaining suppliers	1	2	3		1	2	3
Reading magazines and papers	1	2	3		1	2	3
Brainstorming new business ideas	1	2	3		1	2	3
Researching what other businesses do	1	2	3		1	2	3
Researching customer desires	1	2	3		1	2	3
Finding new/improved products	1	2	3		1	2	3
Finding new markets	1	2	3		1	2	3
Going to the dry cleaner	1	2	3		1	2	3
Shopping for business clothing	1	2	3		1	2	3
Getting coffee	1	2	3		1	2	3
Mining your customer database	1	2	3		1	2	3
Interviewing possible assistants/experts	1	2	3		1	2	3
Waiting in lines	1	2	3		1	2	3
_____	1	2	3		1	2	3
_____	1	2	3		1	2	3
_____	1	2	3		1	2	3
_____	1	2	3		1	2	3
_____	1	2	3		1	2	3
_____	1	2	3		1	2	3
_____	1	2	3		1	2	3
_____	1	2	3		1	2	3
_____	1	2	3		1	2	3
_____	1	2	3		1	2	3
_____	1	2	3		1	2	3
_____	1	2	3		1	2	3
_____	1	2	3		1	2	3
_____	1	2	3		1	2	3
_____	1	2	3		1	2	3
_____	1	2	3		1	2	3

Why are you doing them? Because, if you are like most of us, you've never really thought about it before.

Now you need to think of strategies to cut back on or eliminate as many of those low-value activities as possible. Can you delegate them to someone? Can you get by without them? Can you spend just a little bit more to get someone to do them or use an efficient service as a substitute? It's often hard to break these habits and change our use of our valuable time, but the struggle is worth it because it frees you up to succeed.

You won't find anybody who is highly successful in business standing around in a long check-out line at the grocery store. They know this isn't helping them develop their business. They know it is in fact hurting their business by keeping them from doing what they do well and make money at. So they've found some way to avoid it. A housekeeper or older child does the shopping. Or they go out to eat or have a meal delivered or they only shop late at night when nobody else does. They don't mess with many of the things you do mess with. So time to get smart. Time to start organizing to expand your capacity and achieve your growth potential!

What About Non-Financial Goals?

If you are not focused on making money, just substitute another goal in the worksheet. Could be "raising great kids" or "improving the world." Whatever it is, you still want to pursue it by doing activities that relate to it—and by doing them well!

> While we stop to think, we often miss our opportunity.
> —PUBLILIUS SYRUS

Organizing for "Opportunity Time"

It is common to overlook what is near by keeping the eye fixed on something remote. In the same manner present opportunities are neglected and attainable good is slighted by minds busied in extensive ranges, and intent upon future advantages. Life, however short, is made shorter by waste of time.

—SAMUEL JOHNSON

As the quote from Samuel Johnson points out, it is easy to overlook an opportunity that is not in the plan or on the schedule. In fact, if you think about it, this is perhaps the most common and dangerous form of time management error. Most people, and especially most managers, are so thoroughly overbooked that they do not have time for much spontaneity in their daily lives. And before I lecture you on the subject, I might as well come clean and confess that this is a major issue for me too.

I find myself busy with a series of contracts with publishers and clients, plus a heavy weight of routine chores and tasks. Today, for example, I am supposed to finish this chapter on time management. I am also supposed to evaluate proposals from several publicity agencies and select one to promote my last book, which is going to be launched in three months and so needs lots of marketing attention right now. Then there are a few scheduled phone calls, and there is the little matter of meeting with my accountant to get last year's records in shape for tax season. Consulting my appointment book, I find it full of messages that need returning. And I need to do some research today to prepare for a first meeting with a new client next week. Sounds like I have about forty hours of work on the calendar for today, in fact.

So when I bumped into an acquaintance who teaches management over at the business school this morning while picking up a cup of coffee on the way to work, I was very tempted to give him a quick nod and smile and keep on going. But then I recalled that he and I had exchanged some ideas over the last year or two about ways of applying some exciting research he's done. And I recalled how much I'd learned about ways of increasing the innovation in businesses the last time I met with him. And I also recalled that I had some interesting ideas about possible collaborations that I never followed up because I forgot to return his last e-mail. And I was reminded of the famous old Latin saying that opportunity has hair in front but is bald behind. If you seize her by the forelock, you may hold her, but if you let her past, not even Jupiter can catch hold of her. Here was an opportunity, an opportunity at least to learn something of interest and, perhaps in the long run, an opportunity to develop a valuable business relationship. So I said to myself, forgot the damn schedule! Stop and talk for a few minutes. No schedule is any good if it has no time in it for seizing opportunity by the forelock.

In fact, the best business plan you and your company could possibly adopt is one which says simply: Seek and find more opportunities than the competition does!

My friend gave me some good ideas—the one I stopped to talk with over my hurried cup of coffee. Maybe one will turn into a new training product for my firm some day. If it does, I'll have to chalk up another success to serendipity. Serendipity is my favorite business partner. Looking back, I find an element of chance and luck in every success. It's that way for everyone, I think. So make sure you leave at least a little time for the unexpected in your daily schedule.

The Financial Management Course

Overview of Course V

I'm going to warn you right up front that this is a challenging and lengthy topic. That's because I've put everything I think you have to learn right now about finance and accounting into five jam-packed sessions:

Session 1: The Psychology of Money

Session 2: Cash Flow

Session 3: Assets, Liabilities, and Net Worth

Session 4: Raising Money to Meet Business Needs

Session 5: Analyzing and Understanding Your Costs

I want to show you how key concepts from all aspects of corporate finance interrelate to give you a valuable management perspective on the financial needs and behavior of your firm. And I want to give you a solid grounding in the ways in which finance allows you to think about business.

In a sense, corporate finance is a philosophy, not simply a business function. Sure, you need to take care of financial matters to keep any organization running smoothly. But more than that, you need to think about personal and business decisions from the powerful perspective of financial management. It adds a rich dimension to your understanding of business. A finance perspective helps you make better choices. And without it, you can get into a lot of trouble in a hurry.

To possess money is very well; it may be a most valuable servant; to be possessed by it, is to be possessed by a devil, and one of the meanest and worst kind of devils.

—TRYON EDWARDS

The Psychology of Money

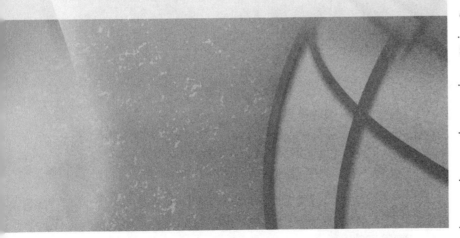

What is money? When you need some, you don't bother with a philosophical question like this. You just try to make a sale, lobby for a raise, or get a loan. But to understand finance, and to truly understand how people and finance interrelate, you need to think about how people perceive money.

Money can represent status and prestige, success or failure, life or death, convenience or inconvenience. Money represents goods, buying power, economic power. Money has virtually no value of itself. It's just paper, nickel, and copper, or electronic traces in a database. But to the economist, money is capital, that wondrous, powerful stuff of which businesses are built and economic cycles created. And in corporate finance, money is valuable because it provides the capital with which to nurture a business and give it the strength to generate enough excess money to pay the workers and owners some return on their capital.

Listen to how one eminent economist talks about money and capital. I find this quote surprising and exciting since it offers a perception of money so different from the ordinary views:

> Capital is powerful only insofar as it continually runs the gauntlet of circulation, each capitalist of necessity distributing his money into the hands of the public (his workers, his suppliers) in order to procure the labor services and materials from which his capital will be reconstituted as a commodity. Each capitalist must win back from the public at large the money capital he has disbursed to various sections of it, and each capitalist is simultaneously trying to win for himself as much as possible of the money capital of other capitalists.
> —Robert Heilbroner, *The Nature and Logic of Capitalism*

Wow. To an economist, then, money is of hardly any consequence at all. It is simply one form capital can take, a form that comes in handy when playing the bold and dangerous game of capitalism. Instead of locking up your capital safely, you must risk it by "running the gauntlet" of business activity—buying and selling, competing with others in the hope that more capital will come back to

Money really isn't everything. If it was, what would we buy with it?
—Tom Wilson ("Ziggy")

you than what you put at risk in the economic system. Now that's an interesting view of money.

Why is it important how people perceive money? What does one's view of it have to do with corporate finance, or success in business and life for that matter?

One's attitude toward money has a powerful effect over one's behavior in business and in life. A healthy, realistic attitude toward money, one that views it as a means to an end and treats it with respect, not adulation or lust, is important in life and in work. People who don't get the psychology of finance right will never master the practice, no matter how sophisticated their understanding. For them, that "gauntlet" of financial risks will always be too much. Somehow, money will slip through their fingers and not return when they need it.

But people who have the psychology of money right are quite the opposite. There are lots of successful entrepreneurs who say something to the effect that, "I just don't know why, but somehow money always comes to me when I need it." Well, it's not really that simple of course. You don't see these folks sitting on their porches, sipping a cold drink and waiting for a truck to come up and dump money on their walk. They are active, even aggressive, in their pursuit of capital and their use of it. But on the other hand, they do seem to have a healthy knack for generating funds. Deals work out in their favor. They seem to be able to get the funding they need for their ideas. And their businesses always make a healthy margin of profit.

> People who don't get the psychology of finance right will never master the practice, no matter how sophisticated their understanding.

How Is Your Financial Judgment?

Good financial management is essential to the survival and success of any business. I guess that's obvious. Yet it's amazing how often you see businesses and individuals exhibit really poor financial judgment. In fact, many people seem to change personalities when they are exposed to money. To prepare yourself fully for business or personal success, you need to acquire a healthy attitude toward money. And you need to learn to spot unhealthy attitudes in others so as to avoid giving them any access to important funds.

How Good Is *Their* Financial Judgment?

One of the things I always look for when evaluating a potential business partner or key employee is whether they are "funny about money." I've known plenty of bright, personable people who seem to be perfect for the job, until they gain some control over the funds. Then a darker side of their personality asserts itself!

Money induces financial intoxication, and you often see people lose their inhibitions, their common sense, or their ethics when exposed to money in quantity. In particular, here are some of the most common forms of dysfunctional financial behavior to watch out for in yourself and others:

- *Wishful thinking.* Lots of people believe that somehow they will "think and grow rich" or that if they just wish hard enough, money will find its way to them. In fact, there are lots of inspirational speakers and trainers who give people advice on the order of, "Write yourself a note saying, 'I'm going to have a million dollars by the end of the year.' Put it in your wallet and carry it with you everywhere. By the end of the year, you should be a millionaire." I figure people who charge good money for advice like that don't plan to be in town at the end of the year. In business, that sort of "faith financing" is pretty dangerous. There are too many cases in which somebody spends more than they've got in the blind hope that somehow the money will come back to them in time to make up the difference. It never does. You don't want someone who takes a superstitious or wishful approach handling any of your money. And you certainly can't afford to be that flaky yourself.
- *Uncontrolled spending.* Some people get overly excited and go on a spending spree whenever they have access to funds. They run up their credit cards and they blow through their budgets. If they can get bank loans, they spend them without regard to how they'll pay the debt. Expenses must always be tightly linked with revenues. Unless you keep an eye on

I've known plenty of bright, personable people who seem to be perfect for the job, until they gain some control over the funds. Then a darker side of their personality asserts itself!

where the return is coming from, money simply won't return. So don't trust uncontrolled spenders—or be one yourself.

- *Pocketing.* A surprising number of people feel a strong urge to put other people's money in their own pockets. I can't even count the number of times I've been approached by someone for advice about how to handle a business partner who seems to be overly possessive about the partnership's funds. The scenario usually goes like this. Both (or all) partners have individual signing power on the company's bank accounts, and they take turns handling financial matters as needed. Everything goes fine, though on occasion the books don't quite balance as accurately as you'd like. Then one of the partners decides to track down some minor sum that's gone missing, and in doing so, discovers a long pattern of unaccounted-for withdrawals by another partner. Confronted, that sticky-fingered partner treats his (or her) behavior as inconsequential. "Oh, sometimes I take out a little cash when I need it, but of course I'll repay it later. Don't you, too?" But in truth, little or none of that borrowed money ever returns to the business. And the other partners view it, quite rightly, as stealing rather than borrowing. There are also lots of employees who think nothing of "borrowing" supplies, equipment, or cash if they can get at it, and rarely bring anything back.

Why do people pocket money or materials that ought to be treated as belonging to the business? I don't really know, but I know it is a common form of behavior and one that often leads to cash-flow crises, lost jobs, breakups of partnerships and marriages, and even to criminal charges. Even individual entrepreneurs often "bleed" their business bank accounts instead of paying themselves a regular and properly accounted for wage. Pocketing is a widespread behavior. Watch out for this all-too-common form of financial intoxication!

> Pocketing is a widespread behavior. Watch out for this all-too-common form of financial intoxication!

- *Bottom-lining.* Obsessive concern with financial matters and measures is all too common among managers and entrepreneurs. People who count their money constantly know just how much they have but usually have little insight into how they'll make more. You can't run a business from the bottom line. You need to run it for the bottom line, but from the top line. The way to produce better profits at the bottom of an income statement is to manage the revenues and expenses that sum to profit or loss.

I've known many managers who constantly harp on bottom-line performance. They sound like stock analysts, not managers. They give their people the strong impression that the numbers have to be made, no matter how. They stimulate lots of inappropriate and short-sighted behavior as a result. People who bottom-line obsessively tend to get their bottom lines in the short term, never in the long term, because their attitude forces everyone to trade off long-term investments for short-term profits. The only way to achieve long-term financial success is to make sure your short-term and long-term plans and goals *are on the same path*. You can't go two directions at once!

- *Overlooking.* To some people, money just doesn't seem very important. Sure, it's nice to have money and make money, and it's really nice to spend money because you can turn it into much more important things. But money itself? Boring. Can't worry about it today. I just talked with an executive who told me she got a call from the bank saying they were overdrawn by a large sum. "That's impossible!" she replied. "We've had the best quarter ever. Our balance should be huge." But when she looked into it, she discovered that her office manager had simply overlooked billing and depositing for a couple months. He'd done a good job of making sure the work got done, but he'd forgotten all about sending out invoices. And he'd left a few checks sitting on his desk without bothering to deposit them. He just overlooked the money part. No big deal, right?

I don't claim to understand this attitude either, but since it does exist you want to keep an eye out for it. Someone who periodically forgets to deposit his or her paycheck should never be put in charge of your company's invoices, for example. No point taking risks by let-

> You can't run a business from the bottom line. You need to run it for the bottom line, but from the top line.

ting anyone who's funny with money handle yours. And if *you* tend to overlook the money part, you need to have a competent and extremely honest bookkeeper in charge of all your finances.

- *Avoiding.* Some people feel anxious about finances and try not to think about them. I do this myself sometimes. I can think of lots of things I need to do instead of attacking my monthly bills, for example, because I just hate to see all those checks go into the mailbox. It pains me to part with thousands of dollars of hard-earned money. When taken to extremes, avoidance leads to a lack of proper accounting, an inability to anticipate and prepare for cash flow or financing needs, and a general lack of proper financial controls and planning.

Let's Get the Attitudes Right!

Like everything in business, financial management requires the right attitude. People who are funny with money are unable to handle financial management, even if they have the technical training to do so. In fact, attitude is especially important when it comes to financial management. Positive persistence and an ability to control one's impulses are vital to successful financial management. It takes significant discipline on the part of individuals and the organization alike to manage finances appropriately. If you lack this discipline, make sure someone who has it is in charge of your finances. If you work with or hire people who lack this discipline, don't let them have access to the petty cash.

Learning from the Psychologist's View of Money

It surprises me that psychologists don't think and write about money more than they do. I've got a lot of psychology textbooks in my office, and I can report that the word "money" is not in any of their indexes. Strange, isn't it? The biggest list of page references in these indexes is often under the term "sexual behavior." I'm certain there is plenty to warrant the attention of psychologists in that subject area, but I have to think that financial behavior is almost as important as sexual behavior and a lot more complex. I don't know

Allegory: The Case of the Free-Spending CEO

I recently evaluated a medical biotechnology company that was having cash-flow problems and on the verge of collapse. Could it be turned around? What had gone wrong? I eventually discovered that the company's president had blown through a $10 million venture capital investment with little to show for it. Rather than stick to the several year research and development budget his plan called for, he had acquired two other companies, hired more managers, and given himself a huge raise. After one year of his free spending the company was broke and had to lay off its researchers. With its R&D funds gone and its top scientists laid off, this company was going down fast. I could not see any way to save it short of replacing the management and starting all over again. And that hardly made financial sense given the depth of the hole left by its free-spending chief executive.

why psychologists have failed to explore the intricacies of how we behave around money. I think they are spending too much time in the bedroom. They need to get out more often, visit a mall, have some fun with their charge cards. Or sit in on a board meeting at any organization that has just received bad financial news. There is plenty to study in the field of financial behavior!

When psychologists do think about money, they treat it as a type of stimulus to behavior. To psychologists, money is interesting because of the behaviors and feelings it is associated with. Human behavior is so often influenced by money. Psychologists ask why and how people learn to respond to money in so many different ways. Their answer is that money is a *generalized reinforcer*. What's that? It's any stimulus that people learn to recognize as a predictor of a wide range of reinforcements—rewards or punishments. And, in the words of psychologists John and Janice Baldwin (in *Behavior Principles in Everyday Life*), "Because money can be used to obtain many positive reinforcers or avoid many punishers in countless different situations, most people learn to respond to money as a generalized reinforcer."

Yes. But what does that mean to you and me? The point I think is most interesting in this psychological view of money is that people do after all have to *learn* their responses to money. We "learn to respond to money" and then follow those learned response patterns. Nobody has a genetic attitude or response when it comes to money. Babies couldn't care less about it, except perhaps as something to teeth on. This is a wonderful thing if you think about it, because it means that anyone can develop healthier, more successful attitudes and behaviors when it comes to money.

Sure, there are lots of unhealthy psychological approaches to money. But they are all presumably learned, and so can be unlearned and replaced with new, improved upgrades. I like to think that we can all acquire the healthy attitudes and habits of those rare few who just seem to be good with money and don't have any trouble handling it appropriately—or making it appear when they wish it to!

> I don't like money, actually, but it quiets my nerves.
> —JOE LOUIS

Cash Flow

Session 2

I'm now going to switch gears for the rest of the finance sessions and focus on the ideas and concepts that finance experts rely upon and that give them such a unique perspective on business. If you are already trained in this area, you may find it redundant. My approach is to explore the handful of powerful concepts that are behind all good financial decision-making and that can improve management decisions in all areas as well.

Core Concept: Cash Flow

There are many reasons for business failure but only one cause. Whatever might go wrong, whatever pressures might exist, the thing that ultimately gets a business is a cash-flow crisis. If you simply haven't got enough money to pay your bills, the vultures will swoop right in and start picking over your carcass.

Cash is the blood of a business, and it must flow through the business to keep it healthy. A small leak won't kill a business right away, but in the long run it will unless stanched. And a major leak will do any business in quite quickly.

Of course, cash is supposed to flow in and out of a business, much like blood flows in and out of specific organs of your body to nourish them. So the key to healthy cash flow is a *balance* between what comes in and what goes out. You need cash to be available whenever you have to pay bills. It's that simple. But to make sure it flows so as to meet that demand can be a bit complex.

For example, let's say a business has $10 million in revenues and $9 million in expenses in the course of one year. Sounds healthy, doesn't it? On paper, this business makes a 10 percent profit, which is nothing to sneeze at. However, it could easily fail under any of the following cash-flow situations:

- Expenses are incurred regularly but revenues are tied up in several large contracts that don't pay until near the end of the year.
- 12 percent of revenues prove uncollectible.
- A balloon loan payment of $1.5 million comes due midway through the year, and management can't roll it over into another loan as they had hoped to.

One should look down on money but never lose sight of it.
—ANDRÉ PRÉVOT

- The business has a fire in its factory, which turns out to be underinsured.
- The business has contracted with several firms to build new facilities on the assumption that revenues would be higher than they are and cannot keep up with the schedule of payments on the construction project.
- Sales suddenly start to grow at unexpectedly higher rates, and the company adds new employees and rents new equipment and facilities faster than it can collect revenues on the new business.
- The cost of several important component parts goes up 25 percent, shrinking the company's profit margin from 10 to 4 percent.

Any of these situations will put a strain on cash flow and perhaps even drive the company out of business. Yet these sorts of things happen all the time. And notice that my list does not include any serious problems such as the entry of new competitors or a new technology that takes away expected sales. Even when a company is doing business successfully, cash-flow problems can and do crop up. In fact, rapid growth, which most managers desire more than anything else, is almost guaranteed to create a cash-flow crisis. You have to scale up to meet the rising demand in advance of collecting on those new sales, and it is hard to fund the scale-up from ongoing business.

Cash-flow crises fall into two important categories, and you need to recognize the distinction because the cures differ for each. There are temporary cash-flow problems, and then there are structural ones.

Temporary cash-flow problems

This category includes anything that produces a temporary shortage of cash in a profitable business: slow payment by customers, the need to ramp up production to meet higher-than-expected orders, the combination of several major expenses coming due at the same time. Such temporary problems can be anticipated by doing projections of the cash you expect to flow in and out each week for the next few months.

> Annual income twenty pounds, annual expenditure nineteen six, result happiness. Annual income twenty pounds, annual expenditure twenty pounds ought and six, result misery.
> —CHARLES DICKENS, *DAVID COPPERFIELD*

The Mystery of the Torn Check

A small business owner ordered three file cabinets from an office supply house. When they arrived with the invoice, he wrote a check, tore it into thirty-six pieces, and sent it back in the mail. Why?

Your business' staying power depends on maintaining a positive cash flow: Money has to come into the business at least as fast as it goes out.

—DAVID H. BANGS, JR., AUTHOR OF THE BUSINESS PLANNING GUIDE AND THE CASH FLOW CONTROL GUIDE

With advance warning, you can try to save up for these temporary cash-flow demands. If you cannot juggle other expenses and save up in order to cope with them, you can seek temporary financing to bridge the gap. Banks may give you short-term loans. Factors (lenders who buy your receivables) may also help out. And often your creditors will be understanding and permit you to renegotiate the terms of payment (always ask them first before trying to line up a loan!). The best insurance against short-term cash-flow crises is to maintain a cash reserve. Set aside a small percentage of each deposit you make in a special savings or money market account in order to build up enough of a cushion to see you through these hard times. Then you can self-finance, which is always easier and less expensive than having to go to the financial markets to raise bridge financing.

Structural cash-flow problems

This category includes anything that produces ongoing pressures on your profit margins: competitive pressures to lower prices or offer discounts, rising labor costs, expensive quality control problems such as errors and rework, rising materials costs, slipping sales volume (which makes fixed costs a larger percentage of each sale and thus cuts profits), routinely late payments on the part of your customers. Any of these problems can lead to a situation in which the business simply fails to make enough profit or actually loses money. Many businesses have structural problems that are gradually bleeding them dry.

Managers often fail to recognize that their cash-flow problems are structural and keep trying to bridge their cash-flow crises with temporary measures. This won't work. It never does; it just makes things worse. Look at it this way. If you are losing one cent on each dollar of revenues, that doesn't seem too bad. It's about the smallest loss you'll ever see in business. What if you do $1 million worth of business? When the dust settles, you will find yourself $1,000 in the hole. Still not too bad. But what if you do $1 billion worth of business? Now you've dug a hole $1 million deep. The more business you do, the more trouble you get into when you have a structural problem.

In this era of hot Internet-based stock offerings, it is easy to believe that losses do not really matter. Amazon.com grew and grew without ever making a profit. In fact, its losses grew faster than its revenues for the first few years of its life. Yet it was honored by the business press as a stellar example of entrepreneurial success. (I never bought a share as I don't like negative cash flows, more fool me!) To understand Amazon.com's cash flow you have to recognize that they were not in the business of selling books in their early years. Sure, they sold books over the Web, but they were *really* in the business of selling stock. They epitomized the promise of a hot new technology, and investors were happy to pay a premium to own a piece of the company in spite of its losses. Amazon.com maintained a healthy cash flow by selling stock whenever it needed to. A nice formula, but not one you can count on for the vast majority of businesses!

Allegory: Franchising for Cash Flow

Once there was an eager young entrepreneur who ran a popular restaurant. It was always crowded and everyone told him he was on to the next big thing. Of course, he was often a bit short on cash since his business was still in its growth phase, but friends and relations believed in his concept and lent him enough to get over the humps. Then one day a slick lawyer came to call with an enticing proposition. Why not let him package up the business and sell franchises? He was confident he could get at least $25,000 per franchise, plus 10 percent of each franchise's revenues. Soon the entrepreneur was busy showing off his restaurant to potential franchises, and it wasn't long before the first few franchises were sold.

Now the money was pouring in! Whopping big checks from each franchise sale made for a healthy bank account, and the entrepreneur was finally able to relax and stop worrying about cash flow, but only for a year or so. Then the old problems began to crop back up. The bookkeeper complained that she didn't have enough money to cover payroll taxes, and the entrepreneur promised to sell another franchise or two to make up the difference. But now it was harder to make those sales because the first few franchisees were complaining that their businesses were not doing as well as promised. They didn't even have enough money to make their 10 percent payments, and in fact, one of them was threatening to sue.

It wasn't long before the whole house of cards came down with a crash. All of the businesses failed, franchisees and franchiser alike. Turns out the basic business concept was not sufficiently profitable. Revenues were too low; expenses too high. Franchising turned a small cash-flow problem into a very big one. In fact, it took years for the litigation to end and the bankruptcy process to conclude.

What happened? The entrepreneur mistook a structural cash-flow problem for a temporary one. And that is a fatal error in any business.

Conclusions

When will you need how much money? Will you have it available when you need it? If it was worth less than the debt, can you easily borrow it on terms appropriate to the timing of the need and at an interest rate lower than what you can make from the money? If not, can you find a way to avoid that expense so that you won't need the money?

These are the basic questions of cash flow management. When you are looking ahead to see what will be happening in and to your bank balances, you are keeping an eye on the most fundamental and important aspect of corporate finance. I know it's overlooked in many MBA programs since it seems so much less sophisticated than double entry bookkeeping, leveraged buyouts, and all those fun topics that make such good chalk talks. But cash flow is the thing that will get you first so you had better manage it closely and well.

Nobody succeeds financially, in life or in business, without healthy, positive cash flows to support their endeavors. So please, if you manage nothing else in corporate finance, at least make it a religious habit to keep a close eye on your cash flow.

In the next session we are going to take a look at where that cash ultimately flows *to*.

Assets, Liabilities, and Net Worth

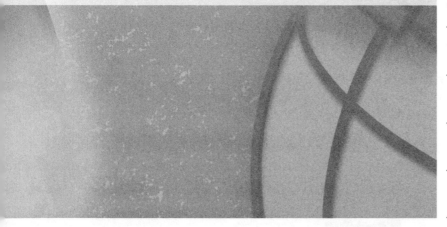

Session 3

A ccountants and chief financial officers tend to look at businesses not in terms of cash but in abstract terms designed to help them see the inherent value and hidden financial structure. For example, to the average car owner, a car loan is thought of from a cash-flow perspective. What's the monthly payment? Can I afford it? But if you were a CFO, you'd look at it differently. You'd ask what the total debt was on the car; how much is still owed. And you'd ask what the car was worth if sold today. Then you'd check to see that it was worth more than the debt on it. If not, then you'd be unhappy. You'd consider that car a financial problem because that car is worth some negative amount in an abstract financial sense. I don't care if it drives well, it's not going to do your business any good if it's on your book as a negative number.

A car loan is a trivial example, to be sure, but businesses are often analyzed the same way I analyzed that car. For example, let's say you are a banker and I just came to you to request a loan for my business. I have a great story about a hot new product that everyone wants to buy. I just need to borrow some money so I can get some molds made and start producing the product. Should you lend me the money? Well, if you are a banker, you don't believe a word I say. Sorry, it's just the way they think. You figure I might have a good product, but then again I might not. And if I don't, how will you get the bank's money back? You won't want the molds for the product if it's no good. So you will have to get the money back some other way. If worst comes to worst, you'll want to be sure the business is worth at least the amount it owes you. You'll need to analyze it in terms of assets, liabilities, and net worth, which are the subjects of this session.

> To the average car owner, a car loan is thought of from a cash-flow perspective. What's the monthly payment? Can I afford it? But if you were a CFO, you'd look at it differently.

Core Concept: Assets and Liabilities

If you own it and it has some value, it's an asset. Money in the bank is an asset. A building is an asset. So is a fleet of delivery trucks, a factory, or an Internet server. All are of value, all could conceivably be sold in exchange for money or even traded for other assets. And if you think about the things a business values as assets, you quickly realize that there may be intangibles of value too. A valuable brand name is an asset if you own the rights to it. A contract worth millions might be a valuable asset, especially if the contract gives you the right to sell it to another party. And receivables, the money owed you in exchange for sale of goods or services, are also an asset. Heck, a credit card can even be thought of as an asset if it has an unused credit balance, because that has value if you need to borrow money to make a purchase.

Assets are valuable, so you can do valuable things with them, such as use them to secure a loan. And if you wish to sell a business, a long list of valuable assets will help justify a high price tag.

Liabilities are the opposite of assets. They are the debts an individual or business owes others. A loan that must be repaid is a liability. A commitment to perform services that have already been paid for is a liability. Money owed on a credit card is a liability. Upcoming tax bills are a liability. And if there are any legal problems, these can also be thought of as liabilities. For example, if customers have filed suits seeking damages as a result of using your company's products, then your company has legal liabilities. You ought to value these liabilities at whatever the most likely settlement or judgment cost of the suits is going to be.

Core Concept: Net Worth

If I have lots of assets—a huge mansion and a million dollars in the bank—am I rich? Maybe, but you can't really say until you find out what my liabilities are. If I have a huge mortgage for that mansion and also owe more than a million dollars in business loans and runaway credit card balances, then I'm not rich after all. In fact, in a month or two I'll probably be flat broke!

Net worth is what's left over when you subtract your liabilities from your assets. It's a very simple calculation, and a very important one. How much are you worth as an individual, financially speaking that is? You can find out by calculating your own net worth. Add up every asset you own. Subtract every debt (don't forget the property taxes you owe this year on your car and home—I mean *every* liability).

Now what's the result? Is your personal net worth a big, hearty number in the six digits or more? Thought not. Is it near zero? Perhaps. In fact, the majority of people have negative net worth

> How much are you worth as an individual, financially speaking that is?

when they do this calculation. How can that be? Because it doesn't account for their future earning power. In fact, you are probably your most valuable asset right now. By investing in your own attitudes, knowledge, and skills, you are taking the single most powerful step toward eventually achieving a high financial net worth. So don't be discouraged if your personal net worth doesn't look like much on paper right now. All in good time!

Core Concept: Balance Sheet

A balance sheet is a standard financial statement that lists both assets and liabilities, then subtracts liabilities from assets to calculate net worth. It is supposed to balance. How? The assets, which are listed on the left side, should equal the liabilities and the owner's equity (or net worth), which appear on the right side of the balance sheet. All balance sheets follow this basic structure:

> You are probably your most valuable asset right now.

BALANCE SHEET

Assets
Current Assets

Itemized List	$xxx
	$xxx
Total current assets	$xxx

Fixed Assets

Itemized list	$xxx
	$xxx
Total fixed assets	$xxx
Total Assets	$xxxx

Liabilities
Current Liabilities

Itemized list	$xxx
	$xxx
Total current assets	$xxx

Long-Term Liabilities

Itemized list	$xxx
	$xxx
Total long-term liabilities	$xxx
Total liabilities	$xxxx

Owners' Equity

Assets minus Liabilities	$xxx

Sometimes the assets are shown in a column on the left side of the page and the liabilities and net worth on the right, since these two categories should be equal in order for the balance sheet to balance.

A balance sheet is a useful tool if you are interested in figuring out how much a business might sell for if liquidated. It is also useful when deciding how much to lend or invest in a business, which is why investors and lenders always want to see the balance sheet. But it tells you nothing about how the business operates or how much money it makes. The income statement is more useful if you are interested in sales, expenses, and profits, since those statistics are reported on the income statement, not the balance sheet. So keep reading; you'll find the income statement covered under the core concept of profit and loss.

Core Concept: Liquidity

Water can be poured from one container to another and can take any form you need it to. Ice cannot.

Money too can be liquid or solid, and it can also be anywhere in between. If it is liquid, you can move it around and put it to any use you wish to; it is more valuable because of its flexibility. Cash is the most liquid form money can take. Cash in your hand can be spent in any way you wish, or it can be saved. But think about other forms money takes in a business. Perhaps you take that cash and buy computer equipment or a vehicle with it. In a sense you still have that cash, but it is not nearly as liquid as it once was. You can't take your

> Water can be poured from one container to another and can take any form you need it to. Ice cannot. Money too can be liquid or solid.

computer into a store and buy office supplies in barter for it. So the money is in a sense frozen when you purchase something with it. It is less liquid.

Any valuables an individual or business possesses can be thought of as money. You can assign a cash value to them (and indeed you do when listing them in the assets column of a balance sheet), but some are more liquid than others. For instance, a CD (certificate of deposit at a bank) that will mature in one month (meaning you can take the money out then) is more liquid than a CD that expires in three months. Your receivables—unpaid invoices due you from customers—are also an asset. They are worth a little less than what they total because there is always the chance that you won't be able to collect some of your receivables. But they have considerable value, and they are a short-term asset because you will presumably collect all of them within the next few months.

When assets are listed on a balance sheet, they are listed in order from most liquid to least liquid. Why? Because the most liquid assets are more valuable from a financial perspective owing to their greater liquidity.

And liabilities are listed from the most current to the least current, so that short-term debts appear higher up on the balance sheet than long-term ones. This reflects a similar logic in that debts you will retire more quickly are less of a negative than ones that you will be paying for a long time to come. Long-term debts reduce your liquidity to a greater extent.

> You can't pay bills with accounts receivable.
> —DAVID H. BANGS, JR.

Raising Money to Meet Business Needs

I n this session of the financial management course, we are going to look at a question that often haunts entrepreneurs and, in fact, is an issue at some point in the life of every business. Where do you get money when you don't have enough from your own cash flow?

Need money? Go to a money store. Well, unfortunately, it's not really that simple. The institutions that provide money for business uses are many and varied, and they are particularly difficult to do business with. You don't just call them up or walk in with your request. You have to make your case first, convince them that you will be profitable to do business with. The problem is no lending institutions are going to lend or give you money unless they think your business is sound enough that you will make a good return on their money. They won't give you a dime until they are sold on how you plan to use that dime.

It makes sense. It's their money. They could invest it in many ways. In fact, the number of ways to invest money is almost infinite in today's complex, global financial system. What makes you a better investment than anything or anyone else? Well, you can often convince them that you are a good investment. But you have to recognize that it will take some effort and insight to make your case. Let's review some core concepts that will allow you to tackle the task of raising funds in a more sophisticated and successful manner.

> The number of ways to invest money is almost infinite in today's complex, global financial system. What makes you a better investment than anything or anyone else?

Core Concept: Bootstrap Financing

My favorite businesses are ones that can finance their own growth out of profits. When you reinvest profits to generate growth, you are "bootstrapping" a business. I like this model because it makes you independent of external financing, which can be hard or expensive to obtain when needed. And I like this model because it is organic. The business grows at a natural rate, in a balanced manner, without ever taking any significant financial risks along the way. However, it takes patience and perseverance to self-finance a business's growth. It is easy to grow impatient and want to swing for a homer instead of hitting bunts and singles month after month.

When I was a young entrepreneur, I worked with a group of entrepreneurs on a biotech startup for a couple of years. We had some of the best technology and attracted some serious venture capital to get us started. But our projects were very big and very long term. We knew there were some shorter-term opportunities to supply the research market with materials based on our technologies, but we didn't think this was as exciting as the long-term chance to introduce revolutionary drug and diagnostic products. So we didn't develop any short-term products. And that was our undoing, because our long-term development efforts slipped over their time and dollar budgets, and we found ourselves without any cash flow. We needed emergency capital in a hurry, and we just couldn't raise it fast enough. The business failed, and years later we sat on the sidelines while other companies brought our technologies to market. Ever since then I've been an advocate of short-term sales. I always look for ways to balance long-term investments with short-term ones. And I try to create profit centers, no matter how small, in every startup. I've become a rabid bootstrapper.

Paul Hawken, a successful entrepreneur and the author of the bestseller *How to Grow a Business*, advocates self-financing and discourages entrepreneurs from building their businesses on a base of investment in exchange for promises. He points out that any successful business concept can be grown using the bootstrapping method, although it sometimes takes creativity to find ways to add capacity incrementally.

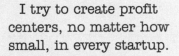

I try to create profit centers, no matter how small, in every startup.

Core Concepts: Debt and Equity Financing

Hawken and other experts may favor bootstrapping and eschew financing for startups, but many other experts argue that you cannot run a business without some financing along the way. These experts tend to be in the financial services industry, so they profit from the strategy, but still, they do have a point. There are many occasions where bringing in some outside investment seems like a sensible thing to do. To finance a business you have two basic options (aside from digging into your own pocket). You can sell ownership interests in the business itself, which is called equity financing, or you can borrow money in exchange for the promise of repayment with interest, which is called debt financing.

Which is better? It depends. Equity financing gives you the most long-term and flexible capitalization since it aligns your interests most closely with the investors' interests. You both profit when the business does well. But on the other hand, you have to give up some of your ownership and control. Here are some equity options:

> Less than 1 percent of U.S. startups are funded by venture capitalists, so you have to realize that real venture capitalists may not even want to talk to you.

- Raising kitchen capital means selling ownership interests to your friends and family. This is often done by entrepreneurs, but seldom with proper contracts. Hire an experienced lawyer to make sure there are fair and reasonable terms and that everybody understands them! (What happens to Aunt Matilda's retirement funds if your business crashes and burns?)
- Raising venture capital means selling ownership interests to professional investors who specialize in young companies with lots of growth potential. Don't even bother submitting your plan to venture capitalists unless this is you. And watch out for con artists who favor this beat. They generally ask you to pay a fee to have your plan evaluated, then you never hear from them again. Real venture capitalists don't charge you money, they give you money. Less than 1 percent of U.S. startups are funded by venture capitalists, so you have to realize that real venture capitalists may not even want to talk to you.
- Taking a company public means financing it by selling equity to the general public, which subjects you to lots of regulations (in the United States the Securities and Exchange Commission will breathe down your neck). You need to go to an investment banking firm with a well-known name and a recent history of taking firms such as yours public in order to do this right.

Those are the main options for equity financing. If they don't work, you can always try to get creative (but have a lawyer clear your schemes first!). Ben & Jerry's, the ice cream upstarts from Vermont, did their initial public offering by selling cheap shares to their consumers via the lids of their ice cream containers. And I'm sure it won't be long before virtual offerings on the Internet become commonplace.

Debt financing takes a great many forms. Several popular independent movies have been financed on their producers' credit cards, for example. (But don't try this at home. The rates are too high and the terms too short. You are much too likely to end up in bankruptcy court!) Credit from suppliers is a wonderful form of debt financing, but again, be careful. It is short term in nature, so don't use it to fund long-term development or you'll soon be out of suppliers—and supplies! Equipment loans are also a great form of debt financing if the rates are reasonable. And I like the fact that they are generally tied to the length of time the equipment is expected to last and the likely resale value of the equipment, so these loans are well balanced against the likely income they will generate.

And then there are all forms of bank financing. Banks generally offer short-term notes and medium- to long-term financing for buildings and equipment. If you are a smaller or newer business, bankers will be quite bricks-and-mortar oriented. They will want to see you purchase something tangible with their money that they can seize and sell if you default. As you get bigger, banks are increasingly willing to lend you funds to help cover short-term cash flow shortages, for example, by securing a loan to your current inventory and asking you to repay it by the time the inventory is turned over (sold). And banks will often provide revolving credit lines for businesses, which can be used to bridge short-term cash flow problems.

But be very, very careful with bank loans. Banks have shut down many a business that got behind on its payments. The best financial managers are even more conservative than their loan officers.

I'm going to include a separate section in a minute on how to get bank loans because there are some tricks to it that every manager should know. But right now I want to make sure you understand the basic principles of borrowing money. They are:

1. Never borrow money today to pay for yesterday's expenses. This is a modern day version of the proverbial pitfall of rob-

> Banks have shut down many a business that got behind on its payments.

bing Peter to pay Paul. If you dug a hole last year, better fill it from this year's profits. If you aren't making profits this year either, better cut expenses in a hurry or, if there is no way to make the darn thing profitable, just shut the business down before it digs your grave. Let's make sure we understand this essential principle of corporate finance because ignorance of it has sunk more businesses than any other cause:

Today's debt must be used to finance tomorrow's profits, not yesterday's losses!

2. Match the term of your loan to the timing of the need and the source of repayment. For example, if you want to buy new equipment that you will use over the next three years to produce a new line of products, don't finance it with a one-year note or a ten-year loan. Neither matches the need or the

Allegory: Patriot Looses a Bet

Patriot American Hospitality Inc. rose rapidly to become a leader in the hospitality industry in the 1990s, with property valued at more than $7 billion by the end of the decade. In just a few years, the company had acquired 450 hotels—a nice trick, and one that impressed a lot of investors and financial analysts as well. Patriot's stock was treated as a "must buy" by many top analysts in early 1998. But by the end of the year the stock had lost 79 percent of its value, burning investors and forcing the company's founder, Paul Nussbaum, to exit with his tail between his legs, nursing millions of dollars of personal debt. What happened? It all came down to a simple but seductive error in financial management. It seems Patriot acquired all those wonderful hotel properties using short-term debt and promises to make good on that debt with Patriot stock.

Hotels can and often do produce a nice return on investment, but nothing so short term as to repay their purchase costs in a year. You need long-term financing to match the long-term nature of an investment in a hotel. Nussbaum had hoped that Patriot's stock would rise rapidly enough to permit him to refinance those short-term loans, but that was a risky gamble. Whenever you make a fundamental error in financial management like Patriot did, you are in essence gambling with your company and your career. And it doesn't matter how smart you are when you gamble. In the end, nobody can beat the odds.

source of repayment. You need financing that is matched to the new line of products. A three-year equipment loan is much more appropriate. If the payments seem too high, then perhaps that equipment isn't such a good purchase after all. You ought to be able to make plenty of money by using that equipment to pay back the loan, invest in developing the next hot line of products, and generate a healthy profit on top of all that. If you can't, then don't borrow the money and don't buy the equipment. Wait until you have a more profitable project.

Let's make sure we understand this essential principle of corporate finance, too, so you don't get stuck with orphan loans that aren't matched to profit centers within your operations:

Each loan must be matched in time to a specific flow of revenues that is large enough to service the debt with ease!

If you follow these two principles, I don't think you will have any serious trouble with debt financing. And you can apply the two principles to equity financing as well. But keep a sharp eye out for cases that violate these principles. I've consulted for many a firm that violates one or both of them, and in every case it's come back to bite them hard.

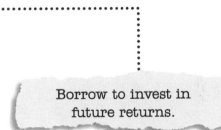

Borrow to invest in future returns.

Break Time

These are challenging concepts. Though seemingly simple at first, they resonate throughout the business and inform every management decision. It takes time and effort to appreciate them fully. I want you to appreciate them fully, so I recommend you take a brief break now. Afterward, I'll take you through another set of financial concepts in the lesson that follows. And I'll also give you some practical tips on how to apply for a loan, because that is one of the most broadly useful of all financial skills.

Analyzing and Understanding Your Costs

Session 5

My business school experience has faded to a dim memory by now, with one exception. I distinctly recall many of the lectures in my first cost accounting course because it was the first accounting course I took in which everything the professor said seemed immediately and obviously applicable in my own business experience. It was obviously valuable stuff. I wanted to rush out and do it right away!

Why? Because cost accounting gives you as a manager wonderful insights into how things work in your own business. Without it, you are actually guessing about a great many things. And when you study cost accounting, you realize that most managers guess far too much and know far too little. They don't have a clear idea of their own cost structures. They don't know whether specific processes, business units, or products are profitable. They don't even know whether they've set their prices at a level necessary to produce profits.

> It's surprisingly hard to know whether you are making any money from specific activities.

It's surprisingly hard to know whether you are making any money from specific activities. For instance, let's say you want to know whether a specific customer is profitable or not. You may be able to estimate fairly quickly how much you'll make from doing business with that customer this year. But how much does it *cost* you to do that business? Hmm. It's hard to know where to begin in allocating costs.

For instance, should you figure out how much of specific people's time that customer will require, then estimate what those people cost per hour? And what about other expenses? Can you readily apply the relevant phone, mail, driving, and other direct expenses associated with communicating with that customer? What about the overhead costs, such as electricity, rent, or heat? Some of those overhead items should be matched to each specific customer, but how much? You can see even from this simple example that cost accounting tackles some pretty tough questions!

Let's look at some core concepts now that will help you tackle such questions more intelligently. In the long run, cost accounting often requires you to make a judgment call. The trick is to make as intelligent and well-informed a judgment as you possibly can.

Core Concept: Cost Accounting

What does it cost you to make a specific product, deliver a specific service, or take care of a specific customer? Well, it depends. Which of your organization's costs are associated specifically with the product, service, or customer in question? This should be an easy thing to calculate, but it's not, and as a result, most managers operate in a vacuum or, worse, with a false sense of confidence about their costs. I've seen many situations in which a company has been losing money for years on a product line, division, territory, or major customer *without knowing it*. The problem is that it can be very difficult to figure out how to allocate costs appropriately.

For example, let's say you are in the training business. You offer workshops in your facility and also rent conference facilities to host workshops in other cities. How can you compare the profitability of these two different scenarios? Is it more or less expensive to offer workshops in your own facility or to offer them in rented space? It depends upon how you assign a large number of difficult-to-allocate expenses. Should the in-house workshops carry all the costs of leasing and running the building? Not if you also house staff who market and put on the off-site workshops. Then some share of the operating costs of your facilities should be allocated to the off-site workshops. And what about staff? Are the office staff more involved in putting on the in-house workshops, or should their expense be allocated evenly over all workshops? One can argue such points ad nauseum. In fact, it's a good idea to do so. The more aware you are of the issues and questions involved in cost accounting, the more likely you are to make reasonable judgments—and to understand that there is always room for reinterpretation and adjustment to any cost accounting system.

Cost accounting is often the tail that wags the dog, because in the long run managers have to make decisions that will produce good bottom-line results. And the assumptions of a cost accounting system determine to a large extent whether a specific activity looks profitable or not. I once taught at a college that allocates overhead expenses across departments based on the number of students taught but credits tuition to departments only for students who are majors signed up with those departments. As a result, departments

> The assumptions of a cost accounting system determine to a large extent whether a specific activity looks profitable or not.

that offer popular courses attracting lots of nonmajors get stuck with extra costs and no offsetting revenues. And because of this quirk of cost accounting at the college, departments are in the habit of turning away nonmajors and minimizing the number of sections to avoid looking unprofitable to the dean's office. Students find the school unfriendly, and teachers are frustrated that they cannot take in all of the students who want to study with them. All because of a quirk of the cost accounting system!

I also recall a consulting project I worked on in cooperation with a hotshot team from the Boston Consulting Group in which we analyzed the costs and revenues of a trucking company route by route. It turned out the trucking company's pricing was off, and some of their routes were losing them money without their knowing it. I've also seen many cases in which the pricing of a specific product is out of line with its costs of production and handling because, for example, it is more labor intensive to sell than other products in the line.

The moral of stories like this is that you should always poke at your cost accounting assumptions. And if you think they are too far off, try reworking them to see if profits are higher or lower than they appear. There are many corporate heroes whose principle claim to fame is that they discovered a major loss center that had been hidden beneath the cost accounting assumptions of their firm!

> You should always poke at your cost accounting assumptions.

Core Concepts: Fixed Costs, Variable Costs, and Break-even

If I sell one more copy of this book, how does it affect my business financially? In an unusual way, because as the author I have no variable costs associated with selling books. All my costs are fixed. Let me explain, and by so doing, hopefully help you clarify your understanding of some essential financial concepts.

A fixed cost is one you have to incur to stay in business, whether you sell anything or not. My publisher has lots of fixed costs associated with publishing this book. They have to maintain a warehouse and staff, and they have to invest up front in printing thousands and thousands of copies of the book in order to have it available. They must also invest in various costs of advertising and selling the book. If the book never sold a single copy, they'd still be stuck with all those costs because those are fixed costs.

There are also some costs my publisher must incur when it sells each book. These are called variable costs because they vary with the number of units sold. Printing, binding and shipping are a variable costs. And so are my royalties because I receive about 10 percent of what the publisher nets in sales. So authors are a variable expense from a publisher's perspective.

Some authors complain that their 10 to 15 percent of the action is too little. But think about no variable costs. What a luxury! I get to keep all the royalties my publisher sends me (well, there are a few taxes, but let's ignore them for now). When you have zero variable costs, *everything* is profit. In contrast, the publisher has lots of variable costs that eat away at the 80 percent of the sale price it keeps.

As an author, all I have at stake are my fixed costs of writing the book. If I spend money on research, staff, publicity, and so forth, then I want to cover those fixed costs before I view the book as profitable. For instance, if I make fifty cents per book, and my fixed costs on the book are, say $50,000, then I have to sell 100,000 copies before I break even on my investment. Every copy I sell from number 100,001 onward is gravy, pure profit.

The break-even point is the point at which your revenues equal your expenses. In the example I just gave there were only fixed expenses, so it was easy to find the break-even point. All I had to do was divide the average revenue per unit (in this case a book) into the total fixed costs. That gives me the number of units I have to sell to reach break-even.

But what if you have some variable costs too? Let's say you sell a product for fifty cents, with a fixed cost of $50,000 and also with a variable (per unit) cost of twenty-five cents. In other words, each unit only contributes half of the fifty cents it brings in, since the other half goes to cover the variable cost of selling that unit. Under this scenario, it will take twice as many units to reach break-even.

The break-even formula reflects the need to subtract out each unit's variable cost before setting the resulting gross profit against fixed costs. Here is the formula:

> The break-even point is the point at which your revenues equal your expenses.

Break-even point in units = total fixed costs ÷ (unit's sales price - unit's variable cost)

The Power of Break-even Analysis

Imagine that you run a very simple business, a fruit stand. You have two expenses. First, you rent the stand for $100 per month. Second, you buy fruit and vegetables from a distributor who has the eccentric habit of charging ten cents for each item, whether it's a peach, apple, a bunch of grapes, or pear. You then mark up the price by doubling it, which gives you a 50 percent margin. (In other words, your gross profit is half of your net price of twenty cents.)

Given the above costs, you can easily calculate your monthly break-even point—the number of units of fruit you must sell to cover your monthly rent plus the purchase cost of the fruit. Start with that $100 rent, a fixed cost that you must pay whether you do any business or not. Then apply to it the contribution each unit makes, after you've covered its variable cost of ten cents. For each unit of fruit, you earn ten cents that can be contributed to covering your fixed costs. Divide the fixed cost of $100 by $0.10 to find out how many units it will take to break even: 1,000 units. If you don't sell at least that number each month, you will lose money from your fruit stand. That's good to know!

Figure 5-1 illustrates the break-even concept. It shows fixed costs, variable costs, total costs, and revenues for different sales levels. Fixed costs are a straight line because they are always $100, no matter how much fruit you sell. Variable costs slope upward, increasing by ten cents with each unit of fruit since that's what it costs you to buy the fruit. Total costs are the sum of fixed and variable costs, so they slope upward starting at the minimum sum of $100 and gaining ten cents with each unit. Revenues start at zero, when there are no sales, and slope upward more rapidly than costs. Why? Because revenues increase by twenty cents with each unit sold, while costs only increase by ten cents. So eventually the revenue line must overtake and cross the total cost line. Break-even occurs where that happens.

Break-even is a fairly simple concept. Once people learn it, they tend to say, "But that's just common sense." It certainly ought to be, but if you look at management behavior it apparently isn't. There are

> Imagine that you run a very simple business, a fruit stand.

far too many examples of cases in which managers press onward, continuing to operate in the hope of making a profit when they are nowhere near their break-even points.

For example, try asking someone you know who runs a retail store what their monthly break-even point is. I've often asked store managers this question when they have come to me for help with business problems. And they never know the answer!

If a store is losing money and having trouble paying its bills, it is obviously below break-even. But how far below? If only a little, then a push next month should put it into its profit zone. But if it is well below break-even, continued effort is guaranteed to produce another losing month. And often retailers face fairly high fixed costs, so their break-evens are surprisingly high. Retail rents are expensive, and utilities, insurance, payroll, and other fixed costs must be met too. High fixed costs require a significant contribution just to break even, but, unfortunately, many retail stores also have fairly small mar-

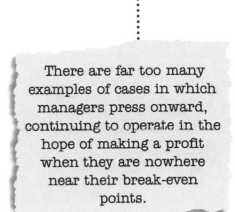

There are far too many examples of cases in which managers press onward, continuing to operate in the hope of making a profit when they are nowhere near their break-even points.

FIGURE 5-1 BREAK-EVEN CHART

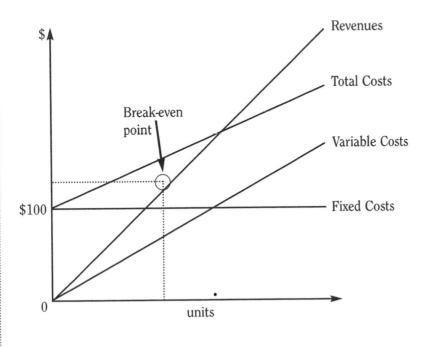

Can Break-even Explain Dumping?

"U.S. Says Japan, Brazil Dumped Steel" declared the bold newspaper headlines when the U.S. Dept. of Commerce ruled recently that these countries should be subjected to penalty tariffs on hot-rolled steel. The evidence suggests that steel imported from these countries was sold at as much as 70 percent off its normal price, which means that U.S. competitors get squeezed out of business. But how can anyone cut their prices by more than half and still stay in business?

One solution to this conundrum is provided by the break-even model. A business that prices to cover only its variable costs does not alter its basic financial equation, for good or for bad. It fails to contribute anything toward its fixed costs, to be sure, but neither does it increase them. The sale of products at variable cost is a wash. So why do it? If the practice builds market share and helps push competitors out, then it can lead to higher sales and prices in the future. The behavior makes sense when examined with the break-even equation. But break-even isn't the only consideration, and this behavior happens to be illegal.

gins. They don't get to keep very much of each sale. Put another way, their variable costs are high too. And the combination of high fixed and variable costs means a dangerously high break-even point. The only way to make most stores profitable is to maintain a high volume of sales.

A great many people try their hand at retailing when they decide to try working for themselves. It seems like so much fun if you love food, imported gift items, books, model trains, clothing, art, or anything at all that might make a nice focus for a storefront. The main street of Amherst, the small college town where I have my offices, is dominated by independent retailers. They are a friendly and interesting lot. Many have exchanged rat race management jobs in New York for the peace and quiet of a New England town. But it's hard to enjoy that peace and quiet unless your store operates well above break-even. And a surprising number of stores fail each year.

The owners are always surprised when their ventures go belly up, but I'm not because I've learned to make a quick eyeball assessment of their break-evens. Amherst does not offer the rush of shoppers that crowd the sidewalks and streets of downtown Manhattan, L.A., London, or Paris. Nor does it have the density of shoppers found in larger malls. There is a trickle of pedestrian traffic and a light stream of cars. So you can assume that *no* store or restaurant will be jam-packed with customers on a regular basis. (In fact, that assumption holds true for the vast majority of store locations around the world. High-traffic retail locations are relatively rare and command impressive rents.)

Because towns like mine don't offer a constant rush of retail shoppers or restaurant diners, volume-oriented businesses cannot succeed. Their break-evens are simply too high to be practical. Yet people continue to open businesses that need long lines at the registers to be successful. The break-even formula tells us what they should do instead. *Here's how to make any business profitable at low to medium sales levels:*

1. Control fixed costs. Keep your basic operating costs considerably lower than average, even if you have to do things on a smaller scale than competitors. Low fixed costs help keep your break-even at a modest level.
2. Mark up prices so that variable costs are very low on a percentage basis. That means you have to do something unique and valuable that people are happy to pay a good price for. Low variable

costs help you reach break-even quickly by maximizing the contribution of each sale.

Now, the interesting thing is that most managers instinctively violate both components of this formula when they run into trouble, regardless of what industry or type of business they are in. When they realize they need more revenues, most people are tempted to invest in upgrading their business on the theory that making the business better will bring in more sales. Perhaps, but leasing more equipment, hiring more expert staff, expanding the facilities, and other such upgrades raise the break-even by adding to fixed costs, so they generally dig a deeper hole instead of filling it.

And when managers realize they need more revenues, they are also very tempted to cut their prices. It seems logical that you will sell more if you cut prices. And you may, but rarely so much more as to make up for

Allegory: Cash-Flow Café

I think of it as the Cash-flow Café, although that's not what the sign outside said. The owner used to talk to me sometimes about his continuing cash flow problems. It was hard to pay the bills. In fact, he had been lending the business money out of his savings for some time in order to keep it open. Surely a little advertising, an expanded menu, or other adjustments would boost sales enough to fix the problem. Yet each month's initiatives failed to stem the tide of losses. I bought as many cups of coffee from him as I could stomach and kept hoping he would find a way to make it work. But eventually, after a long and expensive battle, the owner gave up and sold the business at an unfavorable price.

What had gone wrong with this entrepreneur's American dream? Out of curiosity I did a little research and worked out estimates of the fixed and variable costs for the business in order to identify its break-even. Given my estimate of the average purchase per customer, I decided that cafe needed twice as many customers per month as it actually had in order to make a profit. And when I stood out front and watched the sidewalk, I realized there were hardly any people in that neighborhood most of the day. It was a quiet street. There was simply no way that business could have doubled its customer base in that location. It was doomed to failure from the get-go because its relatively high fixed and variable costs demanded a high-traffic location.

The only restaurant concepts suited to such low-traffic locations are ones with relatively expensive food at high margins and a specialized, high-quality approach that will draw diners from beyond the immediate area. The Cash-Flow Cafe was not right for this location, as a simple break-even analysis could have revealed up front.

the relatively higher break-even resulting from your price cut. (I recommend calculating the new break-even at the proposed price cut to see if it is realistically attainable. Compare break-evens *before* deciding to cut those prices.)

Other managers reason the opposite way. They figure that if they need more money they will just raise their prices. Great idea, but unfortunately it's rarely that simple. The same product or service at a higher price will generally sell more slowly, if at all, which is likely to be counterproductive. *Higher prices are great, but only if the product legitimately warrants a higher price*. What is generally needed is a new line of products that naturally sell at a higher price point so that the break-even equation is adjusted to suit the local conditions. You need to think creatively about your business formula before you try to boost prices significantly.

> The combination of high fixed and variable costs means a dangerously high break-even point.

The Psychology of Break-even

What these points reveal is something I call the *psychology of break-even*. We naturally tend to react to business difficulties in ways that no doubt make psychological sense but run counter to the logic of break-even. The psychology of break-even is the interesting but destructive tendency of managers the world over to react to financial stresses in ways that increase instead of decrease their business's break-even point. If you make a point of understanding the mathematics of break-even, you do not have to fall prey to this psychological trap.

Your knowledge of break-even can help you change your psychological response to financial pressures in your business. As a tool for disciplining our natural but often unhelpful reactions, break-even analysis is good psychotherapy.

How Break-even Analysis Can Make You Rich

Here's a question nobody can answer but everybody ought to: *What is your household's break-even point?*

Once you know that, you know how much money you have to bring in each month in order to cover expenses. And a practical way to think about wealth is as having extra money after clearing your monthly expenses. If you reach break-even early in the month, you'll feel wealthy because you will not have to worry about money and you'll have lots of extra cash to spend or save as you wish. But if you don't reach break-even until the end of the month, then you will always feel poor, no matter how much you earn.

A simple but powerful way to feel richer is to work on reducing your fixed costs. But we tend to overlook this obvious fix, perhaps because our consumer society keeps pushing us toward larger home loans, car payments, credit card balances, and the like. In other words, toward maximum fixed costs instead of minimum.

Financial resiliency is also a direct result of low fixed costs. If you have low fixed costs, you can weather financial storms like the loss of a job, a bad investment, an illness, or a temporary layoff. If your fixed costs are high you will not be resilient enough to cope with such setbacks. So low fixed costs inoculate you against hard times even as they make you feel wealthy in good times.

How do you cut your fixed costs? You simply start chipping away at any and all of your regular monthly expenses. Conserve heating oil or electricity. Pay a little extra toward your principal whenever you make a loan payment. Refinance debts to lower monthly costs if you can find a lower interest rate. Buy in cash, not on credit. Drive used cars instead of new ones. See if you are over-insured in certain areas, and if so, reduce your coverage. Avoid the temptation to move into a larger house or apartment. And if you've purchased any costly recreational items like boats, snowmobiles, RVs, or airplanes on borrowed funds, *get rid of them*. If you are like most of us, you don't use such products often enough to make it pay off to own instead of rent.

If you reduce your fixed costs, you might not *look* as rich, but you will *feel* a great deal more wealthy! In the great game of finance, those who die with the most toys lose. Those who die with the most discretionary income won long ago.

It can take some time to lower your fixed costs appreciably, but each little chip makes a big difference in how wealthy you feel. Think of it this way. Can you cut fixed costs enough to allow you to reach break-even a day earlier each month this year? Or how about two or three days earlier? Then everything you clear above income taxes and the modest variable costs you incur in order to work is free money you can do with as you like. Just don't spend it on downpayments on more loans, okay?

> Low fixed costs inoculate you against hard times even as they make you feel wealthy in good times.

Core Concepts: Profit and Loss

This concept's pretty obvious, but let's just make sure we are clear on it. When you subtract all your expenses from your income, the result is either a positive or negative number—a profit or a loss. Profits (or losses) can be expressed in more than one way. The simplest way is to subtract the direct costs of doing business (such as your costs of goods sold) from your revenues for a specific period. This gives you *gross profit*, which is generally your revenues minus your variable costs (see above).

If your gross profit is a positive number, then you are at least making some contribution toward covering your fixed costs. But to find out if you cover all of them and then some (as you want to do), you need to subtract the rest of your expenses from your revenues. When you subtract operating expenses from gross profit, you get a bottom-line measure of profit, which is *net income*.

Why Saving Is Stupid

Many people save money toward retirement or for a rainy day. They may have a portion of each paycheck contributed toward a pension fund. They may make periodic deposits in a savings or mutual fund account. And they may contribute once a year to an IRA or other tax-deferred retirement account. That's all well and good. But they probably also *borrow* money. The average American adult has both savings and loans, lots of loans, such as credit card back balances, credit lines on banking accounts, car loans, home loans, student loans not yet paid off. The list of loans goes on and on. I don't even want to think about it.

Here's the problem with saving and borrowing at the same time. In general, *you pay a far higher rate of interest on your loans than you earn on your savings.* For example, your savings may earn two-thirds of the interest rate you pay for a home loan, half of what you pay for a car loan, and a fifth of what you pay for credit card debt. It costs you more to borrow money than you can earn by investing it. But if you have both savings and loans, you are in essence borrowing money to invest it, which guarantees a loss. Why do we keep doing things like that?

The sensible thing to do, if you can manage it, is to invest those savings in retiring your debts. Each time you take a dollar from savings and use it to eliminate a dollar of debt, you come out ahead. As long as you have loans that charge higher rates than you can earn on savings, the best form of savings is reduction of debt. Once you get rid of all your debt, *then* you can start saving for real.

So profit (or loss) is the net result of subtracting all your variable and fixed expenses from your revenues. It is usually reported in a statement called a "P&L" (for profit and loss) or, more commonly, an *income statement*. The income statement's basic structure is as follows:

REVENUES

Source A	$500,000	
Source B	$500,000	
Total Revenues		$1,000,000

COST OF GOODS SOLD (OR SERVICES PROVIDED)

Item A	$100,000	
Item B	$50,000	
Item C	$50,000	
Total Cost of Goods Sold		$200,000
Gross Profit		$800,000

OPERATING EXPENSES

Item D	$100,000	
Item E	$200,000	
Item F	$100,000	
Total Operating Expenses		$400,000
Income Before Taxes	$400,000	
Less Income Taxes	$100,000	
Net Income		**$300,000**

> Profit (or loss) is the net result of subtracting all your variable and fixed expenses from your revenues.

Note that I've used the common convention of underlining negative numbers in the right-hand summary column. You need to subtract these from the positive numbers, which aren't underlined, to get the correct net income on the bottom line.

You will see much more complex income statements on occasion. They may itemize more types of revenues and expenses. They may add lines for other forms of income (principally from investments, which aren't operating income unless you're in the investment business). But they always follow this basic structure, so you can always read them with ease. And you can always work out the variable and fixed expenses, and thus find the break-even point, for any business since you now know that gross profit is revenues minus variable costs. Right?

Core Concept: The Time Value of Money

Would you rather I gave you $100 today or a year from now? Today, of course, because money that is available today is more valuable to you than money you can't touch for a year. That's an easy computation; you can do it in your head.

Let's say I offer you a choice of $100 today or $108 next year. Which is more valuable? Which will you choose? If we assume that both are 100 percent certain, then it is just a question of whether that $8 difference is sufficient to make next year's payment of $108 more valuable than this year's payment of $100.

(Did I hear someone say they'll take both? Sorry, that's not an option!)

You might think the puzzle I've posed is trivial. But in truth, business presents lots of more important puzzles that take the same form.

For instance, let's say you are considering making a business investment. Perhaps you have a chance to buy a piece of commercial real estate for $1 million today. Let us assume you have the cash at hand to do so. Your best projection is that by investing another $200,000 in fixing the building up you could sell the building for roughly $1,300,000 in a year's time. Is this a good idea? Well, the profit made is $100,000 on an investment of $1,200,000, which yields a return of 8.33 percent on your investment over a one-year period.

Is that a good use of your money? One way to look at this question is to say that it depends upon what your money might be worth if you *didn't* invest it. If you cannot earn more than, say, 4.5 percent from investing your money in a money market account at the bank, then the 8.33 percent you get from investing in that building begins to sound pretty good. So the first thing managers need to think about when considering the time value of money is what their money

> Time is the measure of business as money is of wares.

would earn in interest if they didn't invest it but simply held onto it in a savings or money market account. If you can beat that rate, then you are ahead of the game. (Of course, there is more risk in fixing up a building than in leaving your money in the bank, so you might want to see a bigger potential return to counterbalance this risk. Most real-estate developers hope to make much more than 8 percent on their investments!)

The scenario above is more realistic and important because it involves a major business investment. But it is still much simpler than the decision scenarios facing many managers. For example, it is much more likely that you would hold onto that building you bought and fixed up for some years, renting or leasing it out to make your money from it. In which case you would project a series of annual revenues from rents extending out far more than one year. Perhaps you might project cash flows from the project for the first five years as follows:

> The first thing managers need to think about when considering the time value of money is what their money would earn in interest if they didn't invest it but simply held onto it in a savings or money market account.

YEAR	$ CASH FLOWS
0 (present)	± 1,200,000 (I'll assume you pay all your costs up front)
1	± 0 (Because you don't have tenants yet)
2	+ 300,000
3	+ 350,000
4	+ 400,000
5	+ 450,000
Net	+ 300,000

I'm going to ignore additional years in order to keep this example simple. Let's just assume that there is a predictable earthquake every five years and all buildings have to be rebuilt at that time.

So your entire return on your investment is $300,000, which is a 25 percent return compared with the 8.33 percent return of the first option (selling after one year) and compared with the 4.5 percent return per year of saving your money instead of investing in the building. Three options: one yields the greatest return. So that's the best, right?

Well, but what about the time value of money? Much of that $300,000 in profit comes in future years, so it shouldn't be considered as valuable as returns you don't have to wait as long for. Now we've got a truly complex puzzle that is going to take some number crunching to sort out. Specifically, what we need to do is discount future cash flows to reflect their lesser value compared to current cash flows. Unless we can somehow adjust all those figures to eliminate the time factor, we are simply comparing apples and oranges. We can't make a sound financial decision until we figure out how to compare the options on a level playing field.

Here's how. We'll adjust future cash flows using that figure for the rate of return we could get by keeping our money in the bank. If the most we can get on our cash is 4.5 percent, then we can use 4.5 percent as our discount factor to adjust future cash flows in order to find their present value.

For example, if we sell the building for $1,300,000 in one year, what is that worth today? This sum's present value is found by dividing it by 1.045, which gives us *a present value of $1,244,019.10.*

What the heck is that number? Well, it's the amount I'd have to invest at 4.5 percent in order to earn $1,300,000 in one year. Here's the formula that I used to find it:

Present value = discount factor × amount of payoff, where discount factor equals $1 / (1 + r)$ and r = my standard rate of return, in this case, 4.5 percent

So now I have an exact way to compare the first two options. The present value of my money right now is simply the amount I have: $1,200,000. And the present value of my money if I fix up and resell the property at the expected price of $1,300,000 is $1,244,019.10, which yields me a profit of $44,019.10 in today's dollars.

And I can do the same sort of calculations to find out what the present value of those five years of cash flows from renting the building are and compare them as well. But when you are adjusting a future cash flow across *more than one year* (or whatever period you are working with), you have to make a small change to the formula. Rather than dividing each future year by 1.045, which wouldn't differentiate between those years, we need to raise the discount factor

> Now we've got a truly complex puzzle that is going to take some number crunching to sort out.

by the number of years. For example, the $300,000 received in rents in year two has to be divided by the *square* of 1.045, which is 1.045 × 1.045, or roughly 1.092. Dividing $300,000 by 1.092 gives us a present value of $274,718.98. That's how much $300,000 in two years is worth to us today given the interest rate we could earn on our money in the bank.

If we adjust each of the cash flows in the five-year table of returns, we can find out how much they add up to in present value:

YEAR	$ CASH FLOWS	DISCOUNT FACTOR	PRESENT VALUE (Cash flow ÷ discount factor)
0 (now)	– 1,200,000	1	– 1,200,000.00
1	± 0	1.045	0
2	+ 300,000	$1.045^2 = 1.092$	+ 274,718.98
3	+ 350,000	$1.045^3 = 1.141$	+ 306,748.46
4	+ 400,000	$1.045^4 = 1.193$	+ 335,289.18
5	+ 450,000	$1.045^5 = 1.246$	+ 361,155.69
Net	+ 300,000		**+ 77,912.20**

It takes a while to run through those computations, so you can always build a spreadsheet on your personal computer if you need to do this kind of thinking very often.

When you compare the net cash flows over five years of $300,000 with their present value in today's dollars of $77,912.20, you can see why failing to adjust for the time value of money can throw off your financial judgment in a big way!

In truth, $222,087.80 of that $300,000 return could be made simply by leaving your funds safely in a money market account. You only realize $77,912.20 of real profit in today's dollars by buying, fixing up, and renting that building for five years. If there is any risk in the endeavor at all, then that relatively modest return would probably decide you against the idea. But still, this return is of greater present value than the other option we evaluated above, in which you sell the property after fixing it up. That nets only $44,019.10 in present value.

> When you compare the net cash flows over five years of $300,000 with their present value in today's dollars of $77,912.20, you can see why failing to adjust for the time value of money can throw off your financial judgment in a big way!

Which is the best decision? You still have to be the judge, but at least you can now compare apples and apples. All three options are expressed in the present value of future cash flows so you can compare them appropriately. Then it's up to you to decide whether the possible returns warrant the risks and trouble of the various options or whether you'd rather leave your money in the bank. Or, even better, go find another investment opportunity that has a higher present value.

Core Concept: Management Information Systems

The whole point of collecting and reporting accounting and financial information is to help make better management decisions. But that purpose is often lost sight of when the traditions of accounting and finance take over. If managers don't understand the numbers they are given, then finance isn't supporting management decision-making adequately. And equally common and problematic, if management isn't getting all the financial information needed to make decisions, finance isn't supporting management properly either.

As a manager or future manager, I want you to *be an assertive consumer* of financial services and information. If you don't understand a report, don't feel bad. Many financial reports are poorly designed and hard even for experts to follow. The majority of managers does not understand the majority of financial statements and reports, which says to me that the reports aren't any good. So please be assertive in asking for clarification.

Also keep in mind that financial statements generally tell you want happened in the past. That's fine if you want to do a post mortem, but it doesn't tell you what you need to know to make good decisions about the future. I like to see more emphasis on financial projections than on reporting of past performance, because as a manager I have to live in the future, not the past. Of course, accountants and bookkeepers don't like projections as much as they like historical statements because they like to be right, and projections are almost always wrong. So you have to keep poking them to get the projections you need. Ask for worst-case, best-case, and straight-line projections of your revenues, income statements, and balance sheets in order to get an idea of how things might play out in the future.

And when you are exploring strategies and options, get your accountant or financial manager to sit in and react to the options. There are often financial or tax implications of management decisions that we non-experts fail to see.

Core Concept: Chief Financial Officers

A CFO is someone who spends his or her days (and sometimes nights) thinking about how to keep a business financially healthy. CFOs are endemic in the largest companies, and they often have extensive staff to support them. But in the vast majority of businesses there is no CFO. That means the bookkeeper, the outside accountant, and the boss share the responsibility for financial management. And as a result, most businesses have pretty bad financial management. They take excessive risks, they don't know about appropriate financing methods, they don't invest excess cash prudently and profitably, they don't prepare or use appropriate financial statements when needed, and they fail to plan ahead for future cash flow and development needs.

If you own or work for a company that lacks a qualified, cautious CFO, then you should recognize that your company is weak in the area of financial management.

What to do? Any company generating more than a few million in revenues will probably find that a CFO is actually a profit center, not a cost. A good CFO should save enough money to repay his or her salary many times over, so the simplest remedy for a lack of financial management is to start interviewing candidates. No reason to let your firm run foolish risks or miss good opportunities for lack of knowledge of this highly technical field.

Another option, this one better suited to smaller firms, is to subcontract for financial management. There are plenty of temp firms and retainer-oriented consulting firms that provide financial management on a part-time basis. Just be careful to check credentials and track records thoroughly so you don't get swindled. And don't give them signing power over anything!

Between full-time and temporary options, there is no reason why any firm needs to be financially undermanaged. Managers are

> Today's business reporting, of course, recapitulates the past.
>
> —ROBERT L. ISRAELOFF, CHAIRMAN, AMERICAN INSTITUTE OF CERTIFIED PUBLIC ACCOUNTANTS

> Companies want to be able to suck it in or puff it out in size quickly, effectively, and in lockstep with changing business conditions. That's exactly what we help them do, and we do it better than temporary help services because we provide a process and not just bodies.
> —Robert W. Weis, President, CFOs2Go

generally plagued by overconfidence. And I can say with a fair degree of confidence that managers are more overconfident about their knowledge of finance than just about anything else. Face it, you probably won't ever make a sufficient investment in studying corporate finance to become truly expert on it. And nor will most executives. CFOs have an important role in any organization that wants to hold onto its money.

Core Concept: Financial Orientation? No Thanks!

Are you working for or running a *financially oriented organization*? If so, you may be headed for trouble. Finance provides the capital to fund business development and tracks the results of operations, but it doesn't have that much to do with what comes in between. The bottom line is on the bottom for the simple reason that it is the *result* of operations, not the cause. Yet many managers focus on bottom-line financial results and thereby fail to manage the things that *drive* those results.

How do you know if you or your organization is overly financial in orientation? The most obvious clue is that everybody is held to "the numbers." That's how managers are evaluated, that's what the boss always wants to talk about, and that's what everybody manages *for*. If you find that you or your people are obsessed with "making their numbers," then you know you have a financial orientation. And while financial management needs to be a core activity in the organization, it cannot be permitted to displace other forms of management.

People and organizations that manage by the bottom line never perform as well in the long run as those that focus on the causes of bottom-line performance. An orientation toward your employees, customers, technologies, and business processes is much more likely to produce good bottom-line results.

For example, take the case of a camping supplies company that hired a new get-tough executive. He insisted that his managers make their numbers, even though they were given unrealistic sales goals. And so they did—by "loading the trade," or overselling product at the end of the year using discounts and other aggressive sales methods. Huge inventories accumulated at distributors and stores so that sales fell and profits evaporated in the subsequent year. So much for rubbing people's noses in the bottom line. It just doesn't produce long-term results.

Financial statements offer one of many possible views into the inner workings and end results of a highly complex business process that is itself just a small part of a complex economic and social system. If you focus only on the bottom line results in your financial statements, you will be managing in the dark because you won't seek out and understand the variables that drive your systems.

How to Get a Loan

Now I want to switch gears and talk about a fundamental management skill: persuading banks to give you their money. In my experience, this is one of the most common goals of entrepreneurs and managers of small and midsize businesses. They are perpetually courting bankers and generally frustrated with the results.

If you are indulging in a bit of entrepreneurship, you are probably eager to get your hands on somebody else's money. Everybody is. I'm often asked by entrepreneurs for advice on how to line up an investor or lender to get their business to the next level. And in truth, this skill is a valuable one in businesses of all sorts. But, BUT, I strongly recommend taking a moment to stop and ask yourself WHY you need to get a loan.

In my experience, the majority of business loans are unnecessary. Borrowing a bunch of money is often the least imaginative and most risky way to address a business problem or opportunity. I'd rather bootstrap and accept the reality of slower development. Or if that's impractical, I'd rather negotiate a partnership or joint venture with a company that already has the capabilities I was thinking of borrowing money to acquire. That way I avoid the negatives associated with borrowing money.

Let's look at the negative effects of any loan:

- A loan commits you to a regular schedule of payments you didn't have to make before, thus raising your carrying costs.

> Ford was finance, finance, finance. It was a very structured company run by tight budgets.
> —Ron Harbour
> (consultant to auto companies)

- A loan gives a bank claims over you and your business, since you have to pledge collateral and often to vouch personally for a loan as well.
- A loan requires you to produce returns on the money borrowed that are higher than the costs of borrowing it, which may be easy if your plans work out but can also be a problem when they don't.
- A loan requires you to run your business to please bankers, who do not necessarily know what is best for a growing business.
- A loan commits you to a business plan that you probably have not tested and developed as fully as you and the bankers think you have.

Okay, don't say I didn't warn you! Now, if you still think a loan is of the essence, here's what you have to do to get one.

Bankers thrive on numbers. If it's numbers they want, numbers they shall get. Unfortunately, however, most real cowboy capitalists are absolutely awful at working up pages and pages of pro forma balance sheets, income statements, and cash budgets. Who has time for paperwork? If that describes you, get yourself a smart number-crunching grunt to put the figures in columns and rows. Hire an MBA who can extract pro formas from a computer, who understands that the game is getting money from the banks, and who doesn't confuse that game with modern financial management (which is a quite different game played largely in MBA programs).

—ENTREPRENEUR DICK LEVIN,
BUY LOW, SELL HIGH, COLLECT EARLY & PAY LATE

> It takes money to make money!
> —AN OLD BUT TRUE SAYING

Placating Your Bankers

Dick Levin recommends that you give bankers plenty of fancy looking financials—the whole suite of forms and projections. Here's why: "The more numbers you have crunched, the more difficult it will be for your banker to find out anything about the assumptions." Levin is a successful entrepreneur and manager who has founded multiple companies and even brought one of them public, so he should know. And it is clear that he does not view bankers as equal partners. With their aversion to risk and lack of in-depth knowledge of your business and its industry, bankers are not likely to view things the way you do. They want to believe that they are lending money to someone who doesn't need it because their business is a 100 percent sure thing.

Levin's Machiavellian view of the loan process is unfortunately a realistic one. You need to put on your marketing hat when you apply for loans, and *make sure you understand what the bankers are looking for* so you can offer it to them. Think of applying for a loan as making a sale to the bank.

To make this sale and land your loan, you need to impress them with the professionalism and solidity of your business. To do so, have a look at the annual reports from a few Fortune 100 companies. Their statements are a great model (but you'll need to do projected, or pro forma, versions of all statements too). To get annual reports you can call a company's headquarters and ask for a free copy—a service they provide for investors—or go to any business school library and view the collection. Also check out company Web sites, some of which have annual reports on-line.

All the financial statements and supporting text of a formal annual report should appear in your loan application. Leave out the fancy four-color photos and other nonessential elements since bankers don't care about the sizzle, only the steak. If you model your submission on the kind of annual report the Securities and Exchange Commission requires of publicly traded companies, you will certainly put your business in the best possible light.

When I say *the best possible light*, I am assuming you understand that I also mean *given the reality of your financial situation*. You cannot misrepresent your business by falsifying facts or leaving them out. When you report on your assets, don't place absurdly high values on them. Use a reasonable market value, one that is generous but also easily defensible. Bankers may have different ways of looking

Impressing bankers is a numbers game.

If you are a smaller or newer business and need to raise more funding than bankers are comfortable lending you, it may be possible to line up federal assistance. The U.S. Small Business Administration funds some programs that can provide loan guarantees to make bankers more open minded. Call up the SBA (it's listed in Washington D.C.) or visit them on the Web. Or better yet, search your local phone directories or ask your bankers how to locate the nearest CDC, or certified development company. Although private and for-profit, they are funded through the SBA and can act as lenders or investors. For example, Center Fresh Egg Farms of Sioux Center, Iowa, was started by entrepreneurs who personally contributed 20 percent of the $2.4 million in needed funds and borrowed 80 percent from a local bank and a CDC, which provided some government funding and guarantees to help make the loan possible. So if your funding is looking like a classic which-came-first problem, look into SBA programs. Maybe you can afford the chicken *and* the egg.

at things, but they are rarely stupid, so don't think you can hoodwink them!

Based on the actual receivables, cash flows, debts, assets, and other details of your business, plus your projections for future quarters of all years during which the loan will be in effect, you should prepare (or have prepared) a full set of balance sheets, P&Ls, and cash budgets.

And then you go begging. Nobody is going to lend you money if you are a young business, a very small business, a business without banking relationships already, a business without significant assets, a business with significant debt already, or a business with a lot of potential but no obvious and steady flow of revenues. In short, anything that might make a banker nervous will keep you from qualifying for a loan. It's hard to get money unless you are a well-established, solvent business with a healthy financial profile. If you aren't, you probably need to work on cutting expenses and increasing your revenues rather than trying to borrow your way out of trouble.

This brings me back to my initial remark about borrowing money, which was that I strongly recommend taking a moment to stop and ask yourself WHY you need to get a loan. The banker is certainly going to ask this question and expect a better answer than, "Um, well, we seem to be short on money right now."

If you think you need a loan to develop and refine your business formula so as to figure out how to make money, then think again. That's supposed to be financed with your own savings and whatever kitchen capital your friends and relations can afford to throw away. The only thing that is worth financing through lenders, from your management perspective or the bank's, is *a demonstrated formula for making money*. If you are currently operating (for example) three stores that sell flowers locally, and each one is profitable, then you have a demonstrated formula for making money. You and the banks can reasonably project the result of borrowing money to open three more stores in similar locations.

But if you have one store that is barely breaking even, then you cannot demonstrate a formula for making money. So don't get in over your head by borrowing money. Even if you could hoodwink some half-witted banker into lending you the money to open three new stores, you'd be putting it at too great a risk for your own comfort, let alone theirs. So let's end this lesson on financing with a final, essential principle of good financial management:

Never, NEVER, borrow to fund an unproved business formula. Develop and demonstrate it first!

Developing Loan-Worthiness

Small businesses and startups have trouble landing bank loans. Initially they may qualify only for personally guaranteed, short-term loans. By limiting you to one year or less, the bank avoids long-term risk. And by making you guarantee your business's loan, the bank also reduces risk by betting on you, not just your business. But who wants to have to personally guarantee a six-month loan when trying to fund long-term growth for a business? It's all wrong.

One way to move away from these constraints is to proceed one step at a time. Start with a very small, short-term, personally guaranteed loan. Pay it back to prove performance. Get another that's a little bigger for a little longer period of time. Pay it back properly too. And keep talking to your banker and maybe to their competitors too. Remind them politely that you want to qualify for business loans that aren't personally guaranteed. Point out (politely) that your business is performing well and repaying its debts. Ask them to try a small loan that isn't personally guaranteed. Ask them about a three-year note or something of the sort. Over time, you should be able to build a record of performance and convince them that your business is a low-risk customer worthy of doing business with them.

Debt rolls a man over and over, binding him hand and foot, and letting him hang on the fatal mesh, till the long-legged interest devours him. One had better make his bed of Canada thistles, than attempt to lie at ease upon interest.
—HENRY WARD, BEECHER

• • •

The only way to get out of making personal endorsements is to convince your banker(s) that you are indeed credit-worthy as a corporation, and the best way to do that is over time.
—DICK LEVIN

The Etiquette of Business Short Course

Overview of Course VI

You might do everything right to get the job, close the sale, or make the presentation and yet if your appearance or manners don't seem right to the audience, all your good efforts are wasted. In this course, we'll look at some of the many subtleties that affect business success in the area of etiquette. From how you smell to how you hold your spoon. The little things can and often do matter.

omedian Will Cuppy once said that etiquette means behaving yourself a little better than is absolutely necessary. In truth, many people go through life and business with little concern for etiquette. They don't worry about the impression they make and expect to be judged by their actions, not their manners. They seem to feel that there is no point in behaving any better than absolutely necessary.

But civility costs nothing, as the old saying goes, and I like investments that don't cost a thing. There is no down side and there is always the chance of a profitable return. A small investment in good manners and personal presentation can make a big difference in how easily you land jobs, makes sales, close deals, and generally get along in business.

It always amazes me that business schools fail to teach the etiquette of business, and I'm heartened to see that MIT's Sloan School of Management, the Daniels College of Business at the University of Denver, and a few others have begun to offer courses in etiquette. Many a graduate of a top business school can calculate the present values of future cash flows in his head but has no idea how to dress or behave in polite company. Eventually, if not at once, all managers find themselves in polite company. And a lack of basic etiquette brings them attention of the sort they cannot afford if they wish to make a good impression:

> "Did you see that guy? He was wearing a knit shirt and gold chain under a three piece suit!"

> "She seemed like a well-qualified candidate, but did you notice what she ate for lunch? A huge bowl of spaghetti and meatballs, and the sauce got all over her silk blouse."

> "I was going to sign a contract with his firm, but you know, it just bugged me how he always let me pick up the bill when we met for lunch. I wasn't sure I trusted him."

> "I know Julia is the most senior person, but I'm hesitant to make her the team leader. Did you see how much she drank when we went out to lunch the other day?"

You might think that these examples are obvious, and that you'd never make a similar mistake. But the truth is that we all make mistakes

Civility costs nothing.
—AN OLD BUT TRUE SAYING

sometimes. No one is immune to the dangers of management manners. No one has perfect business etiquette all the time.

The main reason why it's an issue for all of us is that the rules of etiquette vary dramatically from situation to situation and from group to group. It takes considerable sensitivity to appreciate the nuances of manners and to pick up on the conventions that apply in any new situation. Yet the path to success in business takes you through a myriad of new situations. You will need to do business with people, organizations, and cultures that are currently unfamiliar to you. You may encounter subtle class and status distinctions that could derail you unless you pick up on them.

You will certainly meet important people who are sensitive to manners and will draw inferences about you from your behavior and appearance. In short, you can expect to be judged by a host of complex and subtle rules of etiquette, many of which you will be unfamiliar with and will need to pick up on as you go.

Therefore the most important rule of business etiquette is to be *sensitive*. Make it a habit to ask yourself how people are behaving and dressing in different business situations. You want to understand and follow their rules in most cases, but you cannot hope to do that unless you pick up on their rules in the first place.

Appropriate? Not!

I remember once, many years ago, I was invited to interview for a job with a leading software firm in Northern California. This was before I'd moved out there and become familiar with the culture of Silicon Valley. I was from back East, where business meant suits. The company was located, I was told, just a short drive south of San Francisco. So I arrived in San Francisco and had a look around the downtown area to find out what men wore to work. Dark suits mostly, just like I'd expected, with white shirts and conservative ties. The suits were wool and fairly heavy because the city is foggy and cool, and the shoe of choice was a black or dark brown Oxford.; conservative and traditional the whole way. So I selected my darkest, heaviest pinstripe suit, a starched white Oxford shirt, dark dress

How Much Personal Space Is Appropriate?

Some people like to be close when they talk, others need distance. If you let the other person adjust the distance, then make a note of their preference, he or she will find you easy and pleasant to be around. If you impose your preference unconsciously, you'll only hit it off with people who have the same personal space preference.

Culture makes a difference, although it's not a sure predictor. In general, North Americans, British, and Scandinavians like lots of distance. Latin Americans, Arabs, and the French like to be closer to each other. But that's not enough to go by. You've got to find out what each individual prefers.

Test someone's preference by talking to them while standing. If you find yourself wanting to back up, they like to be closer than you do and you should try to make the adjustment. If you find yourself chasing them around the room, they need more personal space than you do. You need to remember to take a step backward to keep them comfortable.

shoes, blue socks, and a conservative tie. It wouldn't do to be underdressed, after all.

Then I got directions and drove south of San Francisco to the office building where I was to meet with my prospective new boss. The lobby and elevator fit in with my appearance: conservative and businesslike. I rode up to the top floor, punctual to the minute, and adjusted my tie as the elevator stopped. A deep breath to maintain my calm and I was ready.

But not for the sight that met my eyes as the elevator doors parted! The entire floor of the building was open, with vaulted ceilings full of glass windows and flowering vines. On the deep pile carpet, as far as the eye could see, stretched informal clusters of desks and terminals interspersed with more plants and the occasional bicycle or leashed dog. And the people dotting this informal landscape were about as relaxed as any I've ever seen. They were in cutoff jeans, sandals, T-shirts, bare feet, caps, bathing suits, maybe even pajamas, but I couldn't be sure. Some were sitting on top of the desks, others in circles on the floor. There was a hum of conversation, interspersed with occasional laughter. I felt like I'd wandered into a grown-up kindergarten, not an office. But perhaps the executives were more formal, I reassured myself.

They weren't. A few minutes later the VP arrived to interview me in an Hawaiian print shirt, untucked, short, ragged cutoffs, and leather sandals. Instead of escorting me to a private office, he gestured toward a small couch in full view of the entire office. I sat gingerly beside him, trying not to sweat as the hot sun baked down on me from a skylight, while he sat cross-legged beside me and subjected me to a barrage of questions. I'm afraid I didn't give those questions my undivided attention because I was too preoccupied with worrying whether it was better to keep my coat on and continue sweating or to remove it and reveal what I feared must be gigantic patches of sweat seeping through my shirt. If only I'd thought to ask someone what the dress code was before going to the interview!

These things happen, and they aren't necessarily disasters either. (I actually got a job offer from that firm, to my amazement, along with a few suggestions about my wardrobe.) In this new era of

> I felt like I'd wandered into a grown-up kindergarten, not an office.

casual dress office environments, I often find myself as a consultant or trainer to be the only person in a formal suit. But now I'm less embarrassed and more confident, and I think nothing of taking my coat off right away and loosening my tie if appropriate, or asking to move to a cooler seat. And I've also found myself underdressed for events on occasion, as when a client makes an unexpected visit to the office and catches me in my writing clothes instead of a suit.

I've learned not to allow such things to upset me. I'm no longer afraid to make a mistake. I figure you can't be tyrannized by etiquette. You'll never have perfect manners, and you'll never manage to dress correctly 100 percent of the time. On the other hand, I've also learned to have more respect for etiquette even as I've learned to be less anxious about it. Good manners can get you out of those inevitable problems for one thing, which makes them very powerful indeed. The person who is underdressed but attentive and polite will get along much better than a poorly mannered person who is perfectly dressed. And I've learned to pay close attention to other people's manners. So often, the way people present themselves is an accurate indicator of how they'll perform in the future. Etiquette does matter.

Business Table Manners

It is easy to run into trouble in the etiquette department when dining out. Many managers and salespeople make a poor impression on others because they exhibit inappropriate or unpleasant table manners. I'm very conscious of table manners and have come to believe that they are particularly important to anyone who wants to get ahead in this world. Why? Because eating is at heart a relatively unattractive thing. Watching someone else eat is not an inherently appealing thing. Eating should probably not be treated as a spectator sport. Yet it is, because meals provide a valuable opportunity to socialize in a less formal and more human environment than at any other time in the average workday.

To make sure you don't disgust those with whom you eat, here are some basic don'ts. They do seem commonsensical, yet they are often violated in business company. I've made all of these mistakes

Always dress for the job you want to have.
—ADVICE FROM CELIA ROCKS, DIRECTOR OF ROCKS COMMUNICATIONS PUBLICITY AGENCY

myself on occasion, and I think it's possible you might too unless you make a special note of them:

- Don't blow your nose at the table (especially in your napkin!). Please excuse yourself if need be and visit the bathroom.
- Don't eat food that has fallen on the table, lap, or floor. Ignore it if possible. If it is a mess that demands attention, pick it up delicately with your napkin and leave it, napkin and all, to the side of your plate. Or, if it's too messy for that, call the waiter over and ask to have it cleaned up in a polite, apologetic, but matter of fact manner.
- Don't get tipsy. Drinking anything alcoholic is almost always a poor idea, and you should never have more than one or two drinks. Even if others are drinking too much, you shouldn't.
- Don't take too long to select your food. If you are not up to deciding what to eat, why should others trust you with major business decisions?
- Don't dominate the conversation. Talking too much or too loudly leaves a durable negative impression. Business meals are opportunities to ask and listen, not to give speeches.
- Don't say what it is you have to do when excusing yourself to go to the bathroom. Just say, "Excuse me, I'll be back in a minute." Nobody needs to know any more than that.
- Don't tell inappropriate jokes. And most jokes *are* inappropriate at a business meal.
- Don't tell jokes you got off the Internet. All of them are inappropriate, even though some of them are quite funny.
- Don't eat a great deal more than anyone else. Ordering a big steak followed by chocolate cake is fine if everyone else is having a big dinner, but it gives an impression of greediness if everyone else is having a light lunch. The goal is to enjoy your meal without drawing undue attention to what you eat or how you eat it.
- Don't criticize your meal or someone else's. Even if you think the liver someone else ordered is disgusting, it's best not to point that out. And complaining about how poorly cooked

> Good breeding consists in concealing how much we think of ourselves and how little we think of the other person.
>
> —MARK TWAIN

your food is makes you seem overly picky and difficult, even if it is poorly cooked. Just don't eat it if you don't like it.

- Don't make or take calls on your cell phone or allow your pager to beep. I know this is the latest power lunch tactic so everyone thinks it's cool. But it's not. It's rude. If you are eating with someone, give them your polite, undivided attention for as long as you can.
- Don't be rude to the waiter, even if the service is terrible. You can be assertive about your needs by making clear requests without being rude, and you should be if you want to make a good impression on your fellow diners.

In addition, you are more likely to improve the service if you ask politely. Waving the waiter over to say "I'm sorry to bother you, but could you please bring me another cup of coffee because there's a fly in this one?" will probably get you a fresh, hot cup of coffee. Saying, "What the hell's the matter with this dump? Can't you see there's a fly in my coffee?" might get the waiter to return the same cup of coffee with fly removed and then forget to bring you your bill for a half hour.

Being rude to people demotivates them. Being polite motivates them. That's a basic principle of good management, and it keeps you out of trouble in the etiquette department too.

- Try not to violate the traditional rules of table etiquette. There are many, and in a fancy restaurant with its complex table settings and multiple courses they can seem excessive, so don't obsess overly about them. But do obsess a little. For example, if you butter your roll with your dinner knife instead of your butter knife, I doubt you'll lose the deal. But if you grip fork and knife with your fists and shovel food in while keeping your mouth at table level, I hope you do lose the deal. You deserve to. The point is that even though the finer points of etiquette are no longer widely known, bad manners are still easily recognized.
- If you want to perfect your table etiquette, remember that napkins belong in laps, that you use the outermost fork,

> Being rude to people demotivates them. Being polite motivates them. That's a basic principle of good management, and it keeps you out of trouble in the etiquette department too.

spoon, or knife first (for example, the salad fork is to the left of the dinner fork), that you should wait for the others to have their food before digging in, that the host, if there is one, should signal when to begin each course, that you should place utensils on the plate (or in the bowl) in the four o'clock position when finished, and that soup should be spooned up by drawing the spoon away from you, not toward you, especially if trying to get the last few drops out of the bottom of the bowl.

- On the other hand, it's inappropriate to affect more sophisticated manners than the other diners. So if they don't mind, you shouldn't either. You don't want them to feel self-conscious because they are eating with someone whose manners are much more sophisticated than theirs. When in Rome, do as the Romans do!

> The Ritz in Boston offers a popular course that takes place largely over expensive meals.

Such rules and many more may be acquired by observing well-mannered executives (if you can find any) or by attending a business etiquette class. The Ritz in Boston offers a popular course that takes place largely over expensive meals. It's a sort of eat-your-way-to-the-top approach. The instructor, Judith Ré, teaches many details of business etiquette but also argues for simple common sense. Don't try to affect the manners of an old-world aristocrat. It's okay too to ask the waiter what a fancy French dish is or how to pronounce its name. "The only way in which you can overdo it," Ré says, "is when you're pretending you're something you're not."

The Etiquette of Payment

Who should pick up the tab for a business meal? I find this question particularly revealing, as it tells me a great deal about the other diners' etiquette and their attitude toward money. For example, I have declined several business opportunities with managers who ate with impeccable table manners but then allowed the waiter to bring me the bill without offering to pay. To my eye, that indicates a suspicious unwillingness to take financial responsibility for our business relationship, and it tips me off to the probability that I'll have trouble collecting on my invoices later on.

Tradition says employers pay, so the highest ranking employee should pick up the tab. And, on the same principle, anyone who is taking out a subcontractor like a consultant or trainer should also pay the bill.

Of course, it's never that simple. Tradition also says you pay if you are trying to make a sale, so if I call on a manager to ask for consulting I should offer to pay for the meal. But if they invite me to lunch to ask me to do consulting, then it's up to them to pay.

What about when you are going out with friends or associates from the office? Then splitting the bill is appropriate. Alternately, you can offer to pick up the tab this time and let them take their turn next time. I like that approach, because I find out at the next meal whether they arc financially trustworthy. If they duck the bill when it comes to be their turn, then I know to stop going to lunch, and doing business, with them!

The Language of Management

Most people believe that you need to learn lots of business school vocabulary to sound like a manager and talk your way to success. Not so. Most executives don't say things like "Have you applied the capital asset pricing formula to that IPO?" or "Tell me about your core competencies" very often. But in my experience, the majority of successful executives, top salespeople, and promotable employees *speak clearly and well*.

The language of business success is grammatical English without a strong accent, at least in English-speaking countries. And I'm sure the same is true in other languages as well. If you can't follow the rules of grammar, it will be hard to talk your way to success.

In English, there are a few widespread errors that signal a lack of education and sophistication. It's easy to avoid these errors if you tune your ear to them. And there are some positive habits of speech that you might want to cultivate as well.

> Good taste rejects excessive nicety; it treats little things as little things, and is not hurt by them.
> —FENELON

Here is a quick overview of ways in which you can talk your way to success—or destroy your chances without realizing what you've done!

Here is a quick overview of ways in which you can talk your way to success—or destroy your chances without realizing what you've done!

- Don't say "me and . . . " The me comes after the other person or people. This grammatical rule is based on the etiquette that you should put yourself last to be polite. For example, it's, "The team report is by Rudi and me," not "The team report is by me and Rudi."
- If you want to refine it even further, remember to say "so-and-so and I" instead of "so-and-so and me" if you are the subject of the sentence. What does that mean? If you are going to do something, then it's I, not me. For example, you should say, "June and I can handle that project," not "Leave that project to me and June." Rather than learning the arcane grammatical rules governing I and me, just let your ear do the work. Ask yourself which you'd use if it was just you. That makes it easy. For example, you wouldn't say "The team report is by I," nor would you say "Me wrote the team report." So apply the same rules if you wrote the report with someone else. That makes the following sentences correct: "The team report is by Rudi and me," and "Rudi and I wrote the team report."
- Don't say "like" when you aren't sure what to say. It's, like, irritating to listen to. Just take a deep breath and decide what you want to say before saying it.
- I doubt you say "ain't" in place of "isn't," but if you do, please break the habit. Millionaire rap stars and multimillionaire athletes are making ain't popular, but it won't get you anywhere in other businesses. It just ain't professional. I mean isn't.
- Minimize slang and swears. Even if you work for an executive who says things like, "Damn it all, who the hell prepared these numbers? I told you bozos not to mess it up," that doesn't make it wise to answer by saying, "Christ, boss-man, what the hell does a guy hafta do to please a jerk like you?" Once you reach the ranks of executives, you can start swear-

ing like a trooper if you like. But don't do it while you're a trooper unless you always want to be one.

- Try to moderate any strong accent or other unusual habit of speech you may have acquired unconsciously. The easiest way to do this is to spend some time with people from other parts of the country or world, which you will find you do more and more anyway as you pursue your business goals. Also consider the simple experiment of recording your voice and listening to it. Then you'll know how you sound to others. When I first heard an interview I recorded for radio, I was surprised to discover that I said "um" quite a bit. Once aware of this bad habit, I was gradually able to, um, reduce it if not um completely eliminate it.

- Use polite phrasing whenever you ask for or receive anything. Thank people for doing things or getting things for you or for sharing information with you. Say please when you make a request. If you are polite to coworkers, employees, and supervisors, you will stand out as better mannered and more considerate. I know most managers don't seem considerate or polite, so you might not realize it is important to success in business. But as I pointed out in the chapters on maturation and leadership, consideration is one half of the secret of good management. (Providing appropriate structure is the other half.) So good manners and a polite attitude are central to management success. Not many managers know that, but those who do have a distinct advantage over others. They find that people are more willing to help them and perform better for them than for other managers.

- Ask questions. Even if you intend to tell someone what to do, try to discipline yourself to ask a few questions first. It shows respect for their knowledge and opinions. It opens you up to viewpoints and information you would overlook otherwise. And it makes people feel that you are more polite and interested in them. Most managers give out directions and orders far more often than they ask questions. But if you read biographies of the most successful businesspeople, you will find that all of them were famous for asking lots of questions.

Even if you work for an executive who says things like, "Damn it all, who the hell prepared these numbers? I told you bozos not to mess it up," that doesn't make it wise to answer by saying, "Christ, boss-man, what the hell does a guy hafta do to please a jerk like you?"

The test of good manners is being able to put up pleasantly with bad ones.
—A PROVERB

Appearance

While we are on the subject of how you present yourself, let's take a moment to consider your appearance. The best manners are wasted if people write you off because you are inappropriately dressed, so dressing for success is certainly part of the success equation.

And I want you to think about your appearance in the broadest possible manner—how you appear to others' senses. Not just how your clothes look, but how they perceive you in full, because that is what determines their reaction.

In fact, I'm convinced that in business we are judged negatively by any small problem that stands out, any little thing that is inappropriate and signals that we aren't fully professional. For example, when I used to teach at a business school, my students would sometimes come to class dressed for a job interview later in the day. And they generally selected conservative dresses or suits for the occasion. But all too often I'd notice some little problem, something that stuck out to my eye as inappropriate. The guys might wear socks with too bold of a pattern for that dark suit, a tie that was tied unevenly and fell too low, or shoes that didn't match because they were too light or informal. The girls had a better batting average, but sometimes they selected a coat that didn't match, wore too risqué a dress, or (too often) loaded on an excessive amount of makeup.

And the interesting thing is that I found I could predict the outcome of those interviews reasonably well based only upon whether I noticed a standout problem or not. Appearance does matter!

Gamblers talk about looking for the "tell," the unconscious signal to give away the fact that you are bluffing in poker. A poorly selected tie, heavy-handed makeup, and other sartorial errors are management tells. They signal that you are not quite comfortable with the management role. To an experienced eye they suggest that you may be in over your head. Of course, not everyone picks up on these subtle signals. But the people who do are usually the ones you need to do business with, so I recommend paying close attention to matters of dress.

It's hard to know how to dress for success these days because everything is changing so rapidly. What should you wear when visiting a stuffy New York bank on Friday, casual day in the city? Is it appropriate to dress for golf if you plan to attend the morning session of a conference then head for the links? How should you dress if you have two meetings in a row, one with a company that still has a formal dress code, another with one that doesn't?

There are correct answers to all such puzzles, but they take a little thinking. For instance, I generally follow the rule that I'd rather be overdressed for an event than underdressed. I don't really mind if somebody whispers behind my back that I'm too professional. It could be a lot worse! So I tend to wear the most formal clothes I think the occasion might demand, then I don't have to worry about being underdressed.

But I know some successful executives and entrepreneurs who make their own rules. One friend who founded a successful company favors comfort over fashion and wears a warm-up suit and sneakers to work and meetings. He gets away with it because he's very impressive and people are eager to do business with him no matter what he wears. You can make your own rules too, but remember that people are more likely to notice and remember inappropriate dress than appropriate dress. The secret to dressing for success is to avoid making a strong statement with your clothing. Let your clothing decorate you, not the other way around.

It used to be that you could walk into a good clothing store and ask an experienced sales clerk to dress you appropriately. Not any more. Those stores and clerks are gone, and today's world of fashion is eager to push the latest upon you with no concern for your welfare. The best rule today is to avoid the latest fashions, especially any that are unique or striking. Keep it simple. Find some clean, professional, attractive styles that won't go out of fashion anytime soon and make them your own. Don't worry about what the designers are pushing this season. If wide, gangster-style lapels are popular on suits today, you can be sure they will be considered inappropriate tomorrow. And the designers are wrong when they say that highly revealing dresses are going to be the fashion in offices. They say that every five years or so and it never happens. Stick to a conservative, clean look and you'll avoid a lot of trouble.

> We must conform, to a certain extent, to the conventionalities of society, for they are the ripened results of a varied and long experience.
>
> —A. A. Hodge

Do You Smell Successful?

By the way, let's get one thing perfectly clear. You need to avoid making a strong impression on the nose when you do business. Any smell that makes others sit up and notice is counted against you and will probably keep you from getting a job, making a sale, obtaining financing, or winning a promotion. People have a strong emotional reaction to intense smells. Avoid stimulating this reaction!

It is surprising how often this rule is violated. Some people do it the old-fashioned way, by not showering or brushing their teeth often enough. And others think they don't need deodorants. But many people find more creative ways of assaulting others' sensibilities. More and more people are falling for the advertisements of the perfume industry and anointing themselves with powerful-smelling lotions, colognes, and perfumes before going to work. I'm amazed at the number of younger men who now feel that a dollop of one of the designer-name colognes is essential to their business wardrobe. I don't care whether you personally like a particular scent or not. If it is strong enough that others are definitely aware of it when you are around, it violates the rule that you should avoid making a strong impression on the nose when doing business.

Almost all of the department-store brands of colognes and perfumes are quite strong to anyone with a sensitive nose. If you feel a scent is truly necessary, pick something much more subtle and use it extremely sparingly. Just a drop, on a cloth, touched to your skin should be enough. Don't spray the bottle at yourself or you will overdue it. It is easy not to notice that you've got too much scent on, since your nose acclimates to it and you no longer notice. But others will.

Strong smells can also come from cigars or an excess of cigarettes, from eating garlic, from stepping in a dog's mess, and from using commercial breath fresheners. Keep in mind that you don't want to bring yourself to the attention of other people's noses, and you should be able to avoid sabotaging your success because of how you smell. You want people to remember you for your business acumen, not your aroma.

It's got so that if a man opens a door for a lady to go through first, he's the doorman.

—Mae West

Coping with Embarrassment

No amount of preparation in business etiquette will keep you out of trouble all the time. There will be times when you find yourself in an embarrassing situation. And when this happens, your natural resiliency and optimism will hopefully turn it into an opportunity instead of a problem. Embarrassing situations are opportunities in two ways. First, they are opportunities to learn. You will never forget an embarrassing lesson in etiquette! And second, they are opportunities to show yourself to be aware, polite, and considerate by apologizing and to show yourself to be reasonably self-confident and self-assured by keeping your cool instead of melting down.

I am reminded of two old stories about embarrassing situations because they illustrate the sort of problems that will happen on occasion.

The first is about a young woman who was suffering from hay fever and decided to bring two handkerchiefs out to dinner with her, just in case. The first she stuck in her purse, but the second didn't fit so she hid it in the top of her dress. She sneezed quite a bit, and half way through dinner decided it was time for that extra handkerchief. But it had slipped down and she had trouble locating it. Engrossed in the search through her dress, she suddenly realized that the table had grown quiet and everyone was watching her in fascination. Startled, all she could think to say was, "I know I had two when I came."

I have no idea how one should recover from that sort of situation, but the second story illustrates the fact one *can* handle most embarrassments with sufficient ingenuity.

This story concerns a guest at a New York dinner party given for a prominent ambassador. At the end of the party, the guest shook hands with the ambassador and said goodnight, then made the rounds of the other guests, shaking a great many hands, until he found himself shaking the ambassador's hand again by accident. "But you've already said good-bye to me once, haven't you?" the ambassador asked. Thinking quickly, the guest replied, "Yes, but it's always such a pleasure to say good-bye to you."

And it's always a pleasure to be around people who have good manners!

May I Present...

It is rude not to introduce people. So make sure you are clear on names if you are going to be in a situation where you know people who don't know each other. If you aren't sure if they are acquainted, check. Simply say, "Joe, do you know Avery?" or something of the sort. If the answer is no, then introduce them properly by giving their full names and, if appropriate, a very brief mention of what they do or who they work for.

There are detailed rules of etiquette governing introductions. Figures, doesn't it?

In general, you present a more junior person to a more senior person, not the other way around. To do so, give the name of the more senior person first. Doing so signals respect, so treat customers, prospects, bosses, and investors as the senior people to show appropriate respect to them. Traditionally, women are given the same respect, so men are presented to women, not the other way around. "Ms. Lansbury, this is Jim Payton, the new intern," is correct. Got that? Good.

Sexual Harassment Short Course

Overview of Course VII

It's amazing how little most people know about the legalities and practicalities of sexual harassment. Anyone in the working world needs to be aware of the issues, risks, and remedies. Both law and practice are evolving quite rapidly, and in this course we'll take a look at their status in the United States.

Larger corporations have been offering courses on sexual harassment at an ever increasing rate, reflecting the fact that this topic is increasingly problematic for them from both a legal and a management perspective. There is nothing quite as disruptive to a work group as a harassment case.

But you aren't a corporation. You are an individual with the potential to go far as a manager, entrepreneur, or salesperson. So what are your personal interests in this subject? A surprising number of people are touched by sexual harassment problems in their careers, either as victims, perpetrators, or bystanders, and aren't sure what to do or how to help resolve the problem. In any of these roles, you need to know a lot more than most people do. You need to act in your own and the other party's self interests and avoid the various pitfalls that sometimes derail a budding career.

The root of the problem, of course, is that any mix of romantic and/or licentious urges with business often ends up causing trouble. It is certainly not realistic to expect people to bring their heads to work and not their bodies. There will be office romance. There will be workplace sex. This course can't stop people from being human, but it can stop them from making damn fools of themselves!

Let's see how.

It CAN Happen Here

Many people view sexual harassment and office romance issues as interesting tabloid reading but not really relevant to their own professional lives. That's not a wise perspective if you want to build a successful career in business as a manager or employer.

Look, let's be clear about this minefield. It *is* a minefield, and you would do well to prepare yourself to be more careful and mindful than most managers are.

Yes, I know the EEOC—that's the Equal Opportunity Employment Commission, which handles employee complaints of harassment in the United States—has a huge backlog of cases and doesn't get around to many of them for years. And yes, I know that many low-level forms of harassment and some high-level forms go

> A surprising number of people are touched by sexual harassment problems in their careers, either as victims, perpetrators, or bystanders, and aren't sure what to do or how to help resolve the problem.

unreported. And yes, I know that some senior executives, including the heads of many of the Fortune 100s, engage in lewd and licentious behavior around their secretaries and staff routinely. I've seen some pretty appalling behavior on the part of senior executives myself. And yes, I know that even when employees complain about harassment, companies don't always take action. It's no wonder that many people assume sexual harassment doesn't apply to them.

Big mistake! Fact: Sexual harassment cases continue to rise. Fact: Society is increasingly intolerant of sexual harassment anywhere, whether in the White House or your workplace. Fact: Sexual harassment is an increasingly serious issue in workplaces today, and one you need to be prepared to avoid. Don't ever risk it. It could easily derail your career. And don't let the people you supervise get away with it. That could derail your career too.

If you read the headlines, you might think that harassment is unlikely to affect you, either as a victim or a harasser. The few cases that make the news are multimillion-dollar class action settlements for widespread and obviously stupid behavior.

Take the Mitsubishi case, settled in 1998. In one of this company's U.S. auto plants, the *Chicago Tribune* reported, "Women at the plant were subjected to crude threats and forced to view pornography, including pictures from sex parties organized on company time . . . Male employees would fire air guns and shoot water at the breasts and buttocks of female colleagues," and "the government said supervisors would make 'unwanted sexual advances with impunity' and routinely ignore complaints about abuse by others." It's no wonder Mitsubishi was slapped with a $34 million settlement.

But you know not to do those sorts of things, right? (Right???) So how can you run afoul of the sexual harassment laws? Well, it's not quite as simple as that, and I'm convinced it's going to get more complicated over time.

The Costs to Harassers Are Greater Than You Think

Sexual harassment is a remarkably common career trap. Many a talented employee or manager is accused of harassment by another

> Whether you are dealing with the factory floor or boardroom suite, sexual harassment can occur unless the leadership team, from CEO to first-line supervisor, acts aggressively to ensure that the company's culture prohibits sexual harassment.
>
> —PAUL M. IGASAKI, EEOC CHAIRMAN

employee, and from that day on is branded as high risk–to be passed over for promotions and laid off at the next convenient opportunity. Perhaps the EEOC never hears about the complaint or never takes action on it even if they do, but the employee is still viewed as a hot potato, and perhaps rightly so. (In fact, I know one guy who was quietly ousted from a good job by a rival in his department who planted a *rumor* about his harassing female employees. It took my friend several months to find out why he'd been dismissed, and by then it was too late in his view to undo the damage that rumor had done.)

> Too far simply means that the behavior made the victim feel uncomfortable.

An Acid Test: Does It Make Someone Uncomfortable?

The majority of those accused of harassment claim that they are innocent, saying the accuser misunderstood their intent or just made it all up. But did they? Usually not. In most cases, the accused has gone too far. And *too far simply means that the behavior made the victim feel uncomfortable*. A little "harmless" flirting or joking might not seem to be in the same class as the behavior in the Mitsubishi case, but if it makes the employee feel harassed, it is.

You and I know perfectly well that sleeping with an employee is going too far. So is making out in a car in the company parking lot, "dirty dancing" at a company party, or "feeling up" that employee you think is so cute. Even a romantic luncheon at a nice restaurant is borderline if the partner reports to you. In fact, anything that qualifies as an affair or fling is likely to lead to trouble later on. You'd think everyone would know that.

Romance on the Job?

Actually, workplace romances are quite common. One expert I know estimates that 70 percent of all marriages are between couples who met at work! It's no wonder many people view workplace romances as harmless. But are they? If you are in a position of authority or could conceivably control any resources your partner desires, then you should know that you are taking a risk that is too big for anyone who is serious about their career. *It's stupid to fool around with an employee. It's destructive to you and unfair to them. That should be the first lesson for anyone going into supervision or management!* And there is also a trend, at least in U.S. companies, toward regulating or forbidding *any* workplace romances. I think that's an unrealistic goal, but you should take it as an indication that this whole area is a difficult one. Be careful. Be very careful.

> Many people view workplace romances as harmless. But are they?

More Fool You?

Now we're going to take a closer look at some of these issues, with the goal of inoculating both you and your organization against problems and legal actions. To do so, we need to look a little more closely at the vagaries of human behavior.

Why Do People Keep Making Such Fools of Themselves?

It's one thing to fall in love with someone who works in another department of your company and end up going steady with or even marrying them. It's quite another to:

- Have a secret affair with your secretary
- Fool around with people in your department even though you are married
- Make a habit of flirting with and trying to pick up anyone you think is cute in the workplace
- Visit pornographic Web sites on company time and download tasteless images that you pin up around the office
- Tell dirty jokes during staff meetings

Behaviors such as these are the bread and butter of lawyers working in the sexual harassment arena. People do this kind of stuff all the time—people who you think ought to know better.

Here are some more classics from recent court cases: provocative e-mail, dirty jokes in memos, posting of provocative pictures in work spaces, joking, office romances that turn sour, unwanted attentions at the water cooler, propositions on Post-it notes, conditional offers of promotion, and, more common than anything else, suggestive looks and comments, which may, day after day, add up to a truly unpleasant work environment for the employee.

How do you avoid these traps? First, you need to make sure you *comply with your firm's sexual harassment policy.* And second, you need to *come to terms with your own behavior,* so that you can bring it under rational control and avoid sabotaging yourself the way so many people do.

> You need a sound policy, appropriate procedures for handling employee complaints, and adequate employee education to insure that everyone understands those policies and procedures.

Does Your Firm Have an Adequate Sexual Harassment Policy?

If not, you are in big trouble. For one thing, you are far more likely to have sexual harassment going on in your firm. For another, you are far more likely to end up at the sharp end of the law. Specifically, you need a sound policy, appropriate procedures for handling employee complaints, and adequate employee education to insure that everyone understands those policies and procedures. If any of these elements are missing, you are running some pretty serious and easily avoidable risks.

Training magazine interviewed a number of attorneys specializing in sexual harassment to find out what sort of policy organizations should adopt. They agreed that a strong policy, clearly communicated to all employees and supported with some basic education and training to make sure employees understand how to comply with it, is a firm's best protection against trouble. The policy ought to include at least the following four points, according to their sources:

- Your organization's opposition to sexual harassment
- Definitions and examples to make clear the full range of harassment covered by the policy

- A realistic and helpful procedure for reporting sexual harassment (such as a hot line, a committee, an advocate, or whatever is needed to make people feel comfortable about coming forward with concerns and complaints). Make sure the policy includes a clear commitment to investigate any complaints fairly and quickly!
- A description of the possible consequences of sexual harassment for the harasser (including the possibility of dismissal). If you don't give people fair warning, then they may sue for wrongful discharge after they've been fired for harassment!

If your employer has a good policy that meets these standards, then you as a manager can simply make sure your people are aware of it and have had sufficient training or education to understand and implement it. (If the firm hasn't explained or trained sufficiently, you might want to pursue this yourself, but clear any training you plan to do with *your* boss first as this is often a touchy issue!)

If your firm lacks an adequate policy and procedure (or if you are in charge of the business and it's up to you to create the policy), then you need to *draft something right away*. And I'd clear it with a competent lawyer (no, that's not *necessarily* an oxymoron) and then check its readability and practicality by having some employees review it too. You don't want to supervise even one individual, let alone a team, department, or entire organization, without a thoughtful policy, an appropriate procedure for handling complaints, and a realistic way to make sure everyone understands the policy and procedure.

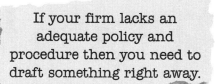

If your firm lacks an adequate policy and procedure then you need to draft something right away.

Report or Else!

As a manager, you are responsible for your employees' conduct as well as your own. What if you observe or receive complaints about sexual harassment? Don't ignore it! You need to take immediate action, as per the reporting procedures of your organization's sexual harassment policy. If the policy isn't specific enough for you to know exactly how to handle the problem, then report that too.

Should you investigate the problem directly yourself? I don't know. It's a little complicated. For one thing, your company may have a formal review procedure that should be followed. Sometimes a special committee or senior human resource executive handles those investigations. And sometimes the well-meaning supervisor creates additional trouble by coming on too strong and accusing people of things they are innocent of. So an aggressive response to those involved is not always wise. But on the other hand, you definitely want any actual harassment stopped as soon as possible. So an intermediate approach that is often more prudent is to:

a) report the problem according to standard procedures, making sure your superior(s) know about it (presuming there is an adequate policy and procedure);

b) when someone comes forward with a complaint, inform them of the company's procedures and encourage them to use them;

c) if you observe actual harassment, let the harasser know in clear terms that the behavior is wrong;

d) make sure the victim feels safe, for example, by separating the people involved; and

e) gather and write down as much and as accurate information as you can. Documentation is important.

> Sometimes the well-meaning supervisor creates additional trouble by coming on too strong and accusing people of things they are innocent of.

What If Your Employer Doesn't Have a Policy?

If you work for a dinosaur that has no policy, consider implementing a policy of your own within your department. One way to do this is to ask your employees in a staff meeting if they think you should have a policy against harassment. They'll say yes. Then suggest that everyone make an effort to get copies of other employers' policies—shouldn't be hard since you all know people who work in other companies. Next week, bring in and review the policies in your staff meeting. Seek a consensus from your staff to adopt one or a combination of them on a provisional basis until your firm develops its own. Then make sure everyone in your department gets a copy of it and agrees to comply with it.

If need be, set up a rotating committee of employees to handle complaints. (You could even send a couple of people to a workshop or seminar offered on the subject.) You could also give your boss a copy of the policy you've adopted and ask him or her to take responsibility for handling any complaints or problems that you can't resolve within your own group. But if you are proactive enough to get your people involved in adopting a policy, you will probably find that this ounce of prevention is worth many pounds of cure!

Amazingly, many harassment cases make it to court every year in which obviously inappropriate and stupid behaviors are involved. In many of these cases, the employees accused of harassment were trained and given copies of a clearly worded sexual harassment policy by their employers. And anyway, the things they did are clearly inappropriate. It's not like you don't know you'll get in trouble if you go around pinching your employees' bottoms. The interesting thing is that *almost everyone knows these behaviors are stupid and inappropriate*. Yet the behaviors persist. Why?

> If need be, set up a rotating committee of employees to handle complaints.

Why Don't People Follow Their Rational Instincts?

Sexual harassment is a bad mix with your career goals, and you certainly know in your rational mind that fooling around with or trying to seduce an employee is off limits. But unfortunately, it can be hard to keep this simple truth foremost in one's mind.

As one expert puts it, "The flirtational operating system appears to kick in without conscious consent." (Joann Ellison Rodgers, *Psychology Today*, Jan/Feb. 1999, p. 41.) When people are engaging in sexual behavior of any sort, research shows that their rational brains are not engaged. They are not thinking, at least not with the part of the brain that pays attention in company training sessions on sexual harassment. In fact, recent studies of flirting behavior indicate that even the most subtle and simple of attraction signals are largely unconscious and innate.

The fact that our higher brains are usually not controlling our flirting behavior leads us to behave in inappropriate ways on the job. Sexual activities, welcomed by another or not, just don't mix well with work. Yet people are constantly flirting and often having affairs on the job. And many bad feelings and charges of harassment arise as the ultimate result. The minute we switch off our rational control of our behavior and start acting on basic instinct, we are liable to do something stupid that could lead to charges of harassment down the road.

So to be successful in your career, you need to watch out for the subtle origins of sexual harassment charges. You need to recognize that sexual harassment charges can generally be traced back to some innocent-looking incident in which one person (usually a supervisor) initiated or reciprocated flirtation with another (usually an employee), even if the employee seemed to reciprocate the flirting.

Flirting: Unconscious Harassment?

If you give or receive any of the basic flirtation signals, you are walking down the nonverbal path toward greater sexual intimacy. That's probably a bad idea in the workplace, especially if you are flirting with someone you supervise or work closely with. Most managers view it as prudent to avoid flirtation. They would prefer not to send such signals to employees at work, and if they receive such signals, they would prefer to respond negatively by not reciprocating the signals.

One reason that flirting is generally best avoided in professional contexts is that it is often perceived as sexual harassment by others. Flirting with someone definitely puts sex on the agenda, and that can be distracting at best and upsetting and harassing at worst. So a very simple rule to follow if you want to stay away from harassment yourself is to remember that flirting is not appropriate in your workplace.

> One reason that flirting is generally best avoided in professional contexts is that it is often perceived as sexual harassment by others.

Select (or Design) Training Carefully!

"Who's harassing whom when I'm forced to attend 'sensitivity train-ing' seminars and reveal my personal feelings to coworkers with whom I don't even exchange recipes?" asked Marianne Jennings, a professor at Arizona State University. I agree. I'm not in favor of the typical formulaic sexual harassment and diversity training put on by organizations for their employees. They try to get all touchy-feely about the topic when the real point is that you shouldn't be all touchy-feely. Privacy is important. People should be permitted to do their work without harassment and should be respected for their work, not singled out for sexual or other selective treatment because of their gender or appearance. So I don't know why trainers should have to probe employees' attitudes and feelings or find out who's gay and who's straight. It's really more than adequate to use the training as a vehicle to *simply explain the policy and tell people what to do and what not to do*. Any trainer who says you have to tell your coworkers what turns you on or who in the office you find attractive is stirring the wrong pot. Just say no to that sort of demand and try to avoid subjecting your own employees to it. Good training never humiliates or demeans!

To keep flirting off the agenda, avoid subtle and often subcon-scious flirtation cues such as the following:

> People should be permitted to do their work without harassment and should be respected for their work, not singled out for sexual or other selective treatment because of their gender or appearance.

Men	Women
Use exaggerated, sweeping gestures.	Toss hair or twist hair with fingers.
Fiddle with tie or collar; square the shoulders.	Swivel hips.
Swivel hips or torso.	Giggle.
Lean toward woman.	Glance "coyly" to the side and down.
"Lint pick" or otherwise clean the other person.	Cover mouth often with hand or touch mouth while giggling.
Touch clothes, eyeglasses, finger-tips, crossed legs, etc.	"Lint pick" or otherwise clean the other person.
Shrug and/or place palm face up on table or knee.	Touch.
Arch body by placing hand(s) behind head and extending chest.	Extend/arch neck.
Extend the chin and jaw.	Arch eyebrows and open eyes wide.
Sit or stand closer than normal.	Sit or stand closer than normal.

Everyone in Western cultures tends to draw from a common set of behaviors when flirting.

(This table is based on studies of heterosexual men and women. Homosexual individuals sometimes use behaviors associated with the other gender, but in general everyone in Western cultures tends to draw from a common set of behaviors when flirting.)

Jargon 101

It's helpful to understand the specifics of legal terminology. The U.S. courts generally recognize two types of sexual harassment in the workplace: *quid pro quo* and *hostile environment*. If you know what they are, then you'll know how to avoid them! The Latin term *quid pro quo* means, literally, "something for something," and it is applied to harassment cases where the victim is pressured for sexual favors in return for a raise, promotion, continued employment, or anything of the sort. It's an obvious no-no for managers. But hostile environment is a no-no too. That's when the employee is forced to endure actions and/or language that would make a reasonable person feel uncomfortable. In other words, if you make someone's work a living hell by being a jerk, you could still get nailed for harassment, even if you don't try to pick them up.

So the bottom line is this: Avoid even the appearance of either bothering someone (hostile environment) or exchanging favors for sex (quid pro quo). In addition, make sure you have a good sexual harassment policy and that you (and everyone else) knows it—and knows what to do when they think it is being violated. And be considerate, empathetic, and sensitive to other people's sensibilities. One person's good joke is another person's hostile environment. Like anything in management, a sensitivity to (and curiosity about) the people around you is essential!

> The U.S. courts generally recognize two types of sexual harassment in the workplace: *quid pro quo* and hostile environment.

Innovating to Lead Your Markets Short Course

Overview of Course VIII

Where does economic growth come from? To my eye, it's roots are always *new ideas*. Progress means coming up with new and better ways to do things. That's true for the individual, organization, and economy as a whole. Innovation is the key driver of success.

But visit the average workplace and you'd never know innovation was the key to success. Creativity and imagination seem to be afterthoughts at best. Perhaps that is why more and more companies are bringing in creativity training for their people.

If there is one thing you absolutely have to do in order to succeed in business now, it is innovate. Why? Because things change. In fact, according to research by Dr. H. Igor Ansoff of United States International University in San Diego (who is so well known in academic circles that he is often referred to as "the father of strategic planning"), about 80 percent of managers at companies in developed countries reported rising levels of turbulence in their business environments in the 1990s.

What's turbulence? That's when things keep changing in unpredictable and hard to see ways. So Ansoff's research—based on studies of hundreds of companies and other organizations in many countries—shows that the environment in which businesses operate became unstable and unpredictable during the '80s and '90s.

More than that, his research and work by like-minded associates created a large database in which it was possible to correlate business approaches on the one hand and environmental conditions—turbulence levels—on the other. And they looked at a third factor of great importance too—how well each business did.

The result? Businesses with traditional or conventional approaches to strategy and management did fine in stable, traditional environments where there was little turbulence. They were efficient and profitable when the environment was stable. But, when turbulence increased—as it has now for most organizations—traditional forms of business did very poorly. They just couldn't make it. They were always doing the wrong thing. It's no good to be the best at something that is no longer needed.

To succeed in the more turbulent, fast-changing world of business that predominates in this new millennium, businesses need to be much more innovative, creative, and entrepreneurial than they traditionally are. This is a pretty big change, and most businesses have not caught up to it fully. Certainly the conventional approaches to teaching and doing business are out of step. MBA students are trained to be great managers, not great innovators. But today, the great managers ARE great innovators. Or maybe it's the other way around. But the point is, unless you are helping your business create changes, you will be a victim of change.

> To succeed in the more turbulent, fast-changing world of business that predominates in this new millennium, businesses need to be much more innovative, creative, and entrepreneurial than they traditionally are.

The Importance of Innovation

Creative ideas and actions produce innovations, and innovations fuel growth and profits. Look at it this way. If you do the same thing, the same way, over and over, who needs you? Even if what you did was clever and unique once upon a time, you will antiquate yourself by not improving upon it. You wouldn't expect to stay employed, let alone qualify for raises and promotions, if you never got any better or learned anything new. The same thing applies to organizations. They too must innovate to stay relevant and vital. And that makes innovation an essential core skill for all managers.

New Products

Look, your business simply has to have something new to sell or it will fail. It's that simple. New products fuel the economy and determine the winning competitors. It's very rare to find a business that can get away with selling the same old thing, the same old way, year after year.

Let's try to think of businesses that don't need to innovate. Maybe oil companies, which can sell the same basic grades of gasoline and fuel oil year after year or perhaps the post office, which doesn't seem to feel the need to introduce new services more than once a century or so (although Federal Express certainly forced some dramatic changes in that industry by introducing the overnight package), are relatively immune to innovation. What about basic commodities like corn and wheat? Well, they may seem pretty constant, but in truth there is constant experimentation with new varieties, as well as improvements to the processing and distribution. And the packaging and branding of commodity products like grains, salt, bottled water, and baking soda are in constant flux. It is pretty hard to find any good examples of product categories in which innovation does not drive competition on a yearly, if not daily, basis.

This means you need to be a champion of innovation and a fountain of fresh new product concepts in order to keep your company competitive. An understanding of product development is an important part of your basic business literacy. And perhaps the most impor-

> Why not go out on a limb?
> Isn't that where the fruit is?
> —FRANK SCULLY

tant part of that understanding is an appreciation of why so many businesses fail to innovate new products as well as they ought to.

New product concepts drive successful businesses. In my many visits to businesses as a consultant, trainer, and speaker, I've noticed that the businesses that seem to be thriving and growing are always focused on developing and introducing new products. Many of them set formal quotas to remind them that it is healthy to have a significant share of revenues come from new products. Others just do it instinctively because they are oriented toward innovation. But all are driven by the urge to innovate. They replace their own offerings with upgrades or new forms before competitors can.

However, many, indeed most, organizations do not have this new product momentum. They seem instead to be wedded to the old. Even when individuals within the organization generate exciting new ideas, nothing much seems to happen. The average organization is conservative and resists innovations of all sorts. Those who strive to update or replace old products face a tough uphill battle.

Lots of researchers have asked what goes wrong to stifle innovation in businesses. There are a great many academic papers and books on the subject. I've read quite a few, and they are interesting to be sure. But I think the most practical results are from the experts who've asked a slightly different question: What to do about the problem, not why it occurs in the first place. That's the difference between the academic and the practical approach to business. The academic approach can inform the practical approach, but on its own is not much use.

Here are some of the things that you can do to break the new products logjam in a conservative organization that resists innovation.

1. Set sales targets for new products. For example, adopt a plan for the next year that commits you to a certain amount in revenues from a new product you have in the pipeline. It won't happen unless you build it into the plan. Organizations that take a wait-and-see attitude instead of committing generally see nothing. Go out on a limb; that's where the fruit grows!

2. Put the best people on the job. If organizations don't commit serious staff to new product development and introduction,

> I've noticed that the businesses that seem to be thriving and growing are always focused on developing and introducing new products.

they won't do it well. The acid test of any organization's orientation is its staffing. Are the most people and highest salaries found in the new product development area? Probably not. But that's an easy fix once you notice the problem.

3. Support innovation with significant funding. Are there funds for creative thinking, new product development, testing, and introduction? These activities are terribly underfunded at most organizations. Unless the organization commits supporting funds to these activities, you can't expect a lot of innovation to occur. Innovation isn't something people do in their spare time. It's hard work, and it requires lots of resources. Fund the status quo and that's what you'll get. Spend more on innovation than competitors and you'll get ahead.

4. Put someone important in charge of innovation. Is someone with real authority in charge of each of the important projects your organization needs to complete in order to develop and introduce winning new products? If not, it won't happen. You can't put a junior team in charge of a company's future.

5. Have a clear, multi-step evaluation process. Organizations in which everyone works hard to develop a new product, only to have the president arbitrarily pull the plug on it at the last minute, aren't fun places to work. Innovation won't last long unless there is a clear, open process for deciding which projects make it to the next step. Everyone working on a project needs to know what criteria are used for deciding when something is worth further development or should be axed.

6. Reward innovators. Incentive pay, recognition, and other rewards encourage people to innovate. If organizations don't recognize and reward innovators, people won't innovate. It's that simple.

7. Learn from mistakes. Things always go wrong when you try to innovate. Most ideas prove unworthy of development. Some that are developed and introduced promptly fail. Others do all right but aren't home runs. And the rare few soar to success. Yet organizations remember and talk about those rare successes, not the many failures. People are afraid they'll be punished for failure. You can't learn from mistakes

If organizations don't recognize and reward innovators, people won't innovate.

unless you acknowledge and study them. A healthy attitude toward mistakes is probably the most important contributor to innovation.

What should you do if your organization falls short on one or more of these seven items? It depends upon the extent of your authority. If you run or own the business, start making dramatic changes right away. If you only manage one little part of it, then make what changes you can in your own area and begin, politely but clearly, to advocate for innovation elsewhere too. Nobody is opposed to innovation. It's just that the practices and customs of the organization get in the way. Raising awareness of the problem generally leads to others wanting to fix it too.

If you work for a business that does few or none of the things in that list of seven innovation essentials, then there is one more thing you might want to work on: your resume, because it is likely that your organization's performance will deteriorate in the next few years. And if you are just another powerless member of your organization's rat race, you definitely don't want to go down with the ship.

Innovation Ripples Can Start with *You*

As a manager, you can stimulate innovation around you. You have far more control over the level and quality of innovation than most people realize. The majority of mangers feel that they are in environments in which innovation is difficult and that they can do little to fix the problem. That's a defeatist attitude that does not harness the manager's own creativity and ingenuity. Rather than giving in, why not get innovative about innovation?

Here are just a few ways in which an individual manager can stimulate innovative behavior in his or her people. And once it gets started, innovation tends to send out ripples. A small innovation in a minor area may eventually stimulate major innovation in a core area. It has to start somewhere. Why not with you? Here are some ways you can make a personal difference (from the Managing for Innovation course, Alexander Hiam & Associates, used with permission):

> The majority of mangers feel that they are in environments in which innovation is difficult and that they can do little to fix the problem. That's a defeatist attitude that does not harness the manager's own creativity and ingenuity.

- Reward. Give out a weekly award for the most innovative idea or action. If you do this every week, the recognition will gradually sink in, and your people will have to admit that you value innovative thinking and doing above routine behavior.

- Change. Change your routines and schedules. Try new approaches to even the simplest things. Are there new ways to run staff meetings? Communicate assignments or ask for progress reports? If you can't think of new ways to try, ask your people for suggestions.

- Praise. Let people know that you want them to think creatively by giving them positive feedback every time they do, even though many of their ideas will be useless at first. Compliment people when they come up with a fresh idea or have the courage to try something new. Even if they came up with something stupid and you have to reject it, make sure you take a moment to praise their willingness to try.

- Question. Most managers tell people what to do. Try asking them what to do for a change. Ask them for their ideas. Ask them to think of better ways. Ask them to try new things. Ask them to tell everyone what happened when they tried something new. Questions are the seeds of all innovation. The more seeds you plant . . .

- Recombine. Creativity is often defined as novel combinations of ideas or things. To get your people to recognize and take advantage of novel combinations, recombine people and tasks. Move people around so they work on different tasks and with different partners. Bring in new information and encourage people to seek new experiences, outside of work as well as on the job. Mix it up whenever you can. For example, try holding your next staff meeting in a different place, even if it's not all that comfortable. A change of viewpoint often produces fresh ideas.

- Evaluate. Keep track of new ideas and approaches. Compare them to the old ones. Jot down some notes so you'll remember the innovations and be able to describe the strengths and weaknesses of each. Evaluation starts with record keeping,

> That is the essence of science: ask an impertinent question, and you are on the way to a pertinent answer.
>
> —JACOB BRONOWSKI

because you have to have some information to evaluate innovations. Even if you just put a few notes here and there in your appointment book, you'll be able to evaluate and learn from your innovations far better than most managers do. And encourage your people to evaluate innovations too by asking them what they think of new ideas and approaches. You have to be critical as well as creative to innovate successfully. New isn't always better after all!

> Innovation has to start somewhere. Why not let yourself be the center?

If you make it a practice to reward innovations, encourage change, praise efforts to innovate, question the status quo, recombine people, ideas, and things, and evaluate the results of innovations, you will create a circle of innovation around you. If you have little authority in the organization, it will be a small circle, but it will be there nonetheless. If you have more authority, the circle will be bigger. But the size is not important, because ripples of innovation will spread out from it no matter how small its center. Innovation has to start somewhere. Why not let yourself be the center?

Living on the Bleeding Edge

Damned if you do, damned if you don't is in some ways a very appropriate saying when it comes to innovation. Or perhaps the old "between a rock and a hard place" saying applies. The problem is this: If you don't keep moving by innovating in all aspects of your business, you'll be trod over by those who do. But on the other hand, if you innovate you face the challenges and risks of introducing something new. And that presents an entirely different and equally difficult set of problems.

In theory, it sounds great. Just be the first to offer a new product or service, the first to distribute through a new channel, the first to do work through a new process, or whatever. And if the new way is better, you'll make a killing. The leading edge is where strategic fortunes are made. Microsoft's the industry giant now, not IBM, because Microsoft led the pack as retail software became the key to success in the computer industry. Now it has translated its leading-edge position into a dramatic strategic advantage and an impressive revenue stream.

When I used to live in northern California in the 80s and consulted to lots of startups, I remember there was a saying that went like this: "You can tell the leaders by the arrows in their backs." And it was true. In many cases, there were dozens of failures before anyone managed to make it big. Innovation is a vital business strategy, but it is also one which needs to be approached with considerable respect and a due sense of humility. There are big rewards on the bleeding edge, but also big risks. So it is important to keep many options open, to experiment and learn as you go, and to try to avoid betting everything on the latest untested idea. The best innovator is a living innovator!

Allegory: Trading on the Web

The World Wide Web is increasingly popular with investors because they can buy and sell securities electronically instead of having to call a broker and wait for the trade to go through. And without people in the middle of the process, fees can be lower, too. So on-line brokerage services are hot, and firms like E*Trade Group Inc., Charles Schwab Corp., and Datek Online Holdings Corp. are doing a brisk business—sometimes too brisk. According to Datek's chief technology officer, "We're on the bleeding edge." And *Wall Street Journal* reporter Scott Thurm says that "Unrelenting growth has made online brokers the guinea pigs of the Internet age, pushing the limits of computer systems and software into uncharted territory."

To put it more simply, these systems fail with alarming regularity. And in this business, even a ten or twenty minute interruption in service is a disaster to some customers. They want to make their trades and get their data now, not in a half hour. And they want to know that their trades will go through with 100 percent certainty and never get lost in a computer glitch. Yet volume is far more variable and difficult to predict for online services than for the old-fashioned broker-driven systems. Brokers can only handle so many calls an hour, so they act as buffers on the system. But modern online systems are expected to handle anyone who wants to call them up. Sometimes that means they must accommodate a sudden surge without crashing their computers. Charles Schwab sometimes handles 60,000 online customers simultaneously, which is a demanding load even for a system that uses six linked mainframe computers as theirs does.

Pioneering Web-based trading is a tough thing to do. There will be problems, lots of them. To survive, you've got to have lots of commitment and plenty of resources to develop leading-edge systems. Very few firms will have the staying power needed to get to the top of this new market and stay there.

I'm going to end this course on innovation by running you through one of my firm's creativity trainings.

Okay, So How Do I Come Up with Innovative Ideas?

So far we've focused mostly on the need for innovation and on building up your courage to be an innovator. There is another key ingredient that many people say they don't have: personal creativity. Innovators need an endless supply of fresh ideas and insightful questions in order to innovate, which means you need to nurture your own personal creativity.

To help you do that, I'm going to end this course on innovation by running you through one of my firm's creativity trainings, a training that is used by businesses and training firms all over the world. It's called Creativity by Design, and the core of it is a self-administered Personal Creativity Assessment, or PCA. The PCA is a neat tool for self-diagnosing issues that affect your ability to be creative in your work (or in the rest of your life for that matter). Basically, it pictures personal creativity as the result of two factors:

- Enablers, things about you and/or your work environment that help you be more creative
- Barriers, things about you and/or your work environment that keep you from being more creative

When you identify specific enablers and barriers, you can generally start modifying them. And when you take control over even a few of your personal enablers and barriers, you can easily help yourself become a lot more creative.

For instance, perhaps you find out by using this assessment activity that you suffer from overconfidence when it comes to making decisions. You might not have realized that this was the case, and you probably hadn't seen that overconfidence hurts creativity by keeping you from looking for alternative approaches. But once you identify this personal barrier, you can begin to work on it.

Specifically, you could look up the advice the Personal Creativity Assessment includes to learn more about how to manage overconfidence. This advice might include something that appeals to you, such as "A good way to fight against the limitations of overconfidence is to try to reverse your basic assumptions. For example, if you are assuming that the traditional way of solving a problem is right, reverse this assumption by saying that the traditional approach must be wrong. Then try to think of explanations to support this new and contrary assumption."

Or you might take a more general, intuitive approach, for example, by vowing to take a little longer to think about decisions and try to consider more viewpoints or alternatives.

The great advantage of the PCA is that it translates a big, messy, tough question—how can I be more creative?—into a handful of very narrow easier questions, such as how can I avoid overconfidence when making business decisions? When you break a messy, difficult problem down into narrow, well-defined problems, then it is far easier to make headway.

But why am I talking about it? I bet you'd rather I just showed you the PCA. So here it is, reproduced by courtesy of training materials publisher Human Resource Development Press (for additional copies, call them at 800-822-2801). I want you to answer the sixty-two questions, then follow the instructions to analyze and interpret your scores. It takes about fifteen minutes to get this far in the activity, and I guarantee it will be the best fifteen minutes you spend today.

Next, follow the instructions to identify the handful of enablers and barriers that make sense for you to target and change right now. Use the detailed descriptions of action steps for personal improvement at the end of the PCA to come up with a personal creativity plan. Your end result should be some specific actions you plan to take to try to overcome barriers, take advantage of your strongest enablers, or build some new enablers. Then you just have to remember to implement your personal creativity plan. I'll leave that part to you!

> The great advantage of the PCA is that it translates a big, messy, tough question—how can I be more creative?—into a handful of very narrow easier questions, such as how can I avoid overconfidence when making business decisions?

The Personal Creativity Assessment (PCA)

PCA

BY ALEXANDER HIAM

WITH LYNNE C. LEVESQUE, ED.D

Published by: HRD Press, Inc.
22 Amherst Road
Amherst, MA 01002
800-822-2801 (U.S. and Canada)
413-253-3488
413-253-3490 (fax)
http://www.hrdpress.com

> Ask yourself whether you agree with each statement.

The Personal Creativity Assessment

Instructions

Read each of the 62 statements included in this two-part assessment.

Ask yourself whether you agree with each statement. Rate your level of disagreement or agreement using the rating scale defined below. Enter your rating in the blank space next to each question.

Please work carefully to make sure you put an appropriate number next to each statement. Don't spend too long on each statement; once you have read and understood the statement, your initial reaction is probably the most accurate.

When you have finished, follow the instructions for Analysis and Interpretation to see what your answers mean in the context of this assessment.

1	2	3	4	5
STRONGLY DISAGREE	DISAGREE	IN THE MIDDLE	AGREE	STRONGLY AGREE

Part A

_____ 1. I am aware of many practical techniques for generating ideas.

_____ 2. I am empowered to be creative because I feel a sense of control over my personal circumstances and fate when at work.

_____ 3. I am confident of my ability to produce valuable new ideas and solutions.

_____ 4. I am drawn to new perspectives, even when they clash with my assumptions or values.

_____ 5. I have often benefited from my own and others' creativity in past work experiences.

_____ 6. I work with a number of people who have succeeded, in part, because of their high levels of creativity.

_____ 7. My leaders (including supervisors, managers or mentors) encourage creativity.

_____ 8. My leaders (including supervisors, managers or mentors) enjoy listening to my ideas.

_____ 9. People who exhibit creativity in my kind of work are traditionally rewarded for their efforts.

_____ 10. I receive plenty of good training to help me be more creative.

_____ 11. I feel resilient. I am ready for anything that my creativity might lead to.

_____ 12. My many activities and interests expose me to a wide variety of new things.

_____ 13. I am viewed as an independent thinker by my peers.

_____ 14. I am not attached to one idea or approach. I like exploring many alternatives.

_____ 15. I like "fooling around" with ideas, so I find creative thinking and problem-solving entertaining.

_____ 16. Once I get thinking about a problem, I don't set it completely aside until I've solved it—even if it takes many weeks.

_____ 17. I am good at sensing what others think and feel. This skill helps me understand and add to the good ideas of people around me.

1	**2**	**3**	**4**	**5**
STRONGLY DISAGREE	DISAGREE	IN THE MIDDLE	AGREE	STRONGLY AGREE

_____ 18. I see myself as a highly creative person.

_____ 19. I often invent new things.

_____ 20. I often come up with fresh ideas by making connections between unrelated things.

_____ 21. I study creativity to make sure I have a solid understanding of what it takes to be creative.

_____ 22. I often think about my own creative strengths and weaknesses.

_____ 23. I apply both logical and intuitive abilities to my creative thinking.

_____ 24. I have the courage to say and do different things if I think they might be better.

_____ 25. I don't mind taking the risk of being wrong when I try to be creative.

_____ 26. Creative activities are a high priority in my life when I make choices about how to spend my time.

_____ 27 I feel a responsibility to use the creative abilities I have.

_____ 28. I take a disciplined approach to creativity in order to keep it focused productively.

_____ 29. I feel that you can never stop working on your creativity skills.

_____ 30. I feel healthy and strong.

_____ 31. I take care of my body by stretching and exercising regularly.

1	**2**	**3**	**4**	**5**
STRONGLY DISAGREE	DISAGREE	IN THE MIDDLE	AGREE	STRONGLY AGREE

Part B

_____ 32. My work requires a narrow, specific set of skills.

_____ 33. My work does not give me many opportunities to develop new skills.

_____ 34. My work does not challenge me.

_____ 35. I don't feel personally responsible for the results of my work because it's hard to see how my own contributions affect overall performance.

_____ 36. I tend to solve problems in certain ways, rather than to explore unconventional approaches.

_____ 37. Most of the time, people around me do not act or think like creative people.

_____ 38. The people around me are not open to new or wild ideas.

_____ 39. If I spend too much time on creative thinking I will be labeled as a trouble-maker or accused of being lazy.

_____ 40. I am afraid to offer too many new ideas of my own.

_____ 41. I am fairly set in my ways. My feeling is, "If it ain't broke, don't fix it."

_____ 42. I prefer to choose between two clear alternatives, so I often find myself thinking in terms of either/or solutions.

_____ 43. I feel that our basic approach is the right one, so I probably don't examine alternatives as often as I could.

_____ 44. There is so much pressure to finish one thing and get on to the next that I rarely have time to take a thoughtful, yet lengthy, approach to a problem.

_____ 45. Ideas about how to do things better are difficult because they violate established policies or procedures.

_____ 46. There isn't much point in contributing creative ideas, because they will just get lost in the bureaucracy.

1	2	3	4	5
STRONGLY DISAGREE	DISAGREE	IN THE MIDDLE	AGREE	STRONGLY AGREE

_____ 47. My leaders (supervisors, managers) are not very open to new ideas. They tend to react defensively.

_____ 48 I'd like to do more creative thinking, but there isn't much opportunity for it in the way we run our meetings and projects.

_____ 49. If you don't look and act the "right" way, you can't succeed in my workplace.

_____ 50. I feel a strong need to make sure my work is perfect.

_____ 51. My fear of failing can keep me from taking on an important challenge.

_____ 52. I am afraid someone will reject me if I voice unconventional ideas.

_____ 53. I worry that if you open things up too much, you can easily lose control.

_____ 54. It is hard for me to accept ideas I didn't develop myself.

_____ 55. I probably filter out lots of creative ideas because they clash with my current views or assumptions.

_____ 56. I often talk myself out of being creative because I can't help thinking about my doubts and fears.

_____ 57. I have chronic aches and pains that bother me when I work.

_____ 58. My back is increasingly weak and inflexible.

_____ 59. I don't feel comfortable with ideas that are too abstract or vague.

_____ 60. I don't feel comfortable with thoughts that skip around without any clear order.

_____ 61. I tend to take a "don't rock the boat" attitude, instead of challenging the status quo.

_____ 62. I don't think the work I do in my job is particularly valuable or worthwhile in the grand scheme of things.

Thank you. Now go to the next page and perform the analysis needed to interpret and apply the information you have just gathered.

Analysis and Interpretation

1. **Please add up your scores for each of the two sections of the assessment.**

   Total Part A: _____ *Total of scores from questions 1–31 of the assessment.*

   Total Part B: _____ *Total of scores from questions 32–62 of the assessment.*

2. **Please divide each subtotal by 31 to obtain the average (mean) score for each part of the assessment:**

   Total Part A ÷ 31 = _____ = *Enabler Score*

   Total Part B ÷ 31 = _____ = *Barrier Score*

3. **Interpret your enabler score.**

   Your score should fall within the range of 1 to 5. A score of 2 or less is low. A score of 3 is medium. A score of 4 to 5 is high.

   An enabler score in the low range means that you don't have enough stimulators around you that help you be creative (sometimes referred to as *enablers*). Enablers stimulate and nurture creativity. Without enough enablers, you will not be able to perform creatively on a sustained basis. Consult Part A of your assessment to see which enablers you lack (look for low scores on specific items). Work on getting more enablers into your life and your work environment. If you aren't sure which enabler an assessment item is related to, look up that item's number in the ***Key to Creativity Enablers and Barriers*** at the back of this assessment. It tells you what each statement in the assessment means, and then provides you with action steps for personal improvement.

   If you have a medium or high enabler score, that's good. You have many positive influences that can help you be creative. However, the odds are that you still don't do as much creative work or as good creative work as you are capable of, because there are barriers that block you. A person with a high enabler score and a high barrier score is like a powerful race car, engine roaring, with big weights tied to its rear bumper. The enablers can't give you the creative power you want until you remove some of the barriers in your way. So, go on to the next step in this interpretation and work on barriers, as well.

4. Interpret your barrier score.

Your score should be from 1 to 5. A score of 2 or less is low. A score of 3 is medium. A score of 4 to 5 is high.

If your barrier score is low, you are cleared for creative take-off. There are few barriers to frustrate your natural creative energy. That's good. However, most people find that they have many barriers blocking their personal creativity.

If your barrier score is medium or high, you will need to reduce or eliminate some barriers in order to be more creative. Work on getting barriers out of your life and your work environment. If you aren't sure which barrier an assessment item refers to, look up that item's number in the ***Key to Creativity Enablers and Barriers*** at the back of this assessment. It tells you what each statement in the assessment measures.

Note: Many of the common barriers measured by this assessment are in our own heads or bodies; we have the power to work on them personally. Others are more dependent upon the work environment or the people we work with, but even these can be controlled and modified.

For example, if you realize that your associates are pressuring you to conform and thus are blocking your creativity, you can ask them to ease up on you so that you can try some creative things. That's a way to alter an external aspect of the barrier. To help you recognize your urge to conform, try consciously being aware of this urge, and practice ignoring it when it is unhealthy. That's a way to alter an internal aspect of the barrier.

The point is, you have a lot more control over both barriers and enablers to your personal creativity than you probably realized. The first and biggest step toward exercising your control is to recognize and identify those enablers and barriers. Once you identify them, you can begin to think about ways of controlling them.

For more information on working with your creativity enablers and barriers, see ***The Manager's Pocket Guide to Creativity*** by Alex Hiam, HRD Press, Amherst, Massachusetts.

> Many of the common barriers measured by this assessment are in our own heads or bodies; we have the power to work on them personally.

Key to Creativity Enablers and Barriers

CREATIVITY ENABLERS	CREATIVITY BARRIERS
1. Knowledge	1. Lack of skill diversity
2. Locus of control	2. Limited opportunities for skill development
3. Confidence	3. Few challenges
4. Open-mindedness	4. Little sense of personal responsibility
5. Experience	5. Limited size of solution sets
6. Role models	6. No role models
7. Leadership support	7. Narrow-minded peer acceptance
8. Leadership openness	8. Sanctions
9. Rewards	9. Fears
10. Training	10. Personal narrow-mindedness
11. Emotional resiliency	11. Bipolar thinking
12. Diverse inputs	12. Overconfidence
13. Independence	13. Time pressure
14. Lack of attachment	14. Procedural constraints
15. Playfulness	15. Red tape
16. Persistence	16. Close-minded leaders
17. Empathy	17. Group-process constraints
18. Self-perception	18. Pressure to conform
19. Inventiveness	19. Perfectionism
20. Boundary-breaking	20. Fear of failure
21. Understanding of creativity	21. Fear of rejection
22. Self-awareness	22. Fear of losing control
23. Balancing thinking and feeling	23. Pride
24. Courage	24. Personal filters
25. Risk-taking	25. Internal voices
26. Priority	26. Physical discomfort
27. Responsibility	27. Unhealthy back/spine
28. Discipline	28. Concrete thinking
29. Self-learning	29. Linear thinking
30. Health	30. Acceptance
31. Self-care	31. Low self-evaluation of work

Key to Creativity Enablers and Barriers
With Action Steps for Personal Improvement

Explanation and Instructions. Each of the questions in the Personal Creativity Assessment measures a specific enabler or barrier that can have an important effect on your creativity. There are a great many possible factors that can affect how creative you are—62 are measured in this assessment. It will be difficult, if not impossible, to work on every factor that might affect your creativity. Instead, you need to focus on a handful of factors that are important right now, based on your individual profile. The assessment will help you identify the most likely candidates for work right now. Here is how to interpret the assessment in order to pick the factors in the list to work on:

1. You should make sure you take advantage of your best enablers. These are questions 1 through 31 on which you received especially high scores. You don't need to change these factors, but you should read up on them to make sure you don't overlook them or let them slip away by accident.

2. You should try to add more enablers if you can. Scan the descriptions of enabling factors on which you received middle or low scores to see if you can do anything to raise your scores on some of them.

3. You should work on reducing any significant barriers. Look for high scores on questions 32 through 62, and focus on those factors in order to develop some action plans.

4. In general, you should focus your efforts where they will do the most good! It's best to pick between one and five factors to work on at any one time. Select those that appeal to you and that you think you can really make progress on. Realistic, appealing goals are essential in building your personal creativity and you must choose them yourself. Think of what follows as simply a lengthy list from which you can make your own selections. It is not a rigid recipe you have to follow.

> You need to focus on a handful of factors that are important right now, based on your individual profile.

Creativity Enablers (Questions 1–31)

1. Knowledge. Awareness of creativity methods, such as brainstorming, idea generation by word association, and the examination or reversal of assumptions. The more knowledge one has about ways to think creatively, the more often one thinks creatively and the more successful one can be generating useful new ideas. To increase your knowledge, read or study the subject or expose yourself to creative people who can model effective methods and approaches. (See *The Manager's Pocket Guide to Creativity* from HRD Press for business-oriented creative thinking methods: The Creatercize Activity, The Magic Toolbox, Three-Step Word Association, Category Expansion, Surfacing Assumptions, The Fault Pair Tree, and What/How Thinking.)

2. Locus of control. A feeling of confidence and control over circumstances helps people gain the confidence to pursue creative alternatives. The opposite, that feeling of being out of control, leads to learned helplessness. So, internal locus of control is important to creativity. Positive thinking and past successes help develop one's sense of control, so if you are suffering from a feeling of helplessness, work on your mood and seek experiences in which you can succeed. External locus of control is associated with depression; if you are depressed, you need to work on that problem (seek professional help if you are stuck) before you can expect to be creative.

3. Confidence. Feeling confident that we are able to generate valuable new ideas or insights boosts creativity. Practice in creative thinking boosts confidence if the practice cases are not too hard, and therefore enables creativity in real life, as well. So, to increase confidence, work on simple problems and try to bring creative thinking to everyday tasks. Also work through examples provided in training materials. Try to add your own ideas to the brainstorming examples in the chapters on idea generation techniques.

4. Open-mindedness. A willingness to consider alternative views and approaches is an important thing to have if one wants to think creatively. To increase open-mindedness, seek out examples of successful people and approaches. Make a point of talking to people you don't know, as well as those you know but aren't comfortable

> Work on simple problems and try to bring creative thinking to everyday tasks.

with. Ask their opinions on topics of importance to them and make a point of trying to listen and understand their thinking, even if you disagree with it.

5. Experience. The positive experiences of others who have applied good creative thinking to solve a problem or develop a better alternative are very enabling. They stimulate future creativity. If you are not very experienced in creativity, you can make up for it by seeking out people who are. Ask them to help you do some brainstorming about the problem you are working on. Their ideas and experience with various approaches will help you learn how creative thinking is done. And, of course, the best way to get experience is to simply take a creative approach to all your work and personal decisions.

6. Role models. Being exposed to people who owe their success to personal creativity is a powerful enabler of creativity in others. However, good role models are hard to find. If you know any successful entrepreneurs who have built businesses, you can be sure they are inherently creative people even if they don't describe themselves that way; they may think only "artists" are creative. Make an effort to spend some time with entrepreneurs, scientists, artists or anyone else who seems creative (some coaches and teachers are very creative at developing new activities). Ask them to let you observe them at work, if possible.

7. Leadership support. Support from supervisors is helpful. If it isn't offered, try asking for it. If the supervisor agrees that creative thinking is part of your job, then he or she should be willing to become more supportive. Otherwise, you will have to practice "closet creativity"; share ideas when they are well developed and you have had time to evaluate them critically; and keep your thought processes to yourself.

8. Leadership openness. Supervisor interest and encouragement in your ideas and suggestions helps enable your creativity. However, many supervisors are not open to unsolicited or outside-of-the-box ideas. Try to find the preferred time and medium for novel ideas—most people are more open at some times than others, and prefer one communication channel over another. Often the supervisor who is not open to verbal suggestions is willing to read them in the form of written proposals or e-mails. If you find a supervisor who is interested in

> Make an effort to spend some time with entrepreneurs, scientists, artists or anyone else who seems creative

new ideas and willing to consider or discuss them, take full advantage of this by submitting as many ideas as you can. Try to get into an "idea dialog" with receptive leaders; it is a shame to waste leadership openness, because it is (unfortunately) a scarce commodity.

9. Rewards. Recognition and/or more tangible rewards for creativity helps encourage it. If your work environment does not provide formal rewards for creativity, seek informal positive feedback from peers and supervisors instead. Try asking them if they think your creative efforts or ideas are helpful; people usually are appreciative of creativity, but just don't think to recognize and reward it. Also try rewarding yourself when you know you've accomplished something as a result of creative thinking.

10. Training. Training exposes you to creativity methods and examples, strengthens your experience, and provides support for creative behavior. Sign up for any available creativity training; sometimes community organizations or local community colleges run inexpensive courses you can take on your own time. If nothing is available, seek self-study options—there are great books on the subject.

11. Emotional resiliency. People who are buoyant in the face of trouble are able to manage their own emotional state and avoid high stress, anxiety or depression. They are better prepared and able to engage in creativity when it is most needed for problem-solving. To boost your emotional resilience, strengthen and use your support network. Also work on lowering your stress through relaxation or counseling. Increase your strength through a healthy diet, exercise, and more sleep, if necessary, so you are at your peak resiliency level more often.

12. Diverse inputs. More and varied exposure to experiences, things, and ideas gives you more material for creative thinking. To increase these benefits, try new things, go new places, read new types of books (or any books if you don't currently do much reading), and make an effort to spend time with people you wouldn't normally spend time with.

13. Independence. The more independent you are in forming opinions and deciding how you want to approach problems, the easier it is to be creative. When you accept someone else's options and allow yourself to be drawn into discussing or using their choices, then you

> Increase your strength through a healthy diet, exercise, and more sleep, if necessary, so you are at your peak resiliency level more often.

are not thinking independently. The independent thinker often tries out a novel option or choice. To increase the independence of your approach, make an effort to always ask yourself if you can think of an alternative viewpoint or approach. And make a point of recognizing when you are using someone else's approach without questioning it.

14. Lack of attachment. People who have an "easy come, easy go" attitude toward ideas, plans, and solutions find it far easier to be creative. They have cultivated a lack of attachment to the old idea, which frees them to consider new alternatives. To achieve this lack of attachment, you must have considerable faith in your ability to come up with and implement new and better ideas. Otherwise, it is a little frightening to "let go" enough to consider chucking everything and starting from scratch. If you lack this courage, it may be because you allow your pessimistic side to sway you. Instead, make an effort to think optimistic thoughts. Remind yourself that there is always a better way, and that things might even be improved if you came up with a different idea.

15. Playfulness. Having a sense of fun and liking to explore new ideas and approaches is a great asset when it comes to creativity. Yet the things that we most need our creativity for are usually things we take very seriously. People who are naturally highly playful are better able to "fool around" with important problems and questions. If you have a hard time being anything but serious, take some "fun breaks" to play games, expose yourself to comedy, or do whatever else helps you recapture your youthful sense of fun. And make an effort to find and learn from people who don't seem to take life as seriously as you do. People whom you avoid because they act goofy or clown around in serious situations are just the people you need when it comes time to do some serious brainstorming.

16. Persistence. There is a myth that creative breakthroughs emerge fully formed as a result of the right inspiration. Nonsense. All great ideas take time to grow and develop. Persistence is essential: If you are in the habit of giving up too soon (as many people are), set yourself some quantitative goals to increase your persistence. Challenge yourself to double the usual number of ideas you generate, or double the amount of time you give to thinking. As you force yourself to practice persistence, you will see the benefits of it and naturally become more persistent at creative thinking as a result.

> Take some "fun breaks" to play games, expose yourself to comedy, or do whatever else helps you recapture your youthful sense of fun.

17. Empathy. People who are skilled at sensing what others feel and think are especially good at group creativity. They are able to pick up on and add to others' ideas. To increase your creative empathy, practice active listening skills (tell people what you think they are thinking or feeling and ask them to correct you if you are wrong). Also work on breaking down any barriers to comfortable collaboration. A stiff, formal setting gets in the way of empathy, for example. It is easier to be empathetic and a good listener when you are in a neutral, relaxed setting.

18. Self-perception. If you see yourself as creative, you are. Much of creativity is based on self-perception: Creativity is a behavior more than a talent, and people who feel creatively act creative. If you don't feel creative (and you won't, unless you are in the habit of being creative), then tell yourself you are going to act like someone who is highly creative. For example, you could tell yourself that you are going to approach a problem the way a painter or filmmaker might approach it. Having a creative role model in your mind's eye helps you learn how to adopt a creative self-perception.

19. Inventiveness. People who are often thinking of new things are naturally good at many other creative tasks too, probably because invention is great practice for all sorts of creativity. If you can think of ten new ways to brew the perfect cup of coffee, you can also come up with lots of novel solutions to a tough "real-world" problem at work or in your personal life. And being inventive is an entertaining game, so practice inventiveness by asking yourself how to redesign simple household or office implements or routine processes. For example, you could spend a few minutes on the way to the office trying to think of new ways of transporting people to and from their offices that would save time and avoid traffic jams. By the time you get to work, you'll be ready to do some more serious creativity. Any ideas yet?

20. Boundary-breaking. When you associate things in familiar ways, you are breaking mental boundaries. Recombining things into unexpected groupings is a basic creative operation, so it helps to be good at this skill. To become better at boundary-breaking, use the combination brainstorming technique described on pp. 76–78 of *The Manager's Pocket Guide to Creativity*. With it, you create many sets

> Recombining things into unexpected groupings is a basic creative operation

Do you always use the same mental strategies? Do you always work in the same time and place? If so, make a conscious effort to vary your routines.

of combinations using the "_____ and _____" format, instead of just brainstorming a list of single items. Pairing them forces you to find new associations by breaking boundaries.

21. Understanding of creativity. People who pursue a deeper understanding of creativity become more creative as a result. To gain this benefit, study and take advantage of resource materials, assessments like this one, seminars, role models, and brainstorming methods.

22. Self-awareness. Understanding one's own creative behavior is essential; it makes self-development possible. People who are highly aware of how they think and what approaches they use are generally more successful at creative endeavors. To achieve high creative self-awareness, watch yourself do creative work. Do you always use the same mental strategies? Do you always work in the same time and place? If so, make a conscious effort to vary your routines. Observe yourself as you change your approach to see how the results change. You will become more experimental in your approach to creativity, and over time will find better and better formulas for your own use. Sometimes it takes just the right environment or background music in order to bring out your natural creativity to its fullest. Know your creative self so you can make useful discoveries like this.

23. Balancing thinking and feeling. Many people fail to get emotionally engaged in a creative problem or challenge. This limits the range of their thinking and prevents them from achieving the level of mental involvement needed to incubate a problem or idea. Similarly, a purely emotional involvement is insufficient for many creative tasks. Unless you are thinking and feeling, your whole mind is not involved in the problem. To make sure you take a more balanced approach, stop periodically and ask yourself a) how you are feeling about the creative work you are doing, and b) what you are thinking. This effort to become aware of both the rational and emotional sides of your creative involvement helps nurture both, and creates a healthy balance between thinking and feeling. Consider inviting someone to work with you who has different strengths; if you are more logical, seek someone intuitive to brainstorm with, or vice versa.

24. Courage. Physical and/or mental courage helps people take the mental leaps required in creative thinking. If you lack courage in other areas, you can still become a courageous creative thinker simply by realizing that the costs of failure are very low. So what if your creative thinking doesn't produce a usable idea? It's not like a mountain climber falling off a cliff, a scuba diver decompressing too fast and getting the bends, or a spy answering a question incorrectly and being discovered by the enemy. In fact, nothing bad happens when you fail at creative thinking. All you've done is waste a little time practicing your creative abilities. So it is not hard to talk yourself into being a courageous creative thinker once you realize that courage is what is really needed.

25. Risk-taking. People who don't mind taking the risk of losing something find it easier to be creative, since they don't talk themselves out of trying new approaches. If you are averse to taking risks, you need to be aware of this and work on it in your own creativity. Seek opportunities to take some planned risks where the down side is not so frightening to you. For example, make a point of trying to change the order in which you perform a routine task, just to see how many different ways you can do it. In essence, this amounts to practicing creative risk-taking, and it should help you overcome your fear of risk in creativity. Also combat this fear by thinking about the risks associated with not thinking creatively. If you avoid creative approaches, you may miss out on valuable opportunities, so it is paradoxically more risky to maintain the status quo than to be creative.

26. Priority. People who make creativity a priority are more successful at creative tasks because they put more time and effort into them. If you don't give creativity enough priority, change the order in which you approach your daily tasks. Identify the more creative ones and make a special point of doing them first. (For example, if you have to do filing, writing, bill-paying, and telephone calls tomorrow, make a point of doing the writing before the other tasks.)

27. Responsibility. Some people feel it is their responsibility to be creative because they sense that they have potential and feel obligated to use it. This is a healthy attitude, leading to commitment to the creative process. The world imposes many competing responsibilities upon us, so it is often up to us to defend our creative responsibility. If you have trouble doing so and find yourself being pushed off creative tasks by the responsibilities others impose upon you, you need to fight back. To remind yourself of your creative responsibility,

> Make a point of trying to change the order in which you perform a routine task, just to see how many different ways you can do it.

just tell yourself that people are remembered for the new things they do, not the routine things everybody else also does! Anybody can do a good job with someone else's ideas, but to really contribute to the world you need to come up with your own ideas. Also, once you develop creative habits and a track record of successful creativity, you will have more respect for your own creative potential and will acquire a greater sense of creative responsibility as a result.

28. Discipline. A sense of fun helps creative thinking, but people who are serious and disciplined about doing creative work are also at an advantage. Even though creativity can feel like play, you need to exercise or practice it long and hard to get a lot out of it. People who are highly disciplined in their approach to creativity have more creative success because they put more time and effort into their creativity and because they practice more creative methods. Discipline is a fairly easy thing to acquire: try tracking what you do in a creativity journal, noting the type of creative work you did each day, how long you spent on it, and how you approached it. Also keep track of any study or reading you do on the subject of creativity or any time you spend talking with others about the topic. Keeping records alone helps you become more disciplined!

29. Self-learning. People who are enthusiastic about developing their own creativity continue to grow creatively and are more successful as a result. If you don't naturally take an interest in developing and refining your creativity, then consider taking a course to help you focus on self-development. Courses get you in the habit of learning about creativity, and afterward it is easier to continue on your own. (Note: A workshop on how to be creative is helpful, but so are any courses you might take in which you do creative things, such as a course in which you study photography, art, creative writing, flower arranging, or musical improvisation or composition.)

30. Health. Good health and well being are a boon to creativity. If you are having trouble with your health, you may not have realized that it is likely linked to any creativity problems you may be experiencing. Rather than try to force yourself to be creative when you don't feel well, make a real effort to invest time and energy into healing first. Rest, relaxation, and proper medical treatment will prepare you for creativity.

> To really contribute to the world you need to come up with your own ideas.

31. Self-care. People who take good care of themselves physically are often better able to think creatively. If you set aside less than 30 minutes a day for exercise and physical fitness, you will not be able to achieve peak levels of creativity. Many people find their exercise routines dull and uninspiring, so they fall out of the habit of doing them. To combat this problem, try being creative about self-care. Seek new and fun ways of exercising and caring for your body.

Barrier Factors (Questions 32–62)

32. Lack of skill diversity. When you do the same thing over and over, it is hard to be creative. In contrast, people who develop and use more than one set of skills are naturally more creative. To benefit from increased skill diversity, seek opportunities to learn and use new skills, either by doing new tasks at work or by pursuing new hobbies in your private life. Take advantage of any training opportunities available to you, especially those that expose you to unfamiliar skills. Job rotation and cross-training opportunities are very good for personal creativity.

33. Limited opportunities for skill development. If your work limits your opportunities for skill development, this will dull your creative imagination. Fight against job stereotyping by seeking cross-training or lateral transfers. Also consider doing volunteer work or taking up a new hobby on your own time in order to find new opportunities for skill development.

34. Few challenges. When you have few challenges in work or life, you are not likely to be creative. Many people avoid challenges, fearing that they will be difficult, inconvenient, or risky. These same people generally say they are bored with their lives, so it is clear that challenges are healthy and necessary for people. Seek challenges by volunteering for an unpopular assignment, forcing yourself to try something new, going somewhere new for vacation, and so forth. Note each challenge you tackle in your daily calendar, and if you haven't anything to write down for a whole week, do something about it right away!

> Job rotation and cross-training opportunities are very good for personal creativity.

35. Little sense of personal responsibility. When people feel that they are just another cog in the wheel, they will not be motivated to be creative. To combat this feeling that your efforts are unimportant, make an effort to get in touch with people who "consume" the results of your work. Find out what they do and don't like. And try to develop more and better feedback from your work: Can you find indicators or measures of the quality of your efforts? Everyone's work makes a difference, but it isn't always easy to see the significance of your personal impact unless you look for it.

36. Limited size of solution sets. When you take a familiar approach to problems, this leads you to "round up the usual suspects" when seeking solutions. It blinds you to unusual alternatives, thus limiting the number of options you consider. To combat this problem, simply try out a variety of creative thinking methods and tools.

37. No role models. Many of us are surrounded by people who are not creative in their behavior. This discourages us from acting creative ourselves. To combat this problem, you should take two steps. First, expose yourself to creative people indirectly by reading about them, renting movies about them, and so forth. Second, make an effort to spend some time with creative people. Do you know any artists, performers, scientists, investigative journalists, or kindergarteners you can hang out with? Even a half-hour of exposure once a week can do much to keep your creative juices flowing.

38. Narrow-minded peer acceptance. In many offices and households, new ideas are either met with criticism or ignored. If this happens in your environment, you will avoid voicing your ideas, and eventually will stop having them altogether. To overcome this barrier, you have to first make note of it. Recognize that your peers are negative about creative ideas and damage your ability to be creative. Find someone who is open and inquisitive to talk with in order to provide some balance. (If there is no one you can trust with your idea, then you are in an unhealthy situation and need to make some changes!) Also consider keeping an idea log in which you record and develop your own ideas; a dialogue with yourself can be a partial substitute for idea dialogues with others.

39. Sanctions. When other people actively discourage creative thinking, it's terribly hard to do it. Sanctions are too often imposed.

> Consider keeping an idea log in which you record and develop your own ideas.

In many organizations, anyone who voices or uses creative ideas is branded a trouble-maker and is censured or punished. (And schools are usually this way too—no wonder most of us are broken of our creativity habit by the time we grow up!) There are only two healthy responses to sanctions: First, you need to work at removing them by advocating rationally for a more open policy on creativity. Second, you need to take your creativity underground. Be creative in ways that don't attract the attention of those who enforce the sanctions. But please, don't stop being creative!

40. Fears. Many people are afraid to volunteer creative ideas. They worry that they will be considered odd or dumb, or that they will be laughed at, criticized, or censured. And all of these possibilities do exist, so there is a legitimate basis for fear about creative behavior.

41. Personal narrow-mindedness. If you are set in your ways and accustomed to familiar paths, it is very, very difficult to think creatively about anything. Habits of mind must be broken. Do something new and different, perhaps just something very small to start with if you can't make any big changes. Try a new route to work or the store. Visit an unfamiliar place. Travel is a wonderful antidote to narrow-mindedness, so you can chalk up the cost of a trip to investing in your creativity! And it's a very beneficial thing to start hanging out with people on the fringe of your network—people whom you have less in common with and might not normally associate with.

42. Bipolar thinking. How many options do you usually think of when considering a decision or problem? Many people frame their decisions as either-or choices. If you do this, it limits the options to the two "forks in the road" you have created for yourself. A simple expedient is to make a list of your options or choices whenever you make a decision. If it's a list of two, don't decide yet. Develop some additional alternatives first. (Also try the fault pair tree in *The Manager's Pocket Guide to Creativity*. It is an easy method for bipolar thinkers because it works with pairs of choices; but it also leads to broader viewpoints by forcing you to generate many pairs.)

43. Over-confidence. If you think you already know the right answer, you don't give any creative thought to alternative approaches. Overconfidence is commonplace, especially when you have some expertise or experience of relevance. But often, past expe-

> Many people frame their decisions as either-or choices. If you do this, it limits the options to the two "forks in the road" you have created for yourself.

rience limits our view of novel alternatives. A good way to fight against the limitations of overconfidence is to try to reverse your basic assumptions. (For example, if you are assuming that the traditional way of solving a problem is right, reverse this assumption by saying that the traditional approach must be wrong. Then try to think of explanations to support this new and contrary assumption. See Surfacing Assumptions in *The Manager's Pocket Guide to Creativity* for details.)

44. Time pressure. It is very hard to be creative in a hurry. Yet we are often under some kind of time pressure. You may not be able to eliminate this pressure in your life, but you can take steps to free up time to think creatively about important matters. The key is to a) identify a single topic for your creativity each day and b) schedule creative time to spend on it. For example, if you feel frustrated about a problem and don't see any really desirable choices, write yourself a note to take an hour off sometime during the day to go for walk and think about it. (If you don't stick with the schedule, discipline yourself by buying an old-fashioned kitchen timer and setting it to the number of minutes you want to give the creative task. Then don't allow yourself to be distracted by anything until it rings.) Also recognize that the fast pace of daily life often leads us to assume we must hurry decisions that do not have as much time pressure as we think. Always ask yourself if you can postpone a decision for a day or a week. If so, please procrastinate! Let the decision incubate for a while and see if you come up with fresh insights that increase your choices. (Other ideas: Some creativity coaches recommend getting up a half hour earlier each morning to write a log of your ideas and concerns—whatever is on your mind. This clarifies your thinking on many of those pressing daily problems and chores, and therefore should lead you to feel you have more time and control in your life instead of less. Another approach is to practice generating ideas rapidly, so as to be able to make better use of the little creative time you do have available in your schedule. See Exercise: Generating and Capturing Ideas on p. 33 of *The Manager's Pocket Guide to Creativity* for instructions.)

45. Procedural constraints. When there are well-established processes and procedures, it is very hard to consider creative alterna-

> Let the decision incubate for a while and see if you come up with fresh insights that increase your choices.

tives. Regulation, habit, or tradition dictates a "no" answer to most suggestions, which discourages us from even thinking about alternatives. This is a hard barrier to fight. When dealing with work processes that have firm procedures to them, you may have to draw a map or flow-chart of the entire process, then prepare alternative process diagrams showing how your ideas would affect the entire system. That way, you can defend a creative idea by showing that it should improve the overall process, even though it violates current procedures—and thereby argue that the procedures could be improved. But often procedure constraints are more perceived than absolute. We do things certain ways for long enough that it seems like there is a rigid procedural requirement, when in fact all there really is is a set of unexamined habits. So it's a good mental discipline to look hardest at any activities that seem to have set procedures, in your work or in your life. In many cases it turns out there are no significant constraints to altering the procedure other than a lack of imagination!

46. Red tape. When there are too many steps and people involved in evaluating a new idea, we are discouraged, rather than encouraged, to present new ideas. For instance, formal suggestion systems often involve complex submission forms and reviews by supervisors and committees, followed by lengthy analyses and planning for the few ideas that trickle through. Committing an idea to such a system is rather like sending a baby off to do the grocery shopping. It will be a miracle if you ever see that idea again! To combat the red tape problem, the best thing to do is to eliminate red tape. Try submitting the suggestion that all red tape be eliminated. At least you'll get a laugh out of it, even if nothing happens as a result. But where there is lots of bureaucracy, you usually find that no one person has the authority to eliminate it without dealing with a lot more red tape. In some organizations, the red tape is actually in charge, not the managers! In such situations, you need to focus on between-the-lines opportunities for creativity. Develop creative approaches to your work that do not fall into anyone's obvious area of authority, and simply implement the ideas yourself. If they are up and working before anyone discovers and reports them, then they are big enough to do the shopping on their own and will probably

> In some organizations, the red tape is actually in charge, not the managers!

> Most people have a preferred channel in which they are better at listening to and considering new ideas.

survive others' efforts to tangle them in red tape. (Oh, and remember: If someone asks you whose idea it was, just shrug and say you don't know, but you think it's always been done that way. Denial is sometimes the best policy for creative thinkers in bureaucracies. But don't tell anyone I told you, okay?)

47. Close-minded leaders. Many people feel threatened when you voice creative ideas or observations. They are closed-minded and don't seem to want to hear what you think if it is different from what they think. Yet if they are in positions of power in your life or work, you need to circumvent their close-mindedness in order to get some ideas developed and adopted. One way to work on this problem is to experiment with different communication channels. Most people have a preferred channel in which they are better at listening to and considering new ideas. It is different for each person, but might be any one of the following: person-to-person conversation in a formal, group setting; person-to-person conversation in a formal, private setting; person-to-person communication in an informal, private setting; written memo; e-mail; voice mail; telephone conversation; a formal, written report; an informal quick note on a message slip or Post-It pad; indirect submission of idea through a third party such as a secretary or assistant; etc. Experiment until you find the channel that works best. Also try different times and settings for delivering creative ideas. But whatever you do, please be politely persistent. Make a joke of it if you must, but keep submitting your ideas and harden yourself to rejection. Eventually even the most pig-headed leaders can be trained to be more open to creative thinking. Treat training your leader as your creative challenge for the next six months, and see how much progress you can make without getting fired. Good luck!

48. Group-process constraints. Strict agendas for meetings, micro-organized team projects and calendars, and formal, over-structured approaches to discussion all get in the way of creative thinking. Unless you loosen up the group process constraints, you can't expect to have many creative ideas. So work more slack into group processes wherever you can. If you can't eliminate constraints, then dodge them by finding other times and places where you and one or two sympathetic associates can re-examine a question in an informal, unregulated atmosphere. Then if you come up with a useful insight, you can relay it to the boss by memo and suggest that it might be worth discussing in the next scheduled meeting. Also, try to do as much creative thinking as you can on your own, outside of the constraining group processes. If you can't do this at work, find time and activities away from work to make sure you maintain your creative fitness.

49. Pressure to conform. If there is pressure to act, dress, think and be like others in an organization or sub-culture, this pressure will inhibit creative thinking. Being "different" is in and of itself a taboo thing, and creativity introduces differences, so we are inhibited from acting and thinking in creative ways. How much conformance pressure is there in the organizations to which you belong? Ask yourself if you are going along with conformance pressures without thinking. Often there is no harm in this—why not dress the way others do in your office or profession? But you will inevitably surface some types of conformance that are unnecessary. You don't have to play golf just because your executives do if your favorite sport is volleyball. That's not a reasonable accommodation to conformance pressure. And although most people fail to recognize it, the sport you choose to play has an impact on how you think about creative problems. Our sports, hobbies, and other interests provide us with many metaphors and images that we bring to the table when we do creative thinking or problem solving. That means it is healthiest for an organization to have diversity in its people. Differences are a hidden source of strength. Remind yourself of this point and permit yourself to express healthy differences between you and "the others" and you will soon find that other people in the organization are unique individuals, too.

50. Perfectionism. If you require perfection you won't like creative ideas because they are often messy and poorly formed. The old approach always seems neater and more perfect because it has been developed and refined. Perfectionism leads us to reject creative ideas prematurely, not giving them a chance to develop enough to know if they ever could have flown on their own wings. To combat this critical tendency, perfectionists can turn their attention to the creative process instead of its products. Fussing to refine the creative process—the way you or a group thinks up and documents ideas— should scratch that perfectionism itch in a more productive and useful manner. There is nothing wrong with the pursuit of excellence.

> It is healthiest for an organization to have diversity in its people. Differences are a hidden source of strength.

It's just that sometimes your perfectionism is best applied to things, and other times to processes.

51. Fear of failure. What if your ideas are wrong and don't work? Thoughts like this can be crippling to creativity. "Nothing ventured, nothing risked" seems to be a popular motto when it comes to creativity. The way to overcome fear of failure is to try and to succeed. That sounds easy, but to make sure it happens for you, give yourself "sure winners" to start with. Tackle creative tasks that are fun and easy, and that have little or no down side in order to build up your own self-confidence until your fear of failure weakens and your urge to create overpowers it. For instance, focus on doing something creative in an area in which you have great confidence with your expertise. If you are a good cook, decide you will cook something new and fun. If you aren't confident enough in anything you do to overcome your fear of failure, then you need to think of new and simpler opportunities for creativity. For instance, try creating your own "mix" of music by selecting tracks from a series of CDs to listen to or put on tape for later listening. If you like the individual songs, the selection you create can't be bad and might be really great. Or rearrange the furniture or pictures in your house or apartment, the clothes in your dresser, or the equipment and supplies at your desk or work-station. Or make a scrapbook of photos and other mementos. Each of these is a creative act with no significant down side, since you can always put things back the way they were if you don't like them later on. It's amazing how even the simplest creative exercises can increase one's confidence for more difficult creative challenges.

52. Fear of rejection. It's one thing to worry that your idea will be rejected—that's a fear most of us can live with. But for many, the anxiety takes a more personal nature, when we find ourselves identifying with our ideas and feeling that their rejection is a rejection of us as people. Taking rejection personally makes each creative suggestion an emotional land mine. Will they reject me or not? Do they still value me? When you approach creativity this way, you don't get very far. Unfortunately, many people contribute to our fears of rejection by giving us person-focused feedback instead of feedback focused on the idea. If your co-workers, managers, or spouse are in the habit of saying, "That's a stupid idea," you need to recognize that they are

> Tackle creative tasks that are fun and easy, and that have little or no down side in order to build up your own self-confidence.

attacking you inappropriately. They just don't realize that they framed the response in the wrong way. Correct them by saying, "Could you please talk about my idea, not me, when you react to it?" The rules of brainstorming provide a good antidote to fears of rejection by outlawing all critical comments until a large number of ideas have been generated by a group and pooled so that they can be considered as a group, separate from the individuals who proposed them. (See Traditional Brainstorming on p. 72 of *The Manager's Pocket Guide to Creativity,* for example.)

53. Fear of losing control. Many people worry that too much creativity is dangerous because it is "out of control." The desire to keep things in control is a strong one for many of us. Even thinking about radically new and different approaches can seem to threaten the current order. To combat this fear of losing control, you need to recognize that true control arises from having choices. The more options you have, the more control you have, because you aren't boxed into any one path or choice. When people realize this, they feel more open to creativity and learn to see it as a source of control rather than a threat to control. Creativity gives us more control over the future, even as it reduces our control over the present. Also, don't feel you have to rush creativity. It can take a little while to get used to the idea that once-solid assumptions may be questionable. Do your creativity in a series of sessions over multiple days or weeks, allowing yourself (and others if a group is involved) to grow used to each wave of new ideas before another is launched. The ability to control the *pace* of creativity does much to make up for our lack of control over the end results.

54. Pride. Pride in one's own ideas often gets in the way of considering other people's ideas seriously. As a result, the creative process is starved for input. Nobody ever developed any great creative idea entirely on their own. Others' ideas and input are vital to healthy creativity. So you need to work hard against pride of authorship and open yourself to good ideas from all quarters. One good way to discipline yourself to listen to and consider other people's ideas is to force yourself to keep a notebook in which you jot down other people's ideas (and nothing else—no ideas of your own!). Make sure you get enough information to describe each idea clearly so you can make a

> Creativity gives us more control over the future.

good entry for it. If you maintain this practice for a week or two, then read back over the journal, you will inevitably find a number of valuable suggestions in it, and that will help you develop a healthier appreciation for other people's ideas. The practice also forces you to work on listening to others' ideas, since you have to "play reporter" to learn enough about any idea to write it up well. (If you don't like writing notes in a notebook, keep an electronic file or carry a small tape recorder with you.) Your efforts to report others' ideas will teach you to listen to them and give you increased respect for them.

55. Personal filters. Most of us are unaware of our personal filters. But we all have them, and they function to screen out ideas and prevent us from thinking about them seriously. It's as if we simply don't hear certain types of ideas, whether they are voiced by others or within our own minds. Usually our filters prevent us from recognizing a new class of ideas or approaches, even though we may consider many new ideas within the existing class or grouping. The chapter on Category Expansion in *The Manager's Pocket Guide to Creativity* walks you through methods that help overcome these personal filters. And a simple thing you can do to work on them yourself is to stop and ask yourself why you don't take certain ideas seriously. Is it for a good, well-considered reason, or is a filter just screening it out thoughtlessly? By making yourself more aware of filters, you can take more control over the process and avoid missing many good ideas by unconscious filtering. (**Example**: Many people assume that only certain "properly qualified" employees in a workplace are legitimate sources of new ideas—the qualified list varies with the topic, but is usually present in the back of our minds. This leads us to filter out suggestions from "inappropriate" people or to simply stop soliciting their suggestions in the first place. This filter is easy to overcome once you are aware of it. Simply make a point of seeking input from at least three unlikely sources whenever you are looking for good ideas!)

56. Internal voices. Many people talk themselves out of being creative because they think of objections to their own ideas, or because they raise doubts about their own ability to perform at creative tasks. ("Oh, that'll never work. You can't come up with a better idea," we tell ourselves. Or we say to ourselves, "It isn't dignified to do brainstorming. I'll let the others do the talking so I won't embar-

> Make a point of seeking input from at least three unlikely sources whenever you are looking for good ideas!

rass myself.") If your internal critic or skeptic is derailing your creativity, make a bargain with yourself. Tell yourself you will postpone critical thinking and just see what you get by thinking creatively. It is a healthy mental exercise, even if it produces nothing of value. After allowing yourself to think creatively for fifteen minutes, you can allow yourself another fifteen minutes to make a list of all your self-doubts and self-criticisms. But you probably won't want to, because after fifteen minutes of creative thinking you are likely to have ideas of sufficient power to subdue those negative inner voices.

57. Physical discomfort. Any physical discomfort or pain distracts from cognitive tasks, and is especially destructive of creative ability. Nobody comes up with breakthrough ideas when they have a headache, for example. So tune in your body's condition before you try to do creative thinking or problem-solving, and work on treating problems or symptoms and making yourself as comfortable as possible first. One common barrier to corporate creativity is uncomfortable meeting rooms. If you are in a room with uncomfortable chairs and no fresh air or light, consider moving the meeting or having everyone take a short walk in order to increase comfort and stimulate creative thought.

58. Unhealthy back/spine. If your back is bothering you, you feel uncomfortable and have difficulty concentrating. In addition, your spinal fluid does not circulate as it should, which interferes with the quality of your thinking. The only way to deal with this problem is head-on, by working on improving the alignment, strength, and flexibility of your spine. Stretching, swimming, walking, yoga, chiropractic care, and medical care are some of the options people use to improve their backs. Also, think about your working posture and make adjustments to chair, desk, and keyboard to avoid slouching postures. Try to vary your posture, take stretching breaks, and walk around more often. And consider getting a headset for your phone to avoid neck strain.

59. Concrete thinking. When you are not in the habit of thinking abstractly about problems, it is harder to be creative about them. Abstract thinking generalizes a problem so that you can see how it is related to other problems which, while literally quite different, are related in abstract ways. Then you can borrow solutions from those

> If your internal critic or skeptic is derailing your creativity, make a bargain with yourself.

> Take a set of index cards, write down the steps in your current approach to a process or problem, and then shuffle the cards.

problems and see if they fit yours. To make your thinking less concrete, force yourself to think of similes and metaphors; then ask yourself in what ways each is like and unlike your problem or area of interest. Also try to build models: Draw a two-dimensional grid or matrix and label each dimension with an important variable, then fill in four or more cells with different possibilities. (The Magic Toolbox method in *The Manager's Pocket Guide to Creativity* helps break through overly concrete thinking.)

60. Linear thinking. People who like to think things through in a methodical, step-by-step fashion often have difficulty thinking creatively because they have trouble making unlikely connections. If you are in the habit of thinking linearly, try to break this pattern of thought intentionally. For example, take a set of index cards, write down the steps in your current approach to a process or problem, and then shuffle the cards. Now try to re-write them to make sense of the order in which the shuffling put them.

61. Acceptance. When you worry that people will reject your ideas out of hand, you tend to withhold them and eventually block yourself from even thinking creative thoughts. To combat the acceptance problem, remove yourself from people who respond negatively to new ideas. Seek a positive physical and emotional environment in which to develop your ideas. If you can't (as when you are stuck in a "hostile" staff meeting), then keep a notebook to record your ideas rather than voicing them and risk getting "slammed." If you must present your ideas to negative people in order to get them implemented, wait until the ideas have matured and you can present them in the form of well-developed, carefully-supported proposals. Don't blurt them out too soon or they'll never have a chance.

62. Low self-evaluation of work. When you doubt the worth or importance of what you do, it is very hard to get "up" enough to tackle it creatively. To combat this negative feeling, remind yourself of what is important about your work. Also think about the potential to make the work more than it currently is by doing it especially well. Even the most trivial-sounding job is important to someone, so also try to talk to the people who "consume" what you produce and ask them what is important about it and what they'd like to see improved. Their desires are a great focus for your creativity, because you know you are working on something that matters to someone else.

Managing Critical Incidents in Sales and Marketing Short Course

Overview of Course IX

If you ask people on a survey to rate their overall level of satisfaction with a company they do business with, you'll get an overall rating. It might be fair, poor, or good. But what does it mean? Will they be loyal or not? Will they spread positive word of mouth or negative?

I learned from doing such surveys that you often get more insight by asking customers to describe a *memorable interaction* with your business. Instead of that overall rating, you get a key memory that is often the driver of overall attitudes—and future purchase decisions too!

When you come across anything that explains purchase decisions, well, it should awaken your marketing instincts right away.

C ritical incidents are the interactions with you, your company, or your products that shape customer perceptions and create loyalty or anger—loyalty if the incident is positive, anger and a desire to become an ex-customer if the incident is negative.

The term "critical incident" is not even in the index of any marketing texts or sales how-tos I've seen. Most people in business don't think about critical incidents. They act as if all customer interactions and all product or service usages are of equal value in shaping customer perceptions. Not so! Occasionally, a specific incident takes on special importance and on its own determines whether that customer will be loyal and profitable for you or disloyal and unprofitable. In this session we'll explore what these incidents are and how to manage them to take advantage of the tremendous leverage they offer the savvy marketer or salesperson.

Critical Incidents: The Make-or-Break Moments in Marketing

I seem to get a lot of letters from unhappy customers. Most of them have read one of my tirades about customer service quality in one of my previous books on marketing and are writing or e-mailing to let me know they appreciate my efforts to get managers' attention. However, they tell me that they could not get managements' attention, or *anyone's* for that matter. You know service must be pretty bad in business when angry customers have to resort to writing letters to authors. It's not like I'm going to give them a refund because they were treated poorly by an airline. But what many of these people want even more than a refund is simple acknowledgment of their plight—recognition that they have been treated poorly, a little empathy and understanding, perhaps even an apology!

Here's a typical example, from someone who wrote me after reading *The Portable MBA in Marketing*:

"I have just survived one of my worst flying experiences, totally unnecessary (i.e., clear day, no weather problems), changing planes on Continental at Newark. One of the most humiliating, unnecessary,

> Occasionally, a specific incident takes on special importance and on its own determines whether that customer will be loyal and profitable for you or disloyal and unprofitable.

inhospitable, inhuman, unconscionable, customer-hating, experiences of my life. Continental is so proud of their new 777's. Well, let me tell you, they should try to hire people who don't hate travelers. I'd like to see every gate person at Newark be forced to travel to the West Coast to see what it's like to be lost and disoriented at a strange airport."

This same person sent another story, demonstrating the power of a little consideration:

"Bought a video from Pentrex, a company that sells railroad videos last year, and paid by check. Never glanced at the shipping papers/invoice. This year, I buy another one. Paid by credit card. Invoice noted that I had overpaid last year by $1.06 and they had deducted it from this year's invoice. Spectacular, eh? Exactly what the world needs. For $1.06 they made a friend for life. If they asked me to send them $10.00 on general principles, I'd do it. They couldn't buy my loyalty through advertising for $1.06, but through competence and honesty, they got it."

These stories reflect the power of critical incidents to shape customer attitudes and behaviors. A critical incident is anything that breaks the pattern, that stands out to the customer. Critical incidents interrupt the routine, making a strong impression in customers' minds. That impression can be strongly negative or strongly positive. The marketer or salesperson can often determine whether the critical incident is remembered in a positive or negative light.

And note that the marketer has the *choice* of making each critical incident positive or negative. It's not just in whether there is a problem or mistake. It's more in how those problems or mistakes are handled. In the two customer stories above, notice that both involved poor performances on the part of the company. Even the positive event started with an error—after all, the company didn't refund the overpayment right away. But because of how the company handled the situation at repurchase, the customer left the incident with a very positive, loyal feeling toward that company.

The good news is that critical incidents don't happen every time someone makes a purchase or uses a product or service.

> A critical incident is anything that breaks the pattern, that stands out to the customer.

Customers aren't usually paying much attention—after all, the average individual engages in dozens of purchases and hundreds of product or service usages each day. Much of the time, things go according to a pleasantly dull routine and the customer does not have to be highly involved, either cognitively or emotionally.

When something goes unusually wrong or unusually right, then the customer's involvement is raised. The routine is broken. The customer is now fully involved and everything about the sales or usage experience will be imprinted strongly on the customer's psyche. The stage is set for a critical incident.

But maybe the company's systems or employees are still blundering along at a far lower level of involvement and interest. Maybe they don't recognize that a critical incident is about to occur. Maybe they are about to dash this customer's expectations and generate frustration, anger, rage, and a strong sense of injustice and unfair treatment. Most critical incidents produce customer disloyalty for the simple reason that the company and its all-important people don't realize they are dealing with a critical incident and don't do anything to make sure it is a positive one.

Oops. Another customer lost.

What's Behind Critical Incidents?

When a company does something notably bad or good, burning a negative or positive impression into a customer's mind, what is behind this critical incident? To understand where and how critical incidents originate is to begin the journey toward managing them. And when you can manage critical incidents, you can tip the balance, insuring that your customers have many more positive than negative incidents.

By the way, positive critical incidents do two wonderful things for your business. The first and most obvious is that they build customer loyalty, thereby insuring that you retain a customer and perhaps even increase the amount of business you get from that customer. But second, they also bring you new customers because customers who have had positive critical incidents want to talk about them. They want to tell their friends and relations about their surpris-

> Much of the time, things go according to a pleasantly dull routine and the customer does not have to be highly involved, either cognitively or emotionally.

ingly nice treatment. It made them feel special, and it's simply human nature to want to let the people around you know just how special you are. So customers who have had positive critical incidents with your company become crusaders and missionaries for you, spreading positive word of mouth. The average customer who has not had high-involvement experiences with you will not talk about your business. But one who has had a positive critical incident will blab about it to everyone—even to strangers like me over the Internet!

And of course, the opposite is true. A negative critical incident loses you a customer and also generates lots of negative word of mouth that prevents other customers from coming on board and may even lead to some defections from your existing customer base. So critical incidents have a high degree of leverage in the areas of customer retention *and* customer acquisition.

But back to the questions of where critical incidents come from. Critical incidents involving your customers can come from a number of sources within your organization, but the most common source is your employees themselves. Here are the most likely sources, the ones you need to manage to insure that incidents are positive, not negative:

Insensitive Systems

If your automated phone system doesn't include the option a customer wants and has no easy way to dial "0" for an operator and ask a real human being for help, then you have an insensitive system. It is just a matter of time before it makes some customer so mad he or she never does business with you again—and tells everyone else not to either. Make sure all your systems that touch customers are friendly, flexible (customers love CHOICE!!!), and have easy-to-find escape hatches in case the customer thinks the system isn't right for him or her. What happens when a customer thinks the bill is wrong? Is there an easy way to talk to someone helpful and friendly to get to the bottom of the question? No? I didn't think so.

Insensitive Personnel

I stopped by the place I get my hair cut this morning and asked when the next opening was. The receptionist, a new one, said 11:30 and wrote my name on the appointment calendar for that time. It

> A negative critical incident loses you a customer and also generates lots of negative word of mouth that prevents other customers from coming on board.

> She blamed it on the new receptionist. And I went across the street to their competition.

was already quarter past eleven, so I did a quick errand and came back. By then the receptionist had gone out and nobody was up front, so I waited ten minutes until one of the stylists came up and asked me what I wanted. I explained I had an appointment that should have started a little while ago. She consulted the appointment book and said, "No you don't." Well, I was a bit puzzled, but I leaned over the desk to show her were I'd seen my name written in. It was covered with fresh white-out. I pointed this out and began to complain, but she cut me off, saying that even if I had been given an appointment it was a mistake because no one was free right then anyway. She blamed it on the new receptionist. And I went across the street to their competition.

Now I'm sure these employees are viewed as "nice" by their manager. They smile and act friendly. But on the other hand, they managed to waste a half hour of my time and send me to the competition. When you have insensitive personnel, it is often the case that they are really perfectly nice people, but they somehow end up acting insensitive toward customers, maybe without realizing it because nobody has taught them how to act. It takes considerable training to get customer service personnel up to speed. However, even knowledgeable, well-trained employees often cause critical incidents and drive customers away. Sometimes they know they are being insensitive, but they don't give a damn. That's because they aren't motivated to be nice because they probably haven't been treated well by their employers (see the next cause of critical incidents).

Insensitive Managers

I've got some amazing statistics from my various studies of companies showing that there are direct links from how managers treat employees to how employees treat customers. I don't think, however, that it takes statistical evidence to convince most people of this link. Of course, management behavior will drive employee behavior. Of course, employees who are treated badly will treat customers badly. It's just how things work. And when it comes to critical incidents, note that most managers aren't very aware of the incidents that might bother their employees. So they aren't modeling good skills for how to handle critical incidents. They are generally ignoring the incidents involving their employees. It's no wonder employees generally ignore incidents involving their customers. And a great way to improve customer relations is to start working on improved employee relations!

Inappropriate Customers

The final cause of critical incidents I recommend you look at is a mismatch between you and your customer. Sometimes you've just got the wrong customer and you're never going to make them happy. It's best to recognize that quickly and send them on their way. Give them suggestions about where to find a company that better fits their needs. Explain that what they want is different from what most of your customers want and that you aren't set up to provide what they want very well. Wish them well, be polite to them, but make it clear you don't think you can help. Better to make the break cleanly and quickly if there has to be a break. Otherwise, they'll take up lots of time and resources because they will always be having problems. And each time they have a problem, they'll spread the bad word about you to all their friends.

> Sometimes you've just got the wrong customer and you're never going to make them happy. It's best to recognize that quickly and send them on their way.

How to Minimize the Damage of Critical Incidents

Here is a simple five-step program you can put in place in any organization to improve customer loyalty by reducing negative incidents and increasing positive ones. It really works. Try it!

1. Manage your employees' critical incidents well. There is plenty of information about how to improve employee attitudes in the courses on leadership and motivation. If your employees are in contact with customers, it's all the more important to manage them sensitively and well. The best advice I can give you is to apply the lessons from those two courses, then keep an ear open for grumblings and complaints.

   Whenever you sense there might be an employee problem, be proactive. Make a point of asking the employee, in a kindly, inter-

> What do customers look like, sound like, act like, and do when they are moving from a routine interaction to a highly involved, critical interaction?

ested manner, if anything is bothering him or her. And if it is, make a point of taking some action right away. It might not be possible to do what a particular employee wants, but it is always possible to do something. Show you care by coming up with a considerate response—pronto. That's how you want your employees to act toward customers, so you better act that way toward them!

2. Teach your people to recognize high customer involvement. Talk to your employees about the importance of critical incidents. Ask them to practice identifying employees who are highly involved in a particular incident, whether because they are unexpectedly happy or unhappy. What do customers look like, sound like, act like, and do when they are moving from a routine interaction to a highly involved, critical interaction? Make sure your people realize they need to recognize these moments and step up with a friendly intervention. These are the make-or-break moments, and your employees need to be trained to RECOGNIZE them before you can ask them to manage such incidents!

3. Teach your employees to manage customers' critical incidents well. As soon as an employee recognizes that a critical incident is under way—perhaps because a customer raises her voice, for example—the employee should then have a routine sequence of responses to fall back upon. For example, you might train employees to:

   a) ask others to handle the routine business so as to avoid distractions and permit you to focus on the critical incident;

   b) smile at the upset customer and reassure her that you want to help and will stick with her until she's satisfied;

   c) encourage her to "vent" and tell her story, listening carefully and never arguing with what she says;

   d) try to mirror the customer's complaint and how she feels about it by saying, "Okay, let me make sure I have this straight. You feel _____ and _____ because we _____ or we didn't _____. Is that right?"

(Phrases always start with how customer feels then go to events that are the root of the feelings.);

e) Let the customer expand upon the complaint or modify it until you have it right;

f) Make an offer, a suggestion, of what you can do to correct the problem and make up for the inconvenience to the customer;

g) negotiate with the customer if necessary until the offer is truly satisfactory;

h) and finally, apologize on behalf of the entire organization and give the customer your name and (work) number and ask for a call if anything else goes wrong or comes up.

This sequence makes a great critical incident intervention plan, a process which you can teach employees to use in order to win over unhappy customers and turn negative incidents into positive ones.

4. Give employees enough control to manage customers' critical incidents well. In the motivation course, I harp on the importance of control as an employee motivator. In the context of customer service, control also has some very important practical benefits. Employees who have control over some of the variables of customer treatment can exercise that control to manage good recovery processes. They can decide that a customer should be offered a discount, a refund, sent some flowers and a note of apology or thanks for their patience, or given a box of chocolates. In fact, employees trained in the handling of critical incidents enjoy taking a creative problem-solving approach. They really get involved in figuring out how to turn around a negative experience and produce a customer who is smiling and thanking them instead of frowning and cursing them. It's a very rewarding thing to do—as long as you have enough control that you can actually DO something to help the customer out. So think about giving employees a budget and some control to go along with their training. Responsibility for

> Since most service is awful, America is ripe for a revolution.
> —HARVEY MACKAY, FOUNDER OF MACKAY ENVELOPE CORP. AND AUTHOR OF *HOW TO SWIM WITH THE SHARKS WITHOUT BEING EATEN ALIVE*

> You can't manage anything you don't measure, because measurements are the eyes and ears of any business.

handling critical incidents isn't real unless you trust them to exercise some judgment too.

5. Keep track of critical incidents. The final step in learning to profit from critical incidents is to develop a simple record keeping system. You can't manage anything you don't measure, because measurements are the eyes and ears of any business. So create a log for employees to make note of critical incidents and record what they did and whether they think the customer was won over. Then review those records periodically. Discuss them in staff meetings, and keep thinking about ways to better handle critical incidents!

Wrap-Up

Well, that's the scoop on critical incidents. They are a subject that most managers don't even think about, yet they shape so many customers' decisions about what to buy and who to do business with—or who not to do business with ever again!

By attending to the critical incidents that stick out in customers' minds, you can reduce customer defections and keep people from badmouthing you and your business or products. And you can begin to build powerful bonds of loyalty by creating positive incidents in which customers are pleasantly surprised by how well you respond to their complaints or needs.

Most people in business do not pay enough attention to those rare situations in which the customer is highly involved and concerned. Yet these are the times when you have their attention, when they really want you to step up and pay attention to them. Most of the time everything is routine and they really don't want to be bothered by yet another marketer, service person, or salesperson. But during a critical incident, the opposite is true. Customers generally feel they don't get enough attention.

So it's a very powerful strategy to shift your focus from the routine to the critical and to begin concentrating on customers at those few times when you have tremendous potential to influence their consumption experiences. A great way to get ahead in business is to become a critical incident manager.

Index

Adams Streetwiseᶠⁱ books for growing your business

Complete Business Plan
$17.05
ISBN 1-55850-845-7

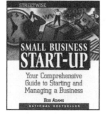

Small Business Start-Up
$17.95
ISBN 1-55850-581-4

Customer-Focused Selling
$17.95
ISBN 1-55850-725-6

Finance & Accounting
$17.95
ISBN 1-58062-196-1

Hiring Top Performers
$17.95
ISRN 1-58062-684-5

Marketing Plan
$17.95
ISBN 1-58062-268-2

Managing People
$17.95
ISBN 1-55850-726-4

Business Forms w/CD-ROM
$24.95
ISBN 1-58062-132-5

Business Letters w/CD-ROM
$24.95
ISBN 1-58062-133-3

Motivating & Rewarding Employees
$17.95
ISBN 1-58062-130-9

Relationship Marketing on the Internet
$17.95
ISBN 1-58062-255-0

Time Management
$17.95
ISBN 1-58062-131-7

Do-It-Yourself Advertising
$17.95
ISBN 1-55850-727-2

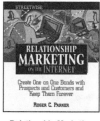

Small Business Turnaround
$17.95
ISBN 1-58062-195-3

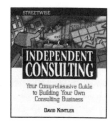

Independent Consulting
$17.95
ISBN 1-55850-728-0

Available wherever books are sold.

How to order: If you cannot find this book at your favorite retail outlet, you may order it directly from the publisher. BY PHONE: Call 1-800-872-5627. We accept Visa, Mastercard, and American Express. $4.95 will be added to your total order for shipping and handling. BY MAIL: Write out the full title of the book you d like to order and send payment, including $4.95 for shipping and handling to: Adams Media Corporation, 260 Center Street, Holbrook, MA 02343. 30-day money-back guarantee.

Visit our exciting small business Website: www.businesstown.com

FIND MORE ON THIS TOPIC BY VISITING
BusinessTown.com
The Web's big site for growing businesses!

☑ **Separate channels on all aspects of starting and running a business**

☑ **Lots of info of how to do business online**

☑ **1,000+ pages of savvy business advice**

☑ **Complete web guide to thousands of useful business sites**

☑ **Free e-mail newsletter**

☑ **Question and answer forums, and more!**

http://www.businesstown.com